W9-BWL-772

Food Culture in
Belgium

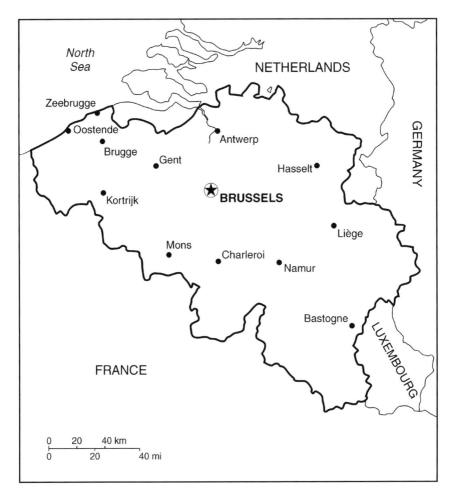

North
Sea

NETHERLANDS

GERMANY

Zeebrugge
● Oostende
Brugge
● Gent
Antwerp
Hasselt ●
⊛ BRUSSELS
Kortrijk
Liège
Mons
Charleroi
Namur
Bastogne ●
LUXEMBOURG
FRANCE

0   20   40 km
0   20   40 mi

Belgium. Cartography by Bookcomp, Inc.

Food Culture in
Belgium

PETER SCHOLLIERS

Food Culture around the World

Ken Albala, Series Editor

GREENWOOD PRESS
Westport, Connecticut • London

Library of Congress Cataloging-in-Publication Data

Scholliers, Peter.
    Food culture in Belgium / Peter Scholliers.
        p. cm. — (Food culture around the world, ISSN 1545–2638)
    Includes bibliographical references and index.
    ISBN 978–0–313–34490–9 (alk. paper)
  1. Cookery, Belgian. 2. Food habits—Belgium. I. Title.
    TX723.5.B4S36 2009
    394.1'209493—dc22   2008031523

British Library Cataloguing in Publication Data is available.

Copyright © 2009 by Peter Scholliers

All rights reserved. No portion of this book may be
reproduced, by any process or technique, without the
express written consent of the publisher.

Library of Congress Catalog Card Number: 2008031523
ISBN: 978–0–313–34490–9
ISSN: 1545–2638

First published in 2009

Greenwood Press, 88 Post Road West, Westport, CT 06881
An imprint of Greenwood Publishing Group, Inc.
www.greenwood.com

Printed in the United States of America

The paper used in this book complies with the
Permanent Paper Standard issued by the National
Information Standards Organization (Z39.48–1984).

10 9 8 7 6 5 4 3 2 1

Every reasonable effort has been made to trace the owners of copyrighted materials in this
book, but in some instances this has proven impossible. The author and publisher will be
glad to receive information leading to more complete acknowledgments in subsequent
printings of the book and in the meantime extend their apologies for any omissions.

The publisher has done its best to make sure the instructions and/or recipes in this book
are correct. However, users should apply judgment and experience when preparing recipes, especially parents and teachers working with young people. The publisher accepts no
responsibility for the outcome of any recipe included in this volume.

9001010922

Contents

Series Foreword

The appearance of the Food Culture around the World series marks a definitive stage in the maturation of Food Studies as a discipline to reach a wider audience of students, general readers, and foodies alike. In comprehensive interdisciplinary reference volumes, each on the food culture of a country or region for which information is most in demand, a remarkable team of experts from around the world offers a deeper understanding and appreciation of the role of food in shaping human culture for a whole new generation. I am honored to have been associated with this project as series editor.

Each volume follows a series format, with a chronology of food-related dates and narrative chapters titled Introduction, Historical Overview, Major Foods and Ingredients, Cooking, Typical Meals, Eating Out, Special Occasions, and Diet and Health (in special cases, these topics are covered by region). Each also includes a glossary, bibliography, resource guide, and illustrations.

Finding or growing food has of course been the major preoccupation of our species throughout history, but how various peoples around the world learn to exploit their natural resources, come to esteem or shun specific foods and develop unique cuisines reveals much more about what it is to be human. There is perhaps no better way to understand a culture, its values, preoccupations and fears, than by examining its attitudes toward food. Food provides the daily sustenance around which families and communities bond. It provides the material basis for rituals through which people celebrate the passage of life stages and their connection to divinity. Food preferences also serve to separate individuals and groups from each other, and as one of the most powerful factors in the construction of identity, we physically, emotionally and spiritually become what we eat.

By studying the foodways of people different from ourselves we also grow to understand and tolerate the rich diversity of practices around the world. What seems strange or frightening among other people becomes perfectly rational when set in context. It is my hope that readers will gain from these volumes not only an aesthetic appreciation for the glories of the many culinary traditions described, but also ultimately a more profound respect for the peoples who devised them. Whether it is eating New Year's dumplings in China, folding tamales with friends in Mexico or going out to a famous Michelin-starred restaurant in France, understanding these food traditions helps us to understand the people themselves.

As globalization proceeds apace in the twenty-first century is it also more important than ever to preserve unique local and regional traditions. In many cases these books describe ways of eating that have already begun to disappear or have been seriously transformed by modernity. To know how and why these losses occur today also enables us to decide what traditions, whether from our own heritage or that of others, we wish to keep alive. These books are thus not only about the food and culture of peoples around the world, but also about ourselves and who we hope to be.

Ken Albala
University of the Pacific

Preface

Sometime during the 1980s, I became engaged in the quantitative historiography of food. I wished to learn about the money people spent on food between 1850 and 1950, the calories they consumed in 1890 and 1910, and the prices they paid for pork, butter, or coffee between 1950 and 1975. This would help me to assess the development of the standard of living of the masses (then, as now, a crucial research theme). Sometime during the 1990s, I started to gain interest in cultural aspects of eating and drinking, realizing that food is much more than a matter of prices and calories. I wanted to learn about the *significance* of foodstuffs and eating habits, which led me to study the role of cuisine in identity formation, the importance of eating chocolate, or the names of restaurants and dishes. This is one way, not necessarily a better way of doing historical research. I think it is more comprehensive and, therefore, more fulfilling.

ACKNOWLEDGMENTS

Taking this route was possible through scientific, mostly cordial but sometimes conflicting, contacts with many people during colloquia, workshops, lectures, teaching, and dining occasions. Also, this book was made possible through the reading of many works on the sociology and ethnology of food, which are quite far from the average social and economic historian's purview. In the Selected Bibliography at the end of this book I refer, and gladly pay tribute, to the work of these diverse scholars. However, this research endeavor was particularly made possible and, moreover, enhanced through my frequent contacts with the members of the Research Unit FOST (Social and Cultural Food Studies) of the Vrije Universiteit Brussel (Brussels Free University), especially with Patricia Van den Eeckhout (my usual sparring partner who, quite luckily, is a great and adventurous cook) and Daniëlle De Vooght, Joeri Januarius, Inge Mestdag, Nelleke Teughels, and Steven Van den Berghe (young researchers with specific approaches, methods, and backgrounds—talks with them are always enriching). I also wish to mention Serge Gutwirth, Marc Jacobs, and Piet Van de Craen, with whom I discuss immaterial as well as material matters (not only about cuisine, nor always at a dinner table). I took most of the photos during long walks (mainly in Brussels), but I sincerely thank the Institute of Social History (AMSAB, Ghent) for permission to use some older photographs.

With regard to the direct development of this book, I would like to thank two wonderful people. Wendi Schnaufer, senior editor at Greenwood Press, read the first version of the text, patiently and efficiently correcting the English of a nonnative speaker. Ken Albala, the series editor, reacted promptly and with great wisdom to the chapters I sent, questioning some of my assertions, correcting mistakes, and making many suggestions. It is great collaborating with proficient, sharp, and flexible people.

Introduction

Writing about Belgium today is tricky. Centrifugal political forces aiming at further federalizing the country, and even splitting it up into three independent parts (Flanders, Wallonia, and Brussels Capital Region), resulted during 2007 and 2008 in eight long months without government and with great doubts about the country's future. Belgium still exists, and many people in the three parts of the country, which today have autonomy in some matters, are quite happy with that. Conflicting forces have far from faded, though. What is this little country that seems to be on its way to dissolving itself?

Elements that may contribute to national sentiments and refer to a distinct image abroad are hard to find. Does Belgium have an identity? What would come to people's mind when the word *Belgium* is uttered? Belgium has no single, shared language. In the north, Flemish (officially, Dutch) is spoken, in the south French is used, and in the east some speak German, while Brussels is a bilingual city (actually, a multilingual place like any other city in Europe). The lack of a common language means that literature, theater, poetry, newspapers, radio, and television fail to address *all* people in the country. Moreover, the regions that make up Belgium do not share a common history. For centuries Flanders developed differently from Wallonia and the Brussels area in economic, social, and political terms, with regions governed by different (often foreign) rulers and with the division of once-united regions. Even nationalistic forces that came into being after the proclamation of Belgium as an independent state in

1830, such as the army, the school, or the Catholic Church, could not forge solid Belgian feelings. Big disasters such as World Wars I and II, rather than uniting the Belgians in their distress, divided them. On top of all that, the national currency (the Belgian franc) disappeared in 2002.

Yet, there are aspects where the country does present unity. Belgium has a king and a royal family, and all things royal fascinate many Belgians. Royal deaths, marriages, and births are impressive moments of Belgianness. Also, Belgians have expressed nationalism at major events such as the 10 world exhibitions between 1884 and 1958 and the anniversaries of the country in 1880, 1930, and 1980. Sports and international film, architecture, or music contests are another field of national pride. At these occasions, the black-yellow-red colors of the Belgian flag appear, putting Belgium on the world map. International contacts are beneficial to national sentiments. When abroad and confronted with other visitors, Belgians tend to stress their Belgianness compared to the Dutch (who cannot eat properly), the Americans (who are too loud), the British (who cannot drink or behave properly), or the French (who are too chauvinistic), implying that Belgians of course do enjoy food, are quiet, know how to conduct themselves, and are unpretentious. Abroad, Belgium seems to exist more than within the country.

According to some theories, food is also an explicit identity marker.[1] Through cuisine, people identify themselves with other people, whether in small units (the family), communities (social or religious groups), regions (the *terroir*), or large areas (the nation). Many households have particular meal habits and preferences, some communities follow strict food rules (no pork, no meat, no alcohol, kosher cooking, etc.), numerous regions cherish particular ways of making and preparing food (e.g., the *European Union geographical protection* of cheese, wine, or ham), and many nations have developed particular foods, like the Italians' pasta or Hungarians' goulash. Many nations and their inhabitants are characterized in terms of food (the krauts or the frogs, for example).[2] Does Belgium have a specific dish, a way of cooking, or an attitude toward food that bonds all regions, classes, ethnic groups, and ages and that is unique to this country and acknowledged abroad? Could food save the Belgian state? People inside and outside the country refer to *Belgian* chocolate, *Belgian* waffles, and *Belgian* beers but definitely not to Brussels chocolate, Flemish waffles, or Walloon beers. Moreover, all Belgians share an interest in good food, not in the sense that it is held in reserve for grand occasions, but that it is part of daily life. Furthermore, there are ingredients, techniques, and dishes that Belgium gave to the world, such as *pommes frites* (oddly, known in the world as French fries), Belgian endives, mussels, beer dishes, and juniper berries. So, there *must* be a Belgian cuisine, and hence, a Belgian state.

Central to this book is the question to what extent Belgium has managed to have a culinary image of its own. There is no simple answer. Gastronomic giants France and Germany are at its borders, and throughout history Belgian regions have been part of the Spanish, Austrian, French, Dutch, and German empires (and earlier in the past, the Celts, Romans, Goths, Franks, and others have settled in these areas) for long or brief periods. Also, for ages, migrating people arrived from faraway regions, bringing along their ways of cooking, ingredients, and culinary habits. Moreover, spices, beverages, and other goods have been widely imported, for these lands have long been important trade centers. Was this small territory able to develop a culinary identity under these varied, worldwide, and nonstop influences? Did these influences precisely shape Belgium's culinary uniqueness? Is Belgium therefore really "Europe's best-kept culinary secret," and if it is, what are its secrets?[3] Chapter 1 answers the first questions, but Belgium's culinary secrets will emerge throughout the whole book.

This book is written "from within," meaning that I am a Belgian trying to narrate what seems obvious to me, which implies the providing of inside information. I would say that one may eat delightfully well as well as appallingly in Belgium. My advantage is the use of archival material and Dutch and French literature that may be unattainable for many other authors. My historical training and a serious attempt to take an ethnological view should ensure a relativist approach, which made me look at things with a naïve eye. Thus, I ask questions about meal routines, ways of cooking, the practice of eating out, mealtimes, shopping habits, the use of ingredients, food at weddings, school and company cafeterias, cooking clubs, male and female chefs, Sunday dinners, family spending on food items, culinary differences between Flemings and Walloons, and many other issues related to ordinary and special food. I compare information with that from other countries. As a historian I try to interpret today's foodways by looking at the past. There are many very old traces (beer production, for example) but also many newer ones (such as potatoes or restaurants) and wholly recent ones (like new exotic foodstuffs). The bulk of attention is of course devoted to recent and present-day developments. Recipes given throughout the book are based on (recollection of) old family recipes that reflect plain Belgian cuisine that, like all national cuisines, is made up of local foodways.

NOTES

1. Peter Scholliers, "Meals, Food Narratives, and Sentiments of Belonging in Past and Present," in Peter Scholliers, ed., *Food, Drink and Identity: Cooking, Eating and Drinking in Europe since the Middle Ages* (New York: Berg, 2001), 3–22.

2. In his *Julie, ou la Nouvelle Héloïse* (1761) the French philosopher Jean-Jacques Rousseau already suggested that "one may find an indication of the nature of people in the food they prefer" (cited in J. M. Bourre, *La diététique du cerveau* [Paris: O. Jacob, 1990], 43–44).

3. The quotation is taken from the back cover of Ruth Van Waerebeek and Maria Robbins, *Everybody Eats Well in Belgium Cookbook* (New York: Workman, 1996).

Timeline

c. 20,000 B.C.	Humans appear for the first time in what now is Belgium.
4000 B.C.	Flint mine is in operation in Spiennes (near Mons).
2600 B.C.	First domesticated animals and farming are introduced.
2000 B.C.	Trade with the British Isles and Southern Europe begins.
250 B.C.	Celts invade this part of Europe.
58–56 B.C.	Julius Caesar conquers Gaul, which gradually becomes Romanized.
256 A.D.	Franks invade northwest Europe.
406	Germans invade what now is Belgium.
455	Roman rule ends.
500	Clovis, king of Franks, is baptized, which starts Christianization and the institution of meatless days (Wednesdays and especially Fridays) and Lent.
c. 510	Anthimus writes *De observatione ciborum*.
751	Pepin the Short becomes the first Carolingian king.
800	Charlemagne is crowned emperor.
843	The Treaty of Verdun divides the Frankish kingdom into three parts, with France and Flanders in the

	western empire, some regions of the Low Countries, Burgundy, and Northern Italy in the middle empire, and Germany in the eastern empire.
c. 1000	Agriculture in Flanders is intensified by applying fertilizer and rotating crops instead of leaving parts of the land fallow.
1000–1300	Population increases markedly, and settlements evolve into significant towns.
1096–1099	The first Crusade is organized, with the count of Flanders and the Duke of Burgundy as important leaders.
1100–1200	Trade revives, thereby increasing production of manufactured goods.
1170	The Great Charter of Flanders gives political and economic rights to certain towns.
1251	The Vleeshuis (Meat House) in Ghent is built.
1278	Italian ships arrive in Flanders. Bruges becomes a major commercial and staple center.
1300–1500	Local courts consume large quantities of food, especially meat.
1302	"Golden Spurs Battle," Flemish guilds and allies defeat the French army.
1337–1453	Hundred Years War. Flemings join the English in a war against French rulers.
1347–1459	Black Death or bubonic plague (with subsequent outbreaks occurring until 1725) kills thousands of people.
1366	Brewery Den Horen (Leuven) established, allegedly the predecessor of brewery Artois and Inbev.
1419–1482	Under Burgundian rule Brabant, Flanders, Hainault, Holland, Sealand, Artois, and Limburg are united.
1490	Antwerp becomes the commercial center of Europe.
1492	Christopher Columbus sets off to explore a new seaway to India, opening commercial roads for new products from the "Americas."
1510	*Een notabel boecxken van cokeryen* (A little notable book of cooking), the first printed cookbook, is published in Brussels.

1519	Charles V unites the Netherlands with Spain.
1523	Execution of Lutherans in Brussels, after outbreak of Protestant reformation.
1566	Iconoclastic fury: Catholic churches are destroyed.
1568–1648	Dutch Freedom Fight leads to the separation between the Spanish Netherlands (Flanders, Brabant, Hainault, etc.) and the Calvinist Republic (Holland, Utrecht, etc.).
1585	Antwerp is taken by the Spaniards, with temporary decline of trade and industry.
1612	Antonius Magirus publishes *Koocboec oft familieren keukenboec* (Cookbook or the everyday recipe book) in Leuven.
1648	The Treaty of Münster recognizes the Dutch Republic.
1695	The French bombard Brussels.
1713	Treaty of Utrecht: the Spanish Netherlands become part of the Austrian Empire. Until 1795 these lands are called the Austrian Netherlands.
1720	First steam engine is installed in Liège.
1745	The French invade the Austrian Netherlands.
1790	The United States of Belgium is proclaimed.
1792	The French invade the Austrian Netherlands, and annex it to France in 1795 (up to 1814).
1803	Code Napoléon introduces French legislation in Southern Netherlands.
1815	Battle of Waterloo: Napoleon is defeated. The United Kingdom of the Netherlands is proclaimed, uniting the southern Netherlands with the Dutch Republic.
1830	Belgian revolution leads to the proclamation of the Kingdom of Belgium.
1834	First train on the Continent runs between Brussels and Mechelen.
1847–1848	High cost of living (again in 1853 and 1855), particularly in Flanders, leads to large migration, increased mortality, and deteriorating living standards.

1861	Philippe Cauderlier publishes *L'économie culinaire* (The economical kitchen) in Ghent.
1867	Delhaize establishes its chain of food stores.
1869	Establishment of the Société philanthropique de secours mutuel des cuisiniers de la ville de Bruxelles (Philanthropic Association for Mutual Aid of Cooks of the City of Brussels).
1873	Import tax on grain is abolished; mass import of American grain leads to structural shifts in agriculture and an economic depression until the 1890s.
1880	Belgium celebrates its 50th anniversary with an international fair in Brussels.
	First bread is baked by the Social Democrat cooperative Vooruit in Ghent.
1885	Belgian Workers' Party is founded.
	The first Belgian World's fair is organized in Antwerp.
1890	The *Abattoir* (central slaughterhouse) in Brussels is built.
1894	Antwerp organizes its second World's fair.
1895	Jean de Gouy publishes *La cuisine et la pâtisserie bourgeoises en Belgique et à l'étranger* (The bourgeois cuisine and pastry making in Belgium and abroad) in Brussels.
1897	Brussels organizes its first World's fair.
1904	*Guide Michelin* includes Belgian restaurants.
1908	Belgium acquires the Congo Free State as a colony.
	First cooking school is established by the Union Syndicale des Hôteliers, Restaurateurs et Cafétiers de Bruxelles (Association of owners of hotels, restaurants and cafés in Brussels).
1910	Brussels organizes its second World's fair.
1913	Ghent and Liège organize their first World's fair.
1914–1918	World War I. Belgium is occupied by the Germans: period of hunger, skyrocketing prices, death, rising inequality.
1919	Eight-hour workday is instituted. Vandervelde Bill severely limits the selling of gin in public places.

1927	The Women's Farmers Association publishes the first edition of *Ons kookboek* (Our cookbook), Leuven.
1930	Antwerp organizes its third and Liège its second World's fair. The economic depression starts.
1935	Brussels organizes its third World's fair.
1936	Paid holidays are introduced for industry workers.
1940–1944	World War II: Belgium is occupied by the Germans. Period of hunger, skyrocketing prices, death, rising inequality.
1952	The Prix Prosper Montagné for the best chef is established.
1955	First cooking program appears on Flemish television.
1957	Belgium is a founding member of Euratom and European Economic Community (the forerunner of the EU, the European Union). Brussels is the unofficial "capital of Europe."
	Test-Achat/Test-Aankoop (Test-Purchase) is launched, an influential consumers' organization.
	The first supermarket opens in Brussels.
1958	Brussels organizes its fourth World's fair.
1960	Congo wins its independence.
	For cooking, 36 percent of Belgians use coal, 35 percent use gas, 24 percent use propane gas, and 5 percent use electricity.
1966	The average lunch takes 34 minutes (compared to 25 minutes in the year 2000).
1974	Jambon d'Ardenne (ham of the Ardennes) is legally protected in Belgium (and since 1996 by the European Union under the status of Protected Geographical Indicator).
1978	First McDonald's restaurant in Belgium opens in Brussels.
1981	The Academie voor Streekgebonden Gastronomie (Academy of Regional Gastronomy), devoted to the history and culture of local food, is established.

1992	The Nutritional Information Centre (NICE) is launched.
1999	The dioxin crisis breaks out, followed by a genuine food scare and political upheaval.
2001	The home espresso machine is launched.
2002	Belgium adopts the euro.
	Public barbecue with thousands of participants introduces large public works in Antwerp.
2003	The annual carnival (Mardi Gras) of the little town of Binche is named a UNESCO world heritage site.
	Belgium wins World Barbecue Championship.
2004	The government's price control for bread is abolished.
2005	The National Food and Health Plan (following the 2004 national food survey) is presented.
	The average family expenditure on food reaches 12.1 percent of total spending.
	Westvleteren Abt 12 is chosen as the best beer of the world.
2007	Food prices increase more than the average price inflation.
	Geraardbergse mattentaart, Vlaams-Brabantse tafeldruiven and Beurre d'Ardenne (respectively, cheese cake from Geraardsbergen, table grapes from Flemish Brabant, and butter from the Ardennes) are put on the EU list of Protected Designation of Origin.
2008	The Week of Taste is organized for the third time, involving dozens of activities related to good food. The TV program *Mijn restaurant* (My restaurant) reaches tens of thousands of viewers, leading to a new gastronomic hype in Flanders.

1

Historical Overview

The country of Belgium came into being in 1830 when the southern provinces of the United Kingdom of the Netherlands revolted against their king. Yet, 2,000 years ago in his *De Bello Gallico* Julius Caesar mentioned the *Belgae* who lived between the rivers Marne and Seine (in present-day France) on the one hand and the river Rhine (in present-day Germany) on the other. He referred to a wider territory than that of modern Belgium (including, for example, the towns of Reims and Trier, today in France and Germany, respectively), but the word *Belgae* and Caesar's line "Out of all of those Gauls the Belgians are the most brave" have been used to show long-term Belgian roots. After the Roman conquest of these lands, a province of the Roman Empire by the name of *Gallia Belgica* existed. A prominent nineteenth-century Belgian historian referred to the Treaty of Verdun in the year 843 to find tangible traces of a Belgian nation, and the term *Belgique* was used in various ways prior to 1830, not in the least with the proclamation of the *Etats Belgiques Unis* (the United States of Belgium) in 1790.[1]

In 1830, thus, a small state of about 12,500 square miles, the size of the state of Maryland, was a new fact.[2] Bordered by the Netherlands in the north, Germany and Luxembourg in the east, France in the south, and the North Sea in the west (with England nearby), the country has three distinct geographical regions—lower, central, and upper Belgium. Since long ago these regions have been relentlessly modified by draining and cultivating land; removing and planting woods; building towns, roads, and bridges; constructing ports; changing waterways' beds; and building work-shops and factories. Lower Belgium is flat (under 350 feet above sea level), with 40 miles of coast and sandy beaches. Right behind the beaches come the *polders*, an area that was once frequently flooded but that has long been dry and fertile because of sluices. The Flemish lowlands run from the polders up to the north toward the Kempen, with some hills but mostly flat; fertile soil alternates with poor soil. Central Belgium (between 350 and 700 feet above sea level) was once part of an extensive forest running from northern France to beyond the Ruhr region in Germany. It has very fruitful clay plateaus and many gentle hills. Upper Belgium (700 feet or more above sea level; the highest point of the country reaches 2,300 feet) is full of woods, with large, fertile valleys and plateaus. Large and small rivers and canals, motorways, and railroads run through the country, con-necting it directly with ports and cities abroad.

Today, Belgium has quite a complex institutional shape. Five state reforms between 1970 and 2001 reorganized the country into three com-munities based on language (Flemish, French, and German) and three regions (the Flemish region, the Brussels Capital Region, and the Wal-loon region). Each has their own parliament and government. These reforms did not abolish the federal parliament and government with its prime minister, so now this little country of about 10 million people has seven parliaments and six governments.

Belgium is one of the most densely populated countries of Europe (340 inhabitants per square kilometer), and it is the fifteenth richest country in the world (gross domestic product per person in 2008 is estimated at $42,000); Antwerp is the third most important harbor of Europe (rank-ing 12th worldwide), and Brussels hosts the headquarters of the North Atlantic Treaty Organization (NATO), the European Union (EU), and many international corporations. Some authors explain Belgium's inter-national role by referring to the country's central geographical location, but actually Belgium's intermediate cultural, economic, social, and politi-cal position amid the big European players is crucial. This intermediary and central position has characterized Belgium since ancient times.

EARLIEST INHABITANTS

Some 20,000 years ago, modern humans entered what now is Belgium.[3] In this period, humans combined hunting with foraging and fishing. The gathering of roots, leaves, berries, and nuts was probably very important in the human diet, but it is hardly documented. Families lived in caves and simple huts. They used axes, knives, spears, arrows, and bows for hunting reindeer, bear, wolf, lynx, and, with the warming of the climate in the Mesolithic period (c. 10,000 B.C.–c. 5000 B.C.), increasingly deer and wild boar. In this period, food was preserved through smoking and drying. Around 4000 B.C. hunting became more difficult because the woods had become much denser. As a result, meat was less available, and people consumed more nuts, roots, mushrooms, wild eggs, and wild fruit (apples and berries), while fishing became prominent, as in the Meuse basin where considerable amounts of freshwater fish were eaten.[4] In the village of Spiennes (near Mons) an extensive flint mine operated between 4000 and 750 B.C., producing spearheads, needles, fishhooks, and other tools for hunting, fishing, and laboring. Migrants, who probably traveled via the rivers running through the continent, such as the Danube and Rhine rivers, gradually introduced agriculture into western Europe. Domesticated animals and farming appeared between 2600 and 1900 B.C. in northwestern Europe (Neolithic period), causing a definite revolution.

Farming implied not only the tilling of land (crops included cereals, peas, lentils, and herbs such as parsley) but also the use of utensils for storing the crop (ceramic pottery) and for milling (grindstones). Moreover, with agriculture the notion of ownership (of land, tools, and know-how) became much more important. Small parcels of land were plowed, and primitive forms of wheat (emmer, einkorn) and barley were harvested. These parcels were abandoned when yields diminished over time, leading to frequent moves in search of new land. These farmers owned cattle, sheep, goats, and pigs. Goats were primarily used for milk (which was drunk as such and used for making white cheese), while sheep were kept for wool; the meat of cattle and pigs was eaten. The growing consumption of vegetable products led to a fall in fish consumption, like in the Meuse basin. Farmers' houses were large and often consisted of three parts: one for people, a second for keeping animals, and a third for storing food and tools. Most people combined foraging, fishing, and agriculture with some hunting and, gradually, trading. Miners from Spiennes, for example, seem not to have produced their own food and most likely traded goods for food instead.

By 1800 B.C. several small settlements could be found near the coast, in the plains of present-day Flanders and in the region between the Sambre and Meuse rivers. By then, farmers had learned about crops and had selected those cereals with the best yields. Domesticated horses were used for transport, riding, and food. New agricultural tools appeared, such as the one-piece wooden shovel, the sickle, and the simple plow; manure was mixed with the soil to increase harvests. Bronze objects (tools, weapons, and jewels) became fashionable around 2000 B.C. and were imported from faraway regions (some coming from Egypt via numerous steps). So-called lords' graves indicate the existence of strict hierarchical communities with rich and poor people; most likely, warriors and their offspring, living in fortified settlements, ruled in particular areas and levied taxes. These families consumed meat regularly, whereas the common people had to make do with legumes, milk, and cereals that were ground, mixed with water, and heated to make porridge or baked into bread (leavened with the foam of beer).

With the use of iron to fabricate tools and weapons, the Iron Age, c. 700 B.C.–1 B.C., began. In contrast to bronze, iron was available locally and thus cheaper and more widespread. The area around present-day Liège became a center of iron making. By 250 B.C. the Celts, people who migrated from central Europe to the west (and up to Ireland), had introduced the wheel plow and the three-field system that consisted of dividing the land into three parts of which two were tilled and one "rested" in a given year. They also introduced chicken, ducks, and geese, as well as mead (a fermented mixture of water and honey) and beer (germinated barley and wheat that was heated and fermented). The Celts in Britain preserved meat, fish, and butter and exported these products to the Continent.[5] On the whole, for thousands of years, the diet of the common people remained simple. Food production did improve, which did not lead to more and varied food but instead allowed the population to increase gradually.

In the first century B.C., Caesar's *De Bello Gallico* informs about the society of the region that forms present-day Belgium. His was the first written account of this region.[6] Caesar referred to its inhabitants as wild, having little contact with merchants or other travelers, and regularly quarreling and fighting among themselves as well as against the people living across the Rhine River, the Germans. They lived in agricultural communities headed by chieftains, which were part of a larger tribe under the command of aristocratic families. Some of these settlements had the aspect of a modest town. Along with the mass of workers, there were druids (or priests) and warriors. Cereals were produced; sheep, goats, and pigs were kept; and pottery, cloth, and iron tools were manufactured. Caesar marched into Gaul in 57 B.C. to defend the Roman Empire against continuing German invasions and Gallic disputes. It took six years, many wars, and tens of thousands of dead to defeat the *Belgae*. Once this was done, a new food revolution was apparent.

GALLO-ROMANS

After protests, revolts, and severe oppression, the *Belgae* lands were incorporated as *Gallia Belgica* into the Roman Empire and remained so for four centuries.[7] This implied the continuing presence of troops and the construction of a dense road network that ran through this province from west to east and north to south, connecting settlements, for example, Boulogne to Tongeren, Maastricht to Reims, and Beauvais to Aardenburg. Some of these, like Boulogne or Tongeren, evolved into important commercial and political towns. These towns were linked to Marseille and Rome via Lyons. Roads were meant for moving troops quickly but were also used for trading goods, a major business. In Tongeren, for example, a salt merchant managed to make a fortune, which shows the importance of trade and of salt as a product to preserve food. In the commercial streets of this town, artisans, bakers (producing simple and elaborate breads with honey, fat, or spices), butchers, brewers, and traders (who imported goods like wine, olives, olive oil, fish sauce [garum], figs, cucumbers, and fine ceramics) sold their goods to town dwellers, foreigners, and country folks. Some of these foodstuffs came from Lyons and southern Spain.

Along the roads vici were established in the countryside. These were small settlements where justice was administered, travelers could rest, and markets were held. Some of these vici developed into local centers (for example, Bruges, Tournai, Ghent, or Namur). In regions with poor soil, houses were built that resembled those of the Iron Age: rectangular dwellings made of wood and loam and covered with straw. In fertile regions, however, a new form of building was introduced. A good example of a flourishing vicus can be found in what is now the town of Tienen, where an estate of 3,800 square feet was established, with several stone buildings used for residences (with modest bath installations) as well as for storage. The estate was also in charge of 125 acres of land. This vicus attracted traders and artisans who manufactured iron objects, cloth, and pottery.

The Romans introduced a new way of farming, in which the villa played a central role. Villae in Gallia Belgica copied the Roman type, with heated floors, bath installations, and nicely decorated rooms for the landowners, living space for the laborers, workshops, stables, and storage rooms. Some of these villae had up to 100 rooms. The landowner organized the farm work, hired hands, distributed foodstuffs, paid taxes, purchased tools and animals, sold products at the market, and leased land out to smaller farmers. The farming was oriented toward the needs of the community, as had long been the case, but an increasing part of the produce was now sold at the market or sent to the local government (to feed the soldiers or to be sent to Rome and other cities). Moreover, grain and salted hams were sent to towns all over Europe. Money, prices, and wages became important. The partition of the land into rectangular parcels (commonly 230 feet by 230 feet) facilitated the use of the plow and the process of harvesting.

On fertile land wheat, barley, and spelt were grown, and on poorer soil legumes were cultivated.

Because of the town dwellers' and soldiers' need for more food, measures were taken around the year 100 to increase yields: land was deforested, rye was cultivated on poor soils, more animals were kept for meat, milk, and manure, and a simple but pioneering harvesting machine was applied. All this resulted in increased production, local and distant trade, the amassing of profit, and an increase in social differences. Beans, lentils, and other legumes were grown in gardens near the *villa*. New vegetables, herbs, and fruit were introduced but only gradually cultivated (like beets, cabbages, carrots, onions, thyme, coriander, dill, plums, and peaches). In the second century A.D. these new varieties became more widespread.[8]

Animals were important: horses and oxen were used for transport and working the land, goats were kept for milk (which was drunk and used for making cheese and butter), and pigs, sheep, and chickens provided meat. Cattle breeding developed smoothly from the last quarter of the first century, as the introduction of Mediterranean breeds made the local sorts heavier, with more meat. Pork was much appreciated (following Rome's habits), and some regions in *Gallia Belgica* specialized in salted ham that was exported to Rome, where it was particularly liked.

The burial place *(tumulus)* near Tienen demonstrates the food variety of the Gallo-Romans during the first and second centuries. In addition to pottery, a multitude of foodstuffs appears: cereals (barley, wheat, spelt), legumes (lentils, beans, peas), fruit (plums, cherries, pears, grapes), nuts (walnuts, hazelnuts), as well as olives, bread, cake, porridge, salt, and fennel.[9] For the vast majority of the Gallo-Romans, however, the daily meals were sober. *Puls*, a porridge, was the main dish: spelt, barley, or millet was mixed with milk and water, then heated, and olive oil was added; it was consumed with peas or lentils.[10] Bread was important, too, and some sorts were enriched with fat, honey, or legumes. The high calorie content of the latter bread was perfect for soldiers and land laborers, although its consumption fluctuated with the price. Meat was eaten only rarely. It was roasted or put in a stew with cereals and vegetables. Freshwater fish (such as eel, trout, or pike) was consumed regularly. Fruit was eaten after the meal. Mostly water was drunk but also milk, beer, and wine (the last was mixed with water and spices). Richer people must have had more meat and wine, although frugality was a common virtue, as in the whole of the Roman Empire. During a *convivium*, or a social gathering, however, abundance was accepted and encouraged. This was primarily a matter of consumption of enormous amounts of fine meats. In Tongeren in the second century, for example, a feast was organized where suckling pig, chicken, lamb, partridge, woodcock, and hare were served, while diners at another feast in the same town had lamb, pigeon, hare, duck, woodcock, trout, perch, and carp. These dishes were prepared according to the much-elaborated Roman style and served to diners lying on beds, eating the food with the right hand, and enjoying entertainment and conversation.

The *Belgae* assimilated many Roman foodways. More food was produced, new foods were introduced, the rich adopted sophisticated food styles, and trade became a source of high profits. The Romans left other traces as well with consequences lasting to the present day. First, in the fourth century Christianity arrived along with the traders and army men. Tongeren got a bishop in the late fourth century, and Tournai in the fifth. Second, the road between Cologne and Boulogne made somewhat of a border, with influence by Celts and Germans north of it, but greater impact of Romans south of it. This led to Belgium's linguistic richness and division up to today.

MONKS AND FEUDALISM

In the fourth century, Rome's authority had weakened owing to internal disputes and wars as well as to permanent efforts to secure the empire's extensive borders. These efforts could not prevent the Germans and Franks from invading *Gallia Belgica*, destroying *villae*, *vici* and towns, killing thousands of people, and disrupting trade and agriculture. The Gallo-Romans consequently deserted settlements such as the *vicus* of Bruges. By then, however, the economy of this province had already encountered great difficulties: the population, agricultural production, and trade had diminished, while social inequality and prices increased. German and Frankish migrants and warriors encountered no great obstacles to settling in these weakened lands. They grew grain and kept animals for meat, milk, and hides in addition to hunting game and gathering wild fruits and nuts. They preferred butter over olive oil, and ale over wine. They disliked some Roman food habits, such as the fish sauce, or frugality.

Gradually, Gallo-Romans came to consider the Germans and Franks as great warriors with noble and fair judgments, as opposed to the relapsing, weak Romans.[11] In the fifth century there was no Roman or other central authority in Gaul. Some Frankish invaders managed to establish lasting power, like Childeric, who had his court in the old Roman town of Tournai in the last quarter of the fifth century. Around the year 500, Childeric's son, known by the Latinized name of Clovis, managed to unite most of the territories of ancient Gallia, which included present-day Belgium.

While the Greek physician Anthimus was ambassador to Clovis's son, he wrote *De observatione ciborum*, in which he adapted recipes from Apicius (*De re coquinaria* [On cookery], late fourth century); it was the last cookbook in the west for almost 1,000 years. Anthimus took into account the likes and dislikes of the Frankish aristocrats, although under the influence of the physician Galen, he also offered health recommendations.[12] Recipes for pork (especially bacon), lamb, veal, and young goat are numerous. Beef, on the contrary, was not recommended, and Anthimus wrote that it should be cooked two or three times before serving. *Cervoise* (or ale) was deemed good for digestion, but butter consumption was discouraged. There are many recipes for fowls and game, which were high in the food hierarchy. Anthimus mentions stylish ingredients (foie gras) and methods of preparation (*afratus*, a delicate poultry dish with eggs that are whipped and then poached). Pepper, *costus* (*Saussurea lappa*), spikenard, and clove were advised for seasoning the meals.

Clovis converted to Christianity and made it the official religion; however, it took centuries before *Francia* was Christianized. The role of monasteries was crucial in the dispersion of Christianity. Monasteries were semifortified places with large gardens, dwellings, stables, and workshops. They were often founded with the aid of nobles and aristocrats who gave land and rights, which made most monasteries strong economic players. For example, Saint-Bavo and Saint-Peter, both in Ghent, evolved into very powerful institutions, producing and trading goods and having important political weight. Christianity combined various elements of old Mediterranean religions, among which were the symbolic significance of bread and wine and regular asceticism. It was forbidden to eat meat on Wednesdays and Fridays, as well as during particular periods in the year, like Lent (the 40 days of fasting and prayer before Easter). This led to a great number of meatless days; for example, Saint John's Hospital in Bruges observed no fewer than 195 fasting days per year.[13] As a consequence, once more and more people had converted to Christianity, less meat was consumed in the tenth and eleventh centuries, while bread, fish, and eggs became more popular. This, however, seems not to have resulted solely from the influence of religion but may also have been linked to necessity, given that meat had become rarer and thus costlier.

People living in the small villages of Torgny (in the present-day province of Luxembourg) and Ciply (near Mons) between the sixth and eight centuries did consume a lot of meat and dairy products but hardly any fish, thus indicating little influence of religion in that area and period.[14] In both villages, men and women consumed similar amounts of animal proteins. A couple of centuries later, nobility and common people in the town of Namur did consume fish: herring for the more modest folks and cod, haddock, whiting, and mussels for the count and his court. A clear difference between both groups also appeared with regard to meat consumption, with the count consuming large amounts of pork, fowls, and game, but the common people small quantities of beef, hare, and wild birds.[15] In the twelfth century, the monks of the Dune monastery in Koksijde, a village on the coast, did eat a lot of fish and crustaceans (reaching up to 30 percent of their total protein intake). The monastery exploited a fishpond and a workshop for salting the fish. These monks also consumed meat, dairy products, cereals, and vegetables, which made them generally healthy people.

By the year 800, Charlemagne ruled over large portions of western Europe, including present-day France, Germany, the Netherlands, Belgium, and parts of Italy. His sons divided this territory into three parts. Feudalism (the exchange of land for military support between lord and vassal) became widespread, and several counts and dukes reigned over territories of different sizes, with different powers and responding to different lords. The Liège area evolved into a prince-bishopric (and remained separate from the neighboring lands for almost 1,000 years), while the counts of Flanders gained power through marriages and alliances (although they were vassals of both the king of France and the German emperor). These lands faced invasions by plundering Vikings, who in 879 sailed up the Scheldt River to Ghent, and their inhabitants dealt with agricultural difficulties and had to cope with roaming poor. In general, for most people, life was hard, with food insecurity, regular starvation, fluctuating prices, and huge social differences that appeared especially through greatly diverging meat consumption.

BRUGES IN THE THIRTEENTH TO FIFTEENTH CENTURIES

In the eleventh century, agriculture had slowly recovered by reusing old techniques and by applying several innovations such as the heavier plow, windmills, or the shoulder collar for draught animals. Draining and deforesting revealed new land. Moreover, and crucially, in Flanders the centuries-old technique of crop rotation gave way to a new intensive method of land use: land was no longer left to rest for one or more years but was instead intensively fertilized to produce clover that enriched the soil and could be used as forage for animals, which in turn provided more manure. This system, later copied in England and many other regions, allowed two harvests per year and alternating crops, which led to more attention to growing vegetables and fruit and raising animals (yielding more meat, milk, dairy products, wool, and leather). More food meant more people and trade, which led to more wealth and power for some. A complex relationship between lords and towns came into being, with towns obtaining rights and lords receiving financial support. Small, almost-forgotten places revived, and other bigger ones developed further, resulting in a dense network of towns and marketplaces like Antwerp, Bruges, Brussels, Dinant, Ghent, Kortrijk, Leuven, Liège, Mechelen, Namur, and Tournai, which were connected by roads and waterways. These places flourished: more people came to live there, towns expanded, and some artisans, bankers, and traders became very rich, paying for exquisite houses, artworks, and feasts. The regular, disastrous bubonic plagues in Europe between 1347 and 1459 did encumber this development to a large extent. However, these left the population with larger food supplies than before, although agriculture met with difficulties due to the lack of workers. The shortage of workers in turn led to increasing wages, which allowed common workers to buy more food, especially meat. As a consequence, in the fourteenth and fifteenth centuries, more meat was consumed.

In the late thirteenth century, the town of Bruges grew to become the most important place in Europe.[16] It had long been a vital market for cloth, but when Italians began to sail directly to Bruges, avoiding the long and costly land roads, and once Italian traders and bankers had become established in town, Bruges became the European center of trade and finance as well. Virtually everything was available for sale, whether spices from India, luxury goods from Tuscany and Córdoba, or the finest local tapestries. Traders from all over Europe met in Bruges. Wealth became apparent in manifold forms, and lavish eating was one of them. When in 1302 the son of the count of Flanders spent 11 weeks in Bruges, he was offered fowls (chicken, pigeon, goose, and partridge), meat (pork, lamb, and beef), and fish (salmon, plaice and sturgeon, mackerel, flounder, lobster, sea hog, and gray mullet). During fast days, poultry, meat, eggs, butter, cheese, and milk were not eaten, which explains the high and varied fish consumption.[17] When the duchess Isabella of Portugal stayed in Bruges in 1450, huge quantities of lamb were served.[18]

A 1473 Ghent manuscript containing recipes mentions several sophisticated ways of preparing dishes. Braised pears, for example, turn into a sophisticated dish: the pears should be served on silver plates to obtain a nice contrast of colors; when the pears are braised, the stalk of the pear should be covered in order not to lose its green color; pears could be cut into four parts, in such a way that each would stand up; cloves would be inserted into each part; a red sauce on top should be sufficiently gluey to hold the sugared aniseed on the pear.[19] The same care as in preparing this dessert is also found in the way the food was presented: white tablecloth, napkins, plants, flowers, and aromatic spices were placed on the table, and knives, spoons, cups, and glasses were on hand. The dishes were full of color with the use of saffron, ginger, or galangal root and were given a finishing touch with chopped hard-boiled eggs and parsley. Sauces were important, and the composition of a dish was meant to be a delight for the eye. Those who could afford it frequently had large and small feasts. The towns' administrators, guild leaders, and clergy enjoyed lavish meals that in general were organized according to strict rules and were meant to confirm social ties and hierarchies. Big, solemn meals consisted of up to six courses, often ending with cheese. Each course had various dishes that were put on the table together. Fresh grapes, oranges, figs, and other exotic fruits were available. Wine, of course, was drunk.

The common people loved to feast too (as a reaction to the many fast days), which the towns' magistrates tried to control (but mostly failed to). These feasts were much simpler: enough bread, beer, and meat were consumed, but fruit pies, pancakes, and waffles were served too. The general welfare of the towns spread to almost all social layers in this period. Affluent consumption by the rich provided jobs and income to many. The proportion of butchers, bakers, brewers, and other caterers increased slowly in Bruges in the first half of the fourteenth century. The textile industry paid well, and poor relief was organized in a far better way than before. In the thirteenth and fourteenth centuries several writers and poets denounced and mocked what they called the opulent eating of the peasants. Most people, however, ate huge quantities of bread, sometimes up to 2.2 pounds per person per day.[20] This high consumption entailed severe regulation of the price and weight of bread by the city administration, because a shortage of bread, rapidly increasing prices, or fraud could lead to social and political turbulence. The high bread consumption also implied that grain traders, millers, and bakers were powerful people in town. The bread of the common folks was made of rye flour that had been sifted to some degree and was eaten with butter, cheese, or some simple meat. Each day a stew was prepared, which consisted of seasonal vegetables (carrots, peas, leeks, beans, cabbages, or turnips), some grains, and, when affordable, salted meat.

People staying in hospitals in Bruges around 1400 had a rather rich and varied diet.[21] These were sick, old, and poor people but also travelers and *proveniers* (country folks seeking safety in town). Despite some difficult years (due to high prices, bubonic plagues, and turmoil), the average diet improved. The dwellers had mostly wheat bread, but bread consumption declined in the early fifteenth century. Beef and lamb were consumed widely, but pork, poultry, and game were nearly absent, which indicates the modest social status of the inhabitants. Butter was increasingly eaten, but cheese consumption declined accordingly. Local vegetables and fruit were eaten according to the seasons, but "exotic" fruit was consumed as well, which implies that it was imported on a large scale and was within the means of the more common people. Milk was rarely drunk, except by some sick people, whereas up to a quart of beer and 10 ounces of wine per day were consumed.

ANTWERP IN THE FIFTEENTH TO SEVENTEENTH CENTURIES

As a result of the silting up of the waterway that linked Bruges to the North Sea, the importance of the town declined in the late fifteenth century. The town's notoriety, however, was such that it took another century before it lost most of its economic and cultural importance (to revive only in the twentieth century). Other towns like Brussels, Ghent, Mechelen, and, in particular, Antwerp were ready to take over the role of Bruges beginning in the late fifteenth century. Brussels, Ghent, and Mechelen frequently hosted a court, but not so Antwerp: this became the city of big merchants, bankers, and insurance agents. If Bruges had been the staple and money market of Europe and the Near East in the fifteenth century, Antwerp became this for the world in the sixteenth century.[22] Backed by a relatively stable political situation—the unification of the Low Countries (broadly present-day Belgium and the Netherlands) under Charles V that became part of an empire "where the sun always shines"—the city kept this role for almost 100 years. Then, its position was taken over by Amsterdam due to the trade and sailing innovations in Amsterdam and, especially, to the religious and social revolt against the Spanish king in the southern part of the Low Countries. This led to the fall of Antwerp in 1585 and the radical repression of the rebellion, after which the Low Countries were divided into two. Yet, even after Antwerp's decline in 1585, the city managed to maintain a dominant role in the Low Countries as an economic and cultural center.

During the sixteenth century, Antwerp served as the marketplace for all possible goods coming in from all over the world, which at that time included new items from the Americas (among them foods that later entered people's diet, such as cocoa, potatoes, tomatoes, and turkey). Also, Antwerp exported many goods to a great variety of places. As with Bruges and later Amsterdam, the fact that Antwerp was a seaport made many goods readily available to well-off inhabitants. Sixteenth-century Antwerp was *the* place of innovation. Trade with the rich hinterland (in woolen and linen cloth, tapestry, cabinets, art, and foodstuffs like butter, cheese, salted meats, and beer) secured booming business in the whole of the Low Countries. The doubling of Antwerp's population within 50 years, the swift expansion of the built area, the superb artistic productions, and the rapid industrial development demonstrate Antwerp's golden age. A telling example of industrial development is the beer industry.[23] Around 1530 Antwerp's beer production was poor, of low quality, and hardly exported, but owing to large-scale investments in water supply and the building of an entire new district that was used for breweries, the beer quality improved and production almost tripled within two decades. By 1570, 25 percent of Antwerp's beer production was exported to three other important beer-brewing areas: Holland, Germany, and England.

The affluence of Antwerp's golden age is reflected in the teeming attention to food. Renowned painters depicted the tables of the city's affluent residents, as, for example, David Teniers's *Kitchen Scene* (1644) showing various fish and meats, decorated fowls, 18 chickens being roasted at once, fruit, hams, little breads, a superbly decorated meat pastry, and fine glasswork, large copper pans, and other utensils, as well as the cooks at work.[24] This is also the period when the first cookbook of the Low Countries was printed: *Een notabel boecxken van cokeryen* (A little notable book of cooking; Brussels, c. 1510), meant for the affluent bourgeoisie and not for aristocratic households.[25] It shows many features of the early Middle Ages, although new interest in beef had appeared, and southern European and Arabic traces (for example, almonds as a thickening agent) are present as well. Out of 169 recipes, the book contains 28 recipes for beef and veal, 6 for mutton and lamb, and only 10 for pork. Recipes for poultry, rabbit and hare, and salted and smoked meats are also given. Milk appears ten times, cream five times, and cheese eight times as an ingredient. In later cookbooks, the proportion of recipes with milk and dairy products increased markedly, which reflected the gradually increasing importance of dairy production in the region. Later cookbooks include milk preparations for fish, cakes, curd, and other sweet desserts.

Antonius Magirus's *Koocboec oft familieren keukenboec* (Cookbook or the everyday recipe book), first published in Leuven in 1612, with two reprints in Antwerp in 1655 and 1663, testifies to the particular foodways of the Spanish Netherlands (as these lands were called after the division of the Low Countries) in the seventeenth century.[26] The author's introduction is telling: in a witty way he opposes the many moralistic treatises against copious food consumption by stressing moderate but tasteful eating and drinking. He translated much of Bartolomeo Scappi's *Opera dell' arte del cucinare* (1570), a then-almost-classic Renaissance cookbook, but selected recipes and adapted these to local habits and tastes. By so doing, he contributed to the diffusion of a new way of cooking in the Low Countries, which was less oriented toward heavy (meat) cuisine, plenty of sauces and spices, and colorful presentations and much more toward light and refined dishes, prepared with herbs and vegetables, and ways to accentuate the flavor of the ingredients. Magirus's cookbook contains 141 recipes (Scappi had published 1,017 recipes), including recipes using vegetables (25 varieties, including artichokes, beans, cucumbers, and asparagus), fruit (pears, cherries, and oranges), pastry and dessert (marzipan, "eggs from Lombardy" or sabayon, and fruit pies), processed meats (sausages and various stews), fish, eggs, sauces, poultry (including the newly introduced turkey), savory pies (*toerten*, with bacon and cheese, but also often with vegetables), and game. Milk, cream, and cheese were used moderately. Another cookbook was *Ouverture de cuisine* (Opening the kitchen; Liège, 1604), published by Lancelot de Casteau, the chef "to three princes," who likewise used and adapted Scappi's recipes, thus diffusing them into the French-speaking parts of the Low Countries.

Interest in food materialized not only in printed cookbooks but also in the practice of eating and drinking lavishly. According to some seventeenth-century writers, this was the case for *all* inhabitants of Antwerp. As in Bruges in earlier times, this lavish consumption was ridiculed and criticized, for example, by the famous Dutch playwright Bredero (1585–1618). The Antwerp guilds (which organized and controlled the city's trades) offer an adequate example of this lavish eating and drinking.[27] Guilds' board members consumed meals that the governor of the Spanish Netherlands considered excessive, comparing the eaters with beasts. In 1659, for example, a dinner included veal, partridge, chicken, duck, ham, sole, savory and sweet pies, vegetables, bread, butter, cheese, fruit, and (sugared) nuts. Other guilds' menus of the seventeenth and eighteenth centuries mention pastries, roasted meats, turkey, hare, smoked sole, carp, and a great variety of desserts (nuts, fruit, cheese, and little pastries). All was digested with beer ("as much as necessary") and wine. Some of these feasts lasted for five days. In 1658 the food and drink consumed by the board members of the Antwerp transport workers' guild represented 38 percent of total spending by the guild (religious expenditures accounted for only 29 percent). Dining lavishly in those years was meant not only to show wealth but also to endorse political power by fostering and renewing contacts with politicians, bankers, other merchants, lawyers, and all other persons who mattered. In the course of the eighteenth century the opulence of the guild meals diminished, which may be explained by generally increasing prices, legal limitation of the guilds' expenses, and their diminishing political influence.

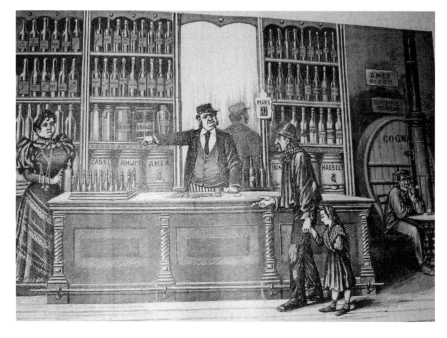

An imagined interior of a Belgian café in the 1890s. A man has no money to pay for a drink and is shown the way out. Note the many tagged bottles (on the right, *Hasselt* stands for gin). From *Le Bien Social*, 1894.

The dinners and banquets of the affluent differed immensely from the fare of the common people. Daily life oscillated around the price of bread. If prices were high (due to poor harvests, political trouble, or war), all resources were directed toward the buying of bread, which limited all other expenses. A low bread price, however, allowed the purchasing of other food and goods.[28] In an expensive year, the cost of bread for simple households amounted to 70 percent of total spending, but in cheap years, it reached only 30 percent. Then, more meat, butter, and cheese could be purchased. A soldier's ration in Antwerp in 1568 included rye bread, two liters of beer, cheese, butter, salt, peas or beans, and some salted meat (for soup), which provided him with a daily energy intake of 3,900 calories.[29] The overwhelming importance of bread, of which each person ate about 2.2 pounds per day, determined daily behavior, expectations, and feelings of satiation. When prices were low, laborers tended to work less and preferred more leisure time, which often implied a visit to a pub. High prices, however, led to discontent, protests, and occasionally brutal outbursts. Local, regional, and central governments were well aware of this relationship and tried to regulate the production and trade of grain and bread as well as the number of leisure days. In the short run, thus, the common people's food fluctuated highly, but in the long run, rye bread, vegetable stews, and cheap beer were the norm.

Due to population pressure in the seventeenth and eighteenth centuries, food became more expensive, and little by little the common people's diet deteriorated: less meat, dairy products, and expensive beer were consumed. In the last quarter of the eighteenth century, however, the influence of bread diminished when the poor started to eat potatoes out of pure necessity. At first, potatoes were seen as pigs' fodder, but under pressure of some extremely costly years and the enduring hunger, they were increasingly eaten. By 1830, they had become a basic food for the poor, and, surprisingly, a regular ingredient in rich people's cuisine as well.

LIÈGE IN THE EIGHTEENTH AND NINETEENTH CENTURIES

Antwerp totally missed the so-called industrial revolution of the eighteenth and nineteenth centuries. It remained a port of some importance but failed to attract mills and workshops powered by steam-driven machines. Only in the late nineteenth century did Antwerp recover as a vital port that attracted new industries. Liège and Mons, and their hinterlands, on the contrary, were extremely successful in the eighteenth and early nineteenth centuries in that they contributed greatly to putting Belgium on the map as the second most industrialized nation of Europe, right after England. By 1900, Belgium was one of the richest countries of the world, with an amazing industrial output for its small size. For ages, Liège had specialized in metalworks (producing products such as guns, nails, tools, and machines), coal mining, and textiles (in the neighboring town of Verviers). The area around Mons had focused on coal mining. These goods have been in demand since the Iron Age, but persisting population pressure throughout Europe during the eighteenth century, and the ensuing greater needs for agricultural tools and cloth, had caused the demand for coal and metal to soar considerably. In 1720, the first steam engine was installed in Liège, in 1734 a steam-driven pump was set up in a coal pit in Pâturages (a village near Mons), and in 1799 two audacious entrepreneurs bought a fully equipped mechanical textile mill in Verviers. These initiatives revolutionized the modes of production of continental Europe.

When the legal limitations of the prince-bishopric disappeared around 1800 and trade was promoted subsequently via the French Empire, the United Kingdom of the Netherlands, and, since 1830, very laissez-faire Belgium, a thriving industrial century began. Industrialization necessitated banking services, a new entrepreneurial mentality oriented toward daring investments, efficient roads and communications, reliable trade arrangements, sufficient skilled and unskilled workers, and the nonstop search for technological, commercial, and labor improvements. All this was at hand in Wallonia in the first decades of the nineteenth century. The provinces of Hainault and Liège utilized 64 steam engines in 1804 but 1,334 in 1850, an exceptional growth in a key component of economic modernization. Liège, Mons, and their hinterlands changed the world's outlook, putting an end to the millennium-old prevalence of agriculture and trade in creating prosperity. Industrialization advanced rapidly in Wallonia but hardly at all in Flanders (where only Ghent had modern mills), initiating a contrast within the young state of Belgium: alongside the language border, an economic split had appeared. Thousands of unskilled Flemish workers left impoverished Flanders for the industrial basins of Wallonia or northern France, and some tried their luck in the United States.

Merchants, noblemen, bankers, some artisans, retailers, and adventurers amassed fortunes that were partly reinvested in the industry, partly used to purchase property, but also to show steps on the road to success. The Warocqué family, living in Morlanwelz near Mons, provides a great example of a rich family with an extravagant lifestyle.[30] By exploiting mines, introducing new machinery, purchasing and selling land and houses, and reinvesting profits, this family became one of the wealthiest of Belgium around 1900. Its members were friends with the most powerful people in Belgium and Europe. Around 1840, this family spent 460 francs daily on food, housing, clothing, and other items, which was half the yearly salary of a miner. A luxury lifestyle including travel throughout Europe and, later, the world, many feasts, specialized hobbies, exclusive sports, magnificent architecture in houses and gardens, several sumptuous redecorations of the manor, and purchases of the latest fads (for example, an automobile in 1895) marked every step of success, strengthened social and commercial networks, and demonstrated the absolutely lighthearted lifestyle.

Dinners, luncheons, celebrations, and soirées were a central part of the Warocqué's lifestyle, although the daily meals were elaborate too. Mutton, beef, game, poultry, fowl, fish, hare, and diverse processed meats (*un pâté de bécasse truffé*, or a pastry of snipes with truffles, costing 30 francs in the 1840s, equivalent to the daily pay of 15 miners) were prepared in large quantities. Huge amounts of fish were bought to prepare in the kitchen as well as to put in the fishponds. Oysters, lobster, and scallops were particularly appreciated. Vegetables were rarely purchased, because they were supplied from the *potager* (the manor's garden where 22 different sorts of vegetables were grown), but exotic fruits like pineapple, oranges, lemons, and melons were bought regularly at extremely high prices.

The scale of eating and drinking appears particularly when people were entertained. When the Duke of Brabant visited the Warocqué family in 1852, he was served foie gras, ortolan (a small fowl), and truffled pheasant, three of the most costly dishes. At the dinner celebrating the 50-year career of a mining engineer in 1897, the 389 diners were served a Portuguese soup, Monglas pastries, cold salmon, *filet de boeuf à la béarnaise* (filet of beef with a delicate herb and butter sauce), potatoes *à la maître d'hôtel*, pork *sauce Vincent* (mayonnaise with herbs and spinach), peas *à l'Anglaise* (cream sauce with pickles), chicken with watercress, ham in jelly, salad, ice cream, cake, and fruit (along with 250 bottles of Bordeaux, 127 bottles of Burgundy, 42 bottles of port, and 112 bottles of champagne). This menu reflected the then-traditional dinner that the French cook and culinary writer Antoine Carême (1784–1833) had conceived and that was launched in the 1800s to become very successful in Europe between 1850 and 1910. It differed from the eighteenth-century luxury cuisine that was linked to the leisurely aristocrats who deemed it unnecessary to work for a living. A crucial distinction was that the nineteenth-century French meal followed the *service à la Russe* (Russian style of serving dinner courses), or the subsequent serving of dishes according to a strict order, as opposed to the *service à la Française* (French style of serving) that was typical of aristocrats' meals throughout Europe during the eighteenth century. The grand bourgeoisie, such as the Warocqué family, copied many features from the eighteenth-century aristocrats' lifestyle.

A model of eighteenth-century luxury dining is to be found in the lifestyle of Charles de Lorraine (1712–1780), governor of the Southern Netherlands, which had become part of the Austrian Empire in 1713. He set a norm for expensive eating and drinking, which served to stress his immense (or absolute) power.[31] In the year 1750 Charles traveled frequently, but when he was in Brussels, he had 142 "fat days" (*jours gras*), 66 "meager days" (*jours de jeûne*), and 35 meatless days (although meat actually was consumed on these days, indicating limited religious concern). In fact, the difference between these categories of days was negligible: Charles's court always ate abundantly and richly, with great variety. Fresh beef, veal, mutton, and lamb were consumed in large quantities, together with ham, meat pies, sausages, and salami that were imported from Bayonne, Mainz, and Westphalia. Animals' kidneys, tongue, and other intestines also appeared on the court's table, primarily in sauces and as ornaments of other meat dishes. Poultry, fowl, and game were very popular, the latter often resulting from hunting on the prince's lands (in some periods, Charles went out hunting three times a week). Twenty-seven different sorts of freshwater fish and sea fish were prepared. Oysters were particularly appreciated.

The list of foods is completed by dairy products, eggs, three sorts of bread (one was baked specially for Charles and consisted of wheat flour and milk), 22 types of fruit (the traditional ones but also melons, peaches, and oranges—the latter produced in Charles's greenhouse), 21 kinds of vegetables (truffles, asparagus, lettuce, carrots, cucumbers, etc.), 12 different herbs (garlic, parsley, onion, etc.), and seven spices (pepper, nutmeg, saffron, etc.). According to the fashion of the day, the cooking was French, which meant that meat was largely predominant, fruit and vegetables were assigned a secondary role, and many small plates and cups of food were put on the table simultaneously, allowing diners to choose whatever they

Pièce montée: The height of eighteenth- and nineteenth-century elitist gastronomy, by the French chef Antoine Carême (1784–1833). This shows a reconstruction during an exhibition on nineteenth-century fancy desserts at the Castle of Gaasbeek (near Brussels), September 2006. Courtesy of the author.

wanted. This was called *service à la Française*.[32] The prince possessed a rich stock of 31 different wines from six countries. Charles drank almost 2 quarts of wine daily; in the 1770s doctors recommended that he limit his consumption, which led him to drink only champagne. According to the records, Charles's energy intake per day amounted to 6,300 calories on a fat day and 5,700 calories on a meager or meatless day, which is impressive, knowing that an adult man can live on about 2,900 calories. However, he did not consume all food served to him, because a great deal of it was part of the theater of appearance.

Aristocratic foodways influenced the nineteenth-century grand bourgeois food culture in another way too: the restaurant. In the late eighteenth century several elements of the manor's noble eating style (tablecloth, maître d'hôtel, luxury food, decor) moved to the fancy restaurant. This public eating place was a Parisian invention, but most Belgian towns quickly adopted this new way of eating. Local and foreign businessmen, administrators, and politicians enjoyed public eating, which was a nice occasion to meet with people, to see and be seen. Soon, tourists joined these wealthy diners. The medieval town of Ghent, for example, which had many cotton mills in the early nineteenth century, had only a handful of fancy restaurants around 1815 but in 1850 had many restaurants, which were highly appreciated by (foreign) travelers' guides. The development of restaurants in Brussels was even more telling. In 1819 this city had 7 Parisian-style restaurants, in 1840 there were 32, and by 1900 there were 312.[33] Not all of these places served the fashionable French cuisine, but those restaurants that labeled themselves as French or Parisian were acknowledged as genuine by patrons as well as by restaurant guides, with the advantage of being cheaper than in Paris.

Middle-class people lived a much more modest life, and they could certainly not afford to go to a restaurant. For business and rarely for pleasure they would eat in estaminets (or pubs) that offered rather coarse food, such as a platter of roast beef with some potatoes, or plenty of bread with cheese, hard-boiled eggs, or some charcuterie (cured meats such as ham, salami, dry sausage, or pâté). Most of the time, members of the middle-class ate at home, where they were particularly concerned with having enough to eat. Whenever they could afford it, they ate meat but without approaching the large quantities consumed by richer people. Their concern with having sufficient food was mirrored in a very high consumption of bread, potatoes, butter, cheese, processed meats, and beer. Fish was eaten rarely, and game, fowl, or poultry was far too expensive, except on a special occasion once a year. After 1850 cookbooks began to appear that were directed to the middle classes and not to the cooks of the bourgeoisie and aristocracy, as had been the case until then. Cauderlier's *Het spaarzame keukenboek* (The economical kitchen book; Ghent, 1861) aimed at "providing a good cuisine to the most modest income groups," although it actually included a great deal of elaborate dishes and luxury ingredients.[34] For example, the book gave 19 recipes for beef, 10 for asparagus, 24 for mushrooms, and no fewer than 45 for chicken. This book was clearly meant for the upper middle classes.

Writings addressed to working-class households were, without exception, moralizing and aimed at frugality and rational management of food expenditures. Nineteenth-century social reformers, medical doctors, and public administrators were convinced that negligent behavior (mostly alcohol drinking by the head of the household) caused shortcomings and even hunger. Therefore, housewives were made responsible for the family's health and happiness: they should prepare thrifty but tasty meals that would keep their husbands away from the pubs. Large-scale inquiries in the middle of the nineteenth century revealed the extent and effects of malnutrition. Malnutrition was caused by a series of enduring misfortunes. Very high prices in the 1760s, 1790s, 1810s, 1840s, and 1850s (due to political upheaval or poor harvests), along with unemployment and diminishing wages (due to uncompetitive production modes, particularly in textiles), lowered the general purchasing power, which resulted in the rapid deterioration of the diet. Between the 1770s and 1850s, working-class people consumed far less dairy products and meat but much more rye bread and, especially, potatoes, which provided cheap and abundant calories. As in many European countries in the first half of the nineteenth century, potatoes saved many people from starvation.

When around 1850 physicians investigated the quantity of food consumed, they arrived at telling results that indicated deficient and unbalanced diets. The average agricultural worker had an intake of about 2,200 calories per day, of which 4 percent originated from animal products, while a mill worker consumed about 1,800 calories, of which only 2 percent came from a little butter and bacon. By way of comparison, in the same period a white-collar employee consumed 2,800 calories, of which 35 percent was of animal origin.[35] By then, working-class families as a rule did not eat fresh meat. A hot meal consisted of a pile of boiled potatoes with onion sauce or vinegar and, during better days, some bacon or, once in a while, meat offal. Only laborers in the new Walloon industries could afford to eat fresh meat regularly. In periods of high wages, as in the early 1870s, metallurgists and miners were accused of eating too many sausages and drinking too much alcohol, instead of saving money for dark days to come. On Fridays workers ate mussels in Flanders and Brussels, and freshwater fish in Wallonia.

Nutritionists pointed out the inadequacy of the diet of most Belgian workers, whether in the towns or the countryside, particularly in Flanders, and stressed its direct consequences for the health of the people and, especially, for their labor productivity. British workers produced much more in a day than Belgian workers, which was believed to result from, among other things, the extremely low meat consumption of the Belgians. In the second half of the nineteenth century, a systematic policy was therefore elaborated to improve the workers' diet. This did not consist of increasing wages, for the general low wage level in Belgium was seen as a valuable advantage for Belgium's economy, but of providing cheap food. Hence, taxes on food imports were lowered or, as for grain during some periods, abolished. Also, consumption taxes in cities were terminated in 1860, and land-development schemes were launched. A radical change occurred in the early 1870s, when massive grain imports from the United States flooded European harbors, causing prices to sink and local farmers to shift production (leaving grain and taking up cattle breeding and fruit and vegetable growing), which led to fundamental changes in the workers' diet. This change appeared particularly in the 1890s, with the upswing of the business cycle, the growing influence of trade unions, and the increase in wages. In Belgium, the growing polarization between Flanders and Wallonia and rich and poor came to an end, with Flanders gradually attracting new, high-paying industries (chemical and automobile factories, for example). By 1900, the average adult worker consumed 2,200 calories (compared to 1,800 in the 1850s), of which 23 percent were obtained from animal products (compared to the meager 2 to 4 percent in the 1850s). The proportion of food costs in total working-class household expenditures started to shrink gradually from more than 60 percent to below 50 percent, which left some room for other expenditures such as fashionable clothing, interior decoration, or leisure activities.

BRUSSELS IN THE NINETEENTH AND TWENTIETH CENTURIES

The swift process of industrialization and commercialization would not have happened without the support of dozens of services such as banks, insurance agencies, schools, wholesalers and retailers, international traders, and other administrative centers. As the capital of Belgium in 1830, Brussels developed these services promptly. By 1900, specific, sizable quarters of the city had acquired a clear administrative character, with harried employees picking up a snack at street stalls or having a quick coffee in a bar. Since the 1900s and up to today, tens of thousands of employees commute daily to Brussels. Employment in Belgium shifted from agriculture to industry and, more recently, to the service sector, which now employs about 75 percent of so-called active people.

Moreover, this city hosted courts, such as Charles de Lorraine's court in the eighteenth century or those of the new kings after 1830. These courts attracted diplomats, aristocrats, businessmen, lobbyists, artists, politicians, scientists, and many other people from all over the country and from abroad. The French particularly loved Brussels, because of its liberal atmosphere, the short distance between Paris and Brussels (with a direct train running since 1847), the same language, and the low cost of living. Administrators, politicians, businessmen, diplomats, and others made use of the many amenities of the city, which were abundant since 1700 but had expanded in the nineteenth century, with the construction of an opera house, theaters, dance halls, public parks, cafés, restaurants, and, later, cinemas, nightclubs, and snack bars. The city center was frequently modernized, and it was conceived not only as a location for living, working, and enjoying but also as a place symbolic of Belgian unity. Hence, all celebrations as well as public protests have occurred in this city. For a long time, this strengthening of a service-oriented city had an international dimension, with many foreigners coming from nearby (not only France but also England, Germany, and the Netherlands) or afar (Poland, the United States, Spain, Italy, and many other countries), and all contributing their skills, habits, and money to Brussels' expansion. This international aspect appeared through the organization of no fewer than four World's fairs in the city (in 1897, 1910, 1935, and 1958), appealing to millions of local and foreign visitors who could see, taste, and try new food products from all over the world. The long-term international significance also shows in the fact that Brussels became the unofficial capital of Europe in the 1950s and that today the city is the third largest conference center in the world.

The presence of many wealthy people, both local and foreign, has particular consequences for food culture. Caterers, restaurants, and stores offering special, exotic, and sophisticated food and beverages have flourished in Brussels since the 1840s. "Belgians show a prodigious interest in cuisine," wrote the French culinary journalists Gault and Millau in 1965, adding "Belgium is the foreign country with the best French cuisine."[36] Twelve years later, they called Comme chez Soi, a Brussels restaurant that had obtained the much-desired three-star rating of the *Guide Michelin*, "one of the best restaurants in Europe." This sign of approval from two authoritative French critics (after all, these two consecrated the nouvelle cuisine of the 1970s) is telling of the quality of Brussels restaurants. They acknowledged the ability of chefs in Brussels and, in general, in Belgium to combine the best of French cuisine with elements of Flemish, Walloon, and Brussels cuisines, evolving into the *Franco-Belge* cuisine that is to be found in most present-day Belgian restaurants. Prior to 1914 this had hardly been the case; at that time, only genuine French restaurants were acclaimed, and "Belgian" cuisine was not appreciated, unless patrons were happy with a democratic *moules-frites* (mussels and fries) and a beer, sitting next to a noisy party of cheerful Bruxellois (inhabitants from Brussels).

When World War I ended, Belgium benefited from international sympathy because of the suffering there, receiving aid from the United States, in particular. This international attention, together with the discovery of regional ingredients and ways of preparation within the luxury cuisine (highly promoted by the legendary chef Auguste Escoffier, 1846–1935), put Belgian specialties on the international culinary map. Hence, the *Larousse gastronomique*, a kind of bible of French haute cuisine from the interwar period until now, states about Belgian cuisine, "Applying enthusiastically and totally the delicacies of the French cuisine, the Belgians, fine gourmets, kept on with their national dishes . . . and even in the posh restaurants one may appreciate eels with green herbs, Flemish beef stew, rabbit with plums, and Brussels meatballs. But the dish that probably is the most liked by both Belgians and foreigners is the Ghent *waterzooi à la poularde*" (a vegetable soup with chicken).[37] Since the 1920s, thus, a proper Belgian cuisine was designated with dishes that are common to all regions. This boosted Belgium's identity within as well as outside the country.

Wealthy people's interest in good eating also shows in many culinary publications. Until the 1930s, mostly teachers in household schools published food recommendations and recipes, but gradually more and more chefs wrote books and published in magazines. In the 1890s, Cauderlier's cookbook was outdated (although it was reissued until the 1920s), and in 1900 Jean De Gouy published *La cuisine et la pâtisserie bourgeoises à la portée de tous* (Bourgeois cuisine and patisserie within reach of all). This book was a best seller with new editions appearing until 1948. It summarized the information about Escoffier's cuisine, mixing it with traditional Belgian recipes and ingredients. De Gouy had launched *Journal de la Cuisine* in 1889 (to become *La Belgique hôtelière* in 1924), which served as the place of culinary innovation and diffusion for both haute and bourgeois cuisine, and for professional as well as home cooking. A common menu in bourgeois cuisine in the 1920s, for example, read omelet *à la Viennoise* (in the Viennese style, with onion and paprika), followed by fillet of hare *à la bordelaise* (in the style of Bordeaux, with white wine sauce) with stuffed eggplant and boiled potatoes, and ending with *madeleines à la crème moka* (spongy cakes with mocha cream). Cookbooks by chefs have proliferated since the 1930s, with influential work by Paul Bouillard in the 1920s and 1930s, Gaston Clément between 1930 and 1970, and virtually all chefs of some importance since the late 1970s. Equally important were the many general and women's magazines that were partly devoted to gourmet cooking, eating, and drinking and that showed how to prepare and serve the food. Although these writings were very close to new developments in the haute cuisine, it took several decades before these were actually applied in home cooking. A 1920s recipe mentioned peppers and eggplant, which were vegetables that could only be obtained at very high prices in exclusive shops. Only when supermarkets supplied these *new* ingredients in the 1980s did more and more people buy and eat them.

Up until the 1960s, gourmet cookbooks addressed a small group of people, but gradually the middle classes and, quite recently, the popular classes started to show interest in gourmet eating, too. This process may be described as the upgrading of food. Workers with decent incomes benefited gradually from the broadening supply of foodstuffs. In the 1920s this included chocolate; canned fish (tuna and sardines), canned meat (corned beef and processed) and canned vegetables (beans in tomato sauce); and more dairy products, whereas in the 1950s this referred to processed food (potato chips, cookies, and frozen foods), alcohol, and particularly fresh meat (steak, chicken). Many workers' wages rose, more women took jobs outside the home, and food prices in general declined as a result of continuing mechanization of production, packaging, transport, and trade. Moreover, social insurance programs (for old age, illness, and unemployment) significantly helped in the course of the twentieth century, guaranteeing a decent income to most people. All this led to a gradual lowering of food's share in the total family budget (from about 40 percent in the early 1950s to about 15 percent in the 1990s), leaving plenty of room for purchasing cars and household equipment, and going on vacations. Together, a shift in the significance of food occurred: what was seen as a luxury product in the 1930s, whether wheat bread or sugar, was seen as ordinary after the 1970s.

Above all, the centuries-old problem of regularly occurring hunger disappeared. Workers' energy intake rose gradually, with the share of animal products in the diet reaching 36 percent in the late 1940s and 45 percent around 1980. Many Belgians prefer a bursting plate filled with familiar food (for example, the combination of plenty of *pommes frites* (fries), a solid steak, and some lettuce is a hit), with a cold beer or two. This diet provides more than enough calories, which some nutritionists already observed in the 1930s, leading them to advise lowering the intake of meat, fat, and sugar while increasing consumption of vegetables and fruit. Prior to 1900, bourgeois women had been sensitive to ideals of slimness and had started to care about healthy eating, but since the 1960s many working-class women have become weight conscious as well. Cookbooks and food recommendations addressed to working- and middle-class households appeared very frequently between the 1930s and 1960s. Up to the 1940s, Belgians were advised to have sufficient and rather plain food. If butter was too expensive, margarine offered a splendid alternative, and if hunger was threatening, as during World War II, it was recommended to chew the food longer to incorporate all nutritive elements well. Specific cookbooks addressed to the working classes disappeared in the 1960s. Since then, all social layers share a common interest in gourmet food. Of course, social differences remain.

Social differences appear especially in the distinct diets of rich and poor households and in food inequalities, which have increased since the 1960s. No doubt the average Belgian benefited from more, enriched, and diversified food since 1950, but groups at the extreme social ends diverge largely from the average. Well-off consumers search for more refinement, new experiences, and different ingredients by exploring exotic cuisines and new ways of preparation, whereas poor consumers stick to familiar and filling food. Thus, blue-collar workers, the unemployed, and retired people consume much more potatoes, bread, pork, and beef than self-employed or white-collar workers, traders, and employers. Some foodstuffs, such as asparagus, veal, or fresh fish, show a direct correlation between social status and increasing consumption of these foodstuffs.[38] These diet differences are linked not only to caloric needs but also to long-established food habits, anxiety about trying new foods, and fear of hunger. Hence, the poorer a person is, the more he or she wishes to have full plates. Since the 1950s, poor people have consumed more than the sufficient number of calories on average and are, as a sign of the times, often overweight. Social differences are found all over Belgium but are the greatest in Brussels, where highly skilled and experienced employees, as well as an army of unskilled workers, are needed.

All in all, plain food of vegetable origin has been the common diet for most of the people for a long time. Prices and income regulated food consumption: the more purchasing power, the more meat and sophisticated preparations. A richer diet was the privilege of the happy few since the

Iron Age. Manifold efforts by agricultural laborers, traders, and workers changed this very gradually, with a breakthrough in the late nineteenth century, when more and more people enjoyed enough food, and in the late twentieth century and early twenty-first century, when they also enjoyed varied and enriched diets.

NOTES

1. For an overview of Belgium's long-term history, see Paul Arblaster, *A History of the Low Countries* (London: Palgrave, 2006).

2. Abundant information is available on Belgium's official Web site (section "About Belgium"), http://www.belgium.be/en/about_belgium.index.jsp (accessed September 15, 2008).

3. Hansjörg Küster, "Northern Europe—Germany and Surrounding Regions," in *The Cambridge World History of Food,* ed. Kenneth Kiple and Kriemhield Conée Ornelas (Cambridge: Cambridge University Press, 2000), 1226–1229; Ruud Borman, *Oude beschavingen van de Lage Landen* (Amsterdam and Brussels: Elsevier, 1980).

4. Hervé Bocherens, Caroline Petit, and Michel Toussaint, "Palaeodiet of Mesolithic and Neolithic Populations of Meuse Basin (Belgium): Evidence from Stable Isotopes," *Journal of Archaeological Studies* 34 (2007): 10–27.

5. Colin Spencer, "The British Isles," in Kiple and Ornelas, *Cambridge World History of Food,* 1217.

6. Arblaster, *History of the Low Countries,* 10–12.

7. Robert Nouwen, *De Romeinen in België, 31 v.C.–476 n.C.* (Leuven, Belgium: Davidsfonds, 2006).

8. Nouwen, *De Romeinen in België,* 120–123.

9. B. Cooremans, "The Roman Cemeteries of Tienen and Tongeren: Results from the Archaeobotanical Analysis of the Cremation Graves," *Vegetation History and Archaeology* 17 (2008): 3–13.

10. Nouwen, *De Romeinen in België,* 161–165.

11. Julia Abramson, *Food Culture in France* (Westport, CT: Greenwood Press, 2007), 7–8.

12. Liliane Plouvier, "L'alimentation carnée au Haut Moyen Âge," *Revue Belge de Philologie et d'Histoire* 80.4 (2002): 1357–1369.

13. Sigrid Dehaeck, Voedselconsumptie te Brugge in de Middeleeuwen. Case study: Het Sint-Janshospitaal en het hospitaal van de Potterie (1280–1441) (master's thesis, Ghent University, 1999), http://www.ethesis.net/sint_jan/inhoud.htm (accessed May 17, 2008).

14. Caroline Polet and M. Anne Katzenberg, "Comportements alimentaires de trois populations médiévales belges: Apports de la biogéochimie isotopique," *Revue Belge de Philologie et d'Histoire* 80.4 (2002): 1371–1390.

15. Ides Boone, Bea De Cupere, and Wim Van Neer, "Social Status as Relected in the Food Refuse from Late Medieval Sites in Namur (Belgium)," *Revue Belge de Philologie et d'Histoire* 80.4 (2002): 1391–1394.

16. James Murray, *Bruges, Cradle of Capitalism, 1280–1390* (Cambridge: Cambridge University Press, 2005); Arblaster, *History of the Low Countries*, 102–108.

17. Raymond Van Uytven, *De zinnelijke Middeleeuwen* (Leuven: Davidsfonds, 1998), 163, 184, and 186.

18. Johanna Maria Van Winter, "The Low Countries in the Fifteenth and Sixteenth Centuries," in *Spices and Comfits: Collected Papers on Medieval Food* (Totnes: Prospect Books, 2007), 107–128.

19. Van Uytven, *De zinnelijke Middeleeuwen*, 159.

20. Raymond Van Uytven, *Het dagelijks leven in een Middeleeuwse stad: Leuven anno 1448* (Leuven: Davidsfonds, 1998), 161.

21. Dehaeck, "Voedselconsumptie te Brugge."

22. On diverse aspects of Antwerp's significance, see Patrick O' Brien, ed., *Urban Achievement in Early Modern Europe: Golden Ages in Antwerp, Amsterdam and London* (Cambridge: Cambridge University Press, 2001).

23. Richard W. Unger, *Beer in the Middle Ages and the Renaissance* (Philadelphia: University of Pennsylvania Press, 2004), 118–119; for a survey on Antwerp's most important brewer and town developer, see Hugo Soly, *Urbanisme en kapitalisme te Antwerpen in de zestiende eeuw* (Brussels: Pro Civitate, 1977).

24. Robert Muchambled, "Aan tafel," in *België in de 17de eeuw*, vol. 2, *De cultuur en de leefwereld*, ed. Paul Janssens (Ghent: Snoeck and Dexia Bank, 2006), 381–394.

25. Van Winter, "Low Countries," 110–111.

26. Jozef Schildermans, Hilde Sels, and Marleen Willebrands, *Lieve schat, wat vind je lekker? Het Koocboec van Antonius Magirus (1612) en de Italiaanse keuken van de renaissance* (Leuven: Davidsfonds, 2007).

27. Harald Deceulaer and Frederik Verleysen, "Excessive Eating or Political Display? Guild Meals in the Southern Netherlands, Late 16th–Late 18th Centuries," *Food and History* 4.2 (2006): 165–185.

28. Etienne Scholliers, *Loonarbeid en honger: De levensstandaard in de 15e en 16e eeuw te Antwerpen* (Antwerp: De Sikkel, 1960).

29. Muchambled, "Aan tafel," 384.

30. Maurice Van den Eynde, *La vie quotidienne de grands bourgeois au XIXe siècle. Les Warocqué* (Morlanwelz: Musée Royal de Mariemont, 1989); Siger Zeischka, "His Majesty, His Miners: Raoul Warocqué's Festivities and Guests," in *The Dining Nobility: From the Burgundian Dukes to the Belgian Royalty*, ed. Paul Janssens and Siger Zeischka (Brussels: VUBPress, 2008), 123–135.

31. Marc Libert, "Les habitudes alimentaires à la cour de Bruxelles au XVIIIe siècle," *Cahiers Bruxellois* 32 (1992): 61–84.

32. Lizet Kruyff and Jonneke Krans, *Mozarts menu: De eetcultuur van de tweede helft van de 18e eeuw* (Bussum: Uitgeverij Pereboom, 2006).

33. Peter Scholliers, "Brusselse restaurants in de 19de en 20ste eeuw: Over koks, eters, schrijvers en luxe: Franse dominantie en Belgische respons," in *Buitenshuis eten in de Lage Landen sinds 1800,* ed. Marc Jacobs and Peter Scholliers (Brussels: VUBPress, 2002), 57–84.

34. Philippe Cauderlier, *Het spaarzame keukenboek* (Ghent: 1861), iv.

35. Peter Scholliers, *Arm en rijk aan tafel: Tweehonderd jaar eetcultuur in België* (Berchem and Brussels: EPO & BRTN, 1993), 32, 58.

36. Herni Gault and Christian Millau, *Guide Julliard de Bruxelles* (Paris: Julliard, 1965), 27.

37. Prosper Montagné and Dr. Gottschalk, *Larousse gastronomique* (Paris: Larousse, 1938), 403.

38. Peter Scholliers, "Roquefort of jonge hollandse? Klassen en eetcultuur in België in de 20ste eeuw," *Tijdschrift voor Sociologie* 18.1–2 (1997): 103–129.

2

Major Foods and Ingredients

Whether in specialty stores, ordinary supermarkets, exclusive restaurants, or small corner shops, foodstuffs from all over the globe are obtainable in Belgium. The daily availability of manioc, ostrich meat, cilantro, Mexican beer, *mozzarella di bufala Campana* (buffalo mozzarella from Campana, Italy), or Thai coconut milk has undoubtedly changed the way Belgians cook, drink, and eat over the past decades. This globalization, however, comes along with huge interest in local cuisine and products. What not long ago was seen as common food or drink is now considered special.[1] The case of *Geuze*, a sweet-sour beer that has been brewed in Pajottenland, very near Brussels, since the fifteenth century is telling. This region hosted over 200 brewers of *Geuze* around 1900, but only a few were left in the 1990s. Contracts between cafés and big brewing companies (in the 1970s especially Scandinavian and Irish brewers made their way into Belgium) pushed small, local beer producers out of the market, and the public lost interest in traditional beers and largely turned toward marketed brands. On top of that, around the year 2000 European legislation about hygienic beer production threatened to bring to an end the traditional *Geuze* production, which uses oak barrels and open-air cooling of wort (leaving bacteria to do what they should). By 2005, however, all this had changed. *Geuze* producers cannot keep up with the ever-increasing international and local demand. The public now highly appreciates the different taste of the beer, the European legislation has been adapted, and producers introduced taste-improving techniques; hence, numerous, small

Geuze producers survive and prosper. This upgrading of a local product is not limited to beer or Belgium, but it also holds for cheese, processed meats, or cookies all over Europe. In this process of rediscovering the authentic, little and big changes in the mode of production are made, thus inevitably changing the nature of the supposedly authentic product. This chapter presents major foods and ingredients that have never gone out of style in Belgium but that have enjoyed renewed attention since the mid-1990s. It will neglect relatively new foods and ingredients such as eggplant or hamburgers, although some of these may be considered major foods in Belgium today, as in the rest of Europe. This chapter shows the way through a Belgian day, starting with the morning coffee and ending with the drop of liquor before going to sleep.

COFFEE

Most Belgians start the day with a cup of coffee. Generally, this bland beverage comes with sugar and (a lot or a little) milk, and people may drink it throughout the day as well. Some households prepare strong, flavorful coffee, whereas others stick to a watery solution. By and large, fresh (or "real") coffee is prepared, not instant (or powdered) coffee. Some people buy small boxes of coffee beans and crush them in a hand-turned or electric grinder, but most purchase ground coffee in a box containing about ½ pound. Each Belgian has a preference for a particular brand, which may show clear regional, deeply rooted differences. Most households use an automatic coffeemaker, although elderly people stick to the kettle and the coffeepot, patiently pouring hot water onto the coffee bag. Some use ready-to-use plastic coffee filters that are more expensive but make a stronger coffee (these were used in cafés and restaurants before the wide diffusion of the espresso machine in the late 1970s). Recently, households have acquired home espresso machines that are mostly used for an Italian-style cup of coffee to end the noon meal or when they have dinner guests.

The drinking of coffee is widespread throughout the morning; coffee is served during office meetings and breaks at work or during the housewife's chores. Factory workers, bus drivers, or trade representatives often take thermos bottles with coffee to get them through the workday. In the afternoon and evening, coffee is drunk less than during the morning. The widespread consumption of this beverage has an old tradition that goes back to the middle of the nineteenth century. Up to the late eighteenth century coffee was a genuine luxury drink, because it was imported from faraway shores and was extremely expensive. Extension of cultivation areas (often at the expense of local crops, thus upsetting food production and consumption) and improved transportation made the coffee price drop, which led to gradual diffusion of coffee drinking. By the middle of the nineteenth century, this drink was widely spread throughout all regions, social classes, and age groups, but most people added chicory or drank a solution of pure chicory. Around 1900, cookbooks and household books recommended that children younger than 10 years of age should not drink coffee, unless chicory was predominant and lots of sugar and milk were added. After World War II, the proportion of chicory in the average cup of coffee slowly diminished, disappearing entirely by the late 1970s. However, in the 1990s, pure chicory surfaced again as a healthy substitute for coffee. Tea, whether in the morning or throughout the day, is far less important, and cocoa drinks (hot or cold) are very much limited to children.

BREAD

With the coffee come slices of bread. As in most European countries, bread holds a special position in Belgium. This is linked to its centuries-old importance in the daily diet, to the social influence of landowners, millers, and bakers, and to bread's symbolic significance in holy occasions, the political implications of the bread price, and the economic weight of grain production and trade. Not that long ago, most of the tilled land was utilized to grow grain (mostly wheat), but today it takes only 20 percent of all agricultural land, and this share continues to decrease slightly year after year.[2] Importation of grain has always been significant, with a crucial breakthrough in the 1870s, when cheap but high-quality wheat was imported in massive quantities from the United States. This caused a revolution in European agriculture, in that tilled fields were turned into grassland and land for growing vegetables and fruit.

Until recently, stale bread was hardly ever thrown away. Instead, it was recycled as crumbs for baked dishes, used to prepare *gewonnen brood* or *pain perdu* (literally, "gained bread" and "lost bread," respectively[3]), and fed to animals (whether domestic animals or ducks in the park). Nowadays, many people still find it impossible to dispose of old bread, unless it is rock hard or moldy. Nevertheless, today bread is thrown away in huge amounts because of its relatively low price. Yet, the importance of bread is still mirrored in the fact that the Dutch word *brood* (bread) appears in many sayings in Belgium, such as *broodnodig* (sorely needed), *broodnuchter* (stone sober), or *brooddief* (unfair competitor). Today, the average Flemish household spends 325 euros per year on bread, but the

Walloons spend only 225 and the Bruxellois a minor 188 euros, or 1.7 times less than the Flemings. Expenditure on other bakery products does not compensate for this.

"Gained" (recuperated) Bread (*gewonnen brood* or *pain perdu*)

4 1/4 cups milk

1/2 cup sugar

1 teaspoon vanilla

salt

6 eggs

butter

stale bread

Bring the milk to a boil with the sugar, vanilla, and a little salt; then let cool. Slice the bread, and soak the slices in the milk for two or three minutes (not too long or the bread will get soggy). Break the eggs, and beat vigorously; add a little salt. Melt butter in a frying pan on the stove. Take a slice of bread, dip it in the egg mix, and fry it on both sides. Serve with plenty of sugar. For a special treat, add rum, cognac, or sweet liqueur to the milk after it has boiled.

Bakers sell diverse sorts of bread and are still expanding and/or specializing their offerings. This is due to the competition between bakers, on the one hand, and the ever-increasing, sophisticated demands of consumers, on the other. In the late nineteenth century, large bread factories produced relatively good-quality bread that was sold at a fair price for an exact weight, which led to a general improvement as well as standardization (for taste, shape, and substance). They produced *huishoudbrood* (*pain de ménage*), bread made of highly refined (or bolted) wheat flour, around 1900, which was by far the most common bread up to the 1970s. Until 2004 the government controlled the price of this bread by setting a maximum price. Famous was the *Expobrood*, rectangular bread that was baked for the 1958 Brussels World's fair (the first after World War II) and that could be purchased throughout the country. Gradually, customers preferred so-called improved (or special) bread, made of a mix of grains or containing raisins or nuts. At first, small, independent bakers who could respond easily to the consumers' demands produced this upgraded bread. Bread factories started to expand their production too, competing with the bread types and quality offered by the *warme bakker* (the hot baker, that is, the small producer making bread and pastry from the flour to the finished product). One hot baker in Waarschoot, a village near Ghent, sells 14 different sorts of bread in his bakery among which are the common wheat bread, raisin bread, and whole-grain bread but also the quite exclusive Black Forest bread, nut bread, and sourdough bread.

Depending on the blend of grains and the shape (round, oval, rectangular, or square), breads have names such as *boulot, galet, stokbrood,* and *plaatbrood* (for wheat breads), and *boerenbrood, hoevebrood, waldkorn,* and fourteen-grain bread (for coarse breads of partly wheat and rye or non-refined grains). These breads sell for widely ranging prices, with the plain wheat bread among the cheapest and the trendy rye bread with raisins and nuts among the most expensive. Within a couple of decades, the hierarchy of bread types (ranging from breads made of refined and non-refined wheat, to a mixture of wheat and rye [*maslin* bread] to plain rye) has totally reversed: today, unbolted, dark bread varieties are much more appreciated and expensive than the wheat bread that used to be the bread of the rich people up to the 1950s. Yet, today even the darkest bread contains wheat, and very dark rye bread (like that common in Germany and central Europe) is hardly to be found in Belgium. At the baker's, most breads are cut into slices and put in a paper bag; at the supermarket, shoppers may themselves put the bread into the bread slicer. Ready-cut bread in plastic bags is rarely purchased, except for the very white, square bread that makes perfect toast.

Most grocery stores sell flour for making homemade bread, but some stores have a special section with wide-ranging offerings. For example, Aveve, a chain store connected to the Belgian Farmers' Association (*Boerenbond*), sells seeds, tools, herbicides, garden clothing, and flour made of wheat, rye, spelt, soy, buckwheat, corn, and oats, as well as enriched or refined flour for pastry, baguettes, biscuits, pancakes, or waffles. At home, bread is made with electric bread makers that became quite fashionable in the early 1990s, although some home bakers do without machines and stick to solid handwork and the traditional oven.

BUTTER AND MARGARINE

Slices of bread are cut into two and stacked on top of each other, which turns them into a *tartine* (French) or *boterham* (Dutch). In both, the word connotes the presence of butter: the Flemish *boterham* includes the word for butter, whereas *tartiner* means "to spread." Butter, or a substitute, makes the bread slice into a *boterham*. Butter was very expensive for quite a while.[4] Turning milk into cream and then into butter is time-consuming and costly when only simple tools are used. Therefore, until the 1950s, many people spread lard on bread slices, and still today some enjoy the taste of salted grease on bread. In the last quarter of the nineteenth century, when more milk was produced and dairy machines appeared, the price of butter fell. Higher milk production was possible because of the so-called agricultural revolution of the late nineteenth century, when many European grain fields were turned into grasslands for pasturing cattle. At the same time, the production of butter was gradually moved from the farm to specialized dairy factories. By the 1920s, the dairy sector was commercialized, with well-organized production, trade, and marketing.

Around the same period, margarine (or "artificial butter") made its appearance. Large factories, which were often established by Dutch people and later became part of multinational corporations like Unilever, manufactured a low-cost substitute for butter. For a long time, margarine was disliked by most consumers, and only the low price and massive publicity campaigns that stressed the healthy aspects of the product led gradually to higher consumption. Butter obtained a bad reputation because of its allegedly unhealthy characteristics: too much fat. Extensive marketing campaigns in the 1960s and 1970s ("Butter makes everything tastier") could not prevent the steady decline of butter consumption in Belgium. Still, Belgian production of butter has been increasing since the mid-1990s to 175,500 tons today (an increase of 20 percent), thus implying that Belgian butter is exported to a greater extent than in the past. Butter and margarine consumption differs in Flanders, Wallonia, and Brussels. In Brussels and Wallonia, consumers prefer butter; in Flanders, they go for margarine (in Flanders butter accounts for 42 percent of total household spending on butter and margarine, compared to 57 percent in Wallonia and 56 percent in Brussels). A classic interpretation of this difference, namely, the lowerincome level in Wallonia, does not help: butter is more expensive than margarine. Taste differences provide the correct explanation (next to Flemings' bigger concerns about healthy food). Not only do the Walloons use butter to spread on bread, but they also prefer to cook with butter (whereas Flemings increasingly use olive oil).

Butter comes in diverse forms. Some people could not do without salted butter, and if there were not enough salt in it, they would add more. Other people profoundly dislike salted butter. Consumers may choose between Belgian and imported butter, the latter coming from Luxembourg, the Netherlands, or France. Delhaize supermarket has its own brand that comes from a highly controlled dairy farm in the small village of Bullange (in the Ardennes).[5] This farm produces three sorts of butter: pasteurized churned butter, unsalted butter, and faintly spiced butter (the last comes in a roll, which, according to the supermarket's Web site, may be sliced and nicely presented on the table). Next, there is gourmet butter from

Brittany and Poitou-Charentes, France; organic butter (also produced in the Ardennes); light butter, in which part of the fat is replaced by water; and ready-to-spread butter, which is the most popular. Prices of these eight types of butter vary widely. Margarine is available in numerous brands and types, and stress is laid on healthy aspects, hence, the launching of margarine with olive oil that is supposed to proactively lower one's cholesterol level.

FRUIT JAM

Very frequently, the morning bread is consumed not only with butter but also with fruit jams. Not so long ago, these were primarily homemade. The aim was to preserve fruit for the winter by heating it, adding sugar, and storing it in jars in a cool, dark place. The process required days of work, including cleaning glass jars and caps, preparing the fruit, and sterilizing it by cooking for at least half an hour. Strawberries and raspberries were popular, because they do not require much work: clean the fruit, add sugar (about the same amount as the fruit), heat this mixture until it becomes syruplike, pour into jars and cap immediately, and put in a cool place. Cherries, plums, or apricots, however, require more preparation: clean the fruit and remove the pit, then heat the fruit for 30 minutes after adding sugar, pass the mash through a filter, and then pour into jars.

If in-season fruit was relatively cheap, sugar was certainly not. Until the late nineteenth century, sugar was a luxury and it was used in pastry, hot drinks, cookies, and desserts. Fruit jams were used in pastry that was served at the end of fancy dinners in the nineteenth century (for example, *carré de confiture de cerises*, a small, square pastry of cherry jam). Common people rarely ate or drank sweet things. When sugar began to be made from beets in big factories around the 1850s, the price gradually dropped, which made it accessible to more people. By 1920, the food of all Belgians had become sweeter, and making fruit jam became a yearly routine in many households. Cookbooks give abundant recipes for making *confitures* (jams). Today, grocers and supermarkets sell a wide variety of fruit jams, although strawberry jam remains one of the most popular. The tradition of making jam at home is quickly disappearing.

Fruit syrup merits a special mention.[6] This is made of apples, pears, and sugar and has been specially produced in Limburg and Liège since the Middle Ages. It is the result of a simple process for keeping fruit throughout winter, which involves cooking fruit juice for a long time until it becomes gluey. Fruit syrup was used as a sweetener, just like honey, and was relatively expensive as long as it was handmade. In the small village of Herve, near Liège, the Meurens family commercialized the production of syrup in 1902, using steam cooking and hydraulic presses and applying consecutive steps (cooking of the fruit, extraction and concentration of the juice). The price of the product dropped considerably, which made it accessible to many. Publicity in the 1920s shows a happy and healthy boy with white teeth digging into a nice *tartine* full of dark, brownish *Vrai Sirop de Liège* (genuine syrup of Liège). This product became a trademark in 1947 and has remained quite popular for breakfast (particularly, among children); it is also eaten with *fromage de Herve,* a pungent and soft cheese made with unpasteurized cow's milk (this cheese has the European Union certificate of Protected Designation of Origin since 1996).

The large-scale production of fruit in Belgium dates from the late nineteenth century.[7] Up to the 1880s, fruit was grown for rich urban dwellers and for export. Some fruits such as apples, pears, cherries, plums, oranges, and peaches were used to construct impressive *pièces montées* (decorative constructions of food), by putting them in jelly and on cakes. Belgian agriculture changed when cheap imports forced many to abandon grain growing. Farmers started to produce fruit, and some regions (Haspengouw, Meetjesland, and Pays de Herve) specialized in growing apples, pears, cherries, or plums. Other regions developed hothouse production, for example, growing strawberries in Pajottenland and grapes in some villages east of Brussels. Production not only became commercialized but also improved generally, which led to rising output and falling prices. Today, apples are the most important product in terms of production and consumption. The Golden variety was very successful up to the 1980s, when severe competition from French apples ended its career. The Jonagold was then launched, which saved this sector. Production of Belgian strawberries (in open air and increasingly in greenhouses) has expanded significantly (more than 30 percent between 1999 and today). Another traditional product, grapes grown in a hothouse, is declining sharply (down by 40 percent compared to 1999), despite the fact that Brabantine grapes (the varieties Colman and Ribier and the most widespread, Royal) have been protected since 2007 by its European Union–protected designation status.

POTATOES

Traditionally, the noon meal consists of three parts: potatoes (or substitutes), meat (or fish), and vegetables, all put on one plate and with gravy on top. Potatoes may come in very diverse forms among which are plain boiled potatoes, mashed potatoes, croquettes, potatoes "in their jackets" (unpeeled boiled potatoes, cut into two, and topped with butter), *pommes allumettes* (match-sized potatoes, or fried potato sticks), roasted potatoes, *pommes frites* (known as French fries even though they are of Belgian origin), potatoes au gratin, and little potato balls. Some late nineteenth-century Belgian cookbooks easily list three dozen potato recipes. Each type of recipe requires a particular sort of potato, and most shoppers know which sort to buy for which potato dish (and if they do not know, a clear indication on the packaging will help). For example, Agria, Astérix, Manon, and Première are excellent for *pommes frites*, Bintje and Désirée are used for mashed potatoes, while Corne de Gatte, Nicola, and Ratte have a solid texture and are perfect for boiling or roasting.[8] Most of these varieties are cultivated in Belgium, although some also stem from France and the Netherlands. About 9,500 Belgian farmers bring in 2.5 million tons of spuds every year, of which half is exported. The area dedicated to growing potatoes rose from 144,800 acres in 1999 to 167,785 acres in 2007. Today, Belgians consume almost 88 pounds of fresh potatoes per person per year (in addition to some 11 pounds of processed potatoes, such as potato chips), which is far less than in the past.

Cookbooks now hardly inform the reader about the characteristics of potatoes before giving recipes, but up to the 1960s this vegetable merited an extensive paragraph, informing about the qualities of the tuber: potatoes are never boring because they may be combined with most other foodstuffs and may be served in various ways, they contain nutritive elements such as carbohydrates and vitamin C, they are easily digestible, and they may be stored for quite a long time (best in a dark, dry, and frost-free cellar, moving them now and then to avoid the growing of eyes). This interest reflects the huge importance of this vegetable. In the eighteenth century, potatoes were scarcely consumed by humans (they were given to pigs as very cheap fodder), but high bread prices forced the poor and the laboring classes to eat potatoes. A statistical survey in 1813, when the Belgian provinces were part of the French Empire, showed the large extent of potato consumption. It rose throughout the nineteenth century, with a peak of about 860 pounds per person per year in the 1850s.[9] Historians see this high intake as a mark of poverty. Yet, the increasing potato consumption around 1850 helped to stop the daily fear of starvation, excessive prices, and dreadful living conditions experienced by the mass of Belgians.[10] Today, poverty has largely disappeared in Belgium, but the daily habit of eating potatoes has remained.

OTHER STARCHES

Until the 1960s, rice was not seen as a substitute for potatoes. It appears in recipe books of the nineteenth century, labeled as a high-quality food-stuff that is used in soups and desserts, for example, rice biscuits, *riz portugais* (sugared rice with cream and almonds), and *rijstpap* (rice pudding); in popular culture *rijstpap* is represented as being eaten with golden spoons in heaven (which reflects the luxury aspect of this sweet). In the 1960s, Belgian cookbooks mention rice as a possible alternative to potatoes, but only very recently is it presented as an integral ingredient of exotic cuisines. Macaroni appeared in nineteenth-century cookbooks as a separate dish (served, for example, *à l'Italienne*, which is with tomatoes, or au gratin with ham), but this was marginal. Pasta was particularly popular in soups (vermicelli and little pasta letters). In Roeselare (a little town in the province of West Flanders), the Soubry family has produced vermicelli since 1921, and today it manufactures diverse hard pasta types. Recent cookbooks publish genuine Italian recipes, although many Belgians simply replace potatoes in traditional Belgian dishes with spaghetti.

MEAT

Belgians may consider potatoes important (with *pommes frites* even a symbol of national identity), but they see meat as the centerpiece of their daily plate. Meat appears in all recipe collections, cookbooks, and manuals for household schools throughout the nineteenth and twentieth centuries and up to today (except in rare vegetarian cookbooks). Today, every Belgian consumes about 220 pounds of meat per year (carcass-weight equivalent, which means that bones, fat, and tendons are included; this quantity comprises fresh as well as processed meats). This may appear huge, but it is equal to consumption in most West European countries and it is less than in the United States (where 270 pounds per person per year are consumed on average).[11] At 110 pounds per person, pork is the most popular meat in Belgium. Belgians are the seventh highest consumers of pork in the world (Denmark is first, with 163 pounds per person). Beef and veal come next at 48 pounds, which is far below the 154 pounds of the number-one consumer (Argentina). Then comes poultry at 44 pounds, again far below the 147 pounds of the world leader (Hong Kong). Lamb and horsemeat, at 4.5 pounds each, are marginal, and goat is hardly eaten, while game, rabbit, and other sorts are limited to particular periods or social groups. This breakdown of the consumption of the three main meat types (50 percent pork and 25 percent for both beef and poultry) has remained fairly stable for the last 25 years. It deviates quite markedly from the breakdown of meat types in the surrounding countries in that France has higher beef consumption, the Netherlands and the United Kingdom higher poultry consumption, and Germany higher pork intake.

Pork

Belgians have always had a preference for pork, which may be "eaten from ear to tail." Bacon (*spek* in Dutch and *lard* in French) was long the only meat eaten by the poor, particularly in the countryside, while the finest processed meats also use pork. Until the mid-nineteenth century pork was very expensive. Between 1800 and 1850 its price was about 25 percent higher than the price of the second most expensive sort (veal), owing to the general better quality of the meat, which was highly appreciated in the towns.[12] Slaughtering a pig at the farm, which was done just before winter, began a feast period when sausages were made, meat was salted, and stews were prepared with the pig's ears, tail, and legs. All meat prices fluctuated heavily throughout the century, according to demand and supply, but gradually pork became relatively less expensive. By 1900, the price differential had totally changed, with pork about 25 percent cheaper than veal, owing to the high supply of pigs, which could be kept in relatively small and simple barns, being fed on cheap rye, beets, and potatoes. Pig breeding commercialized fast, with the arrival of semi-automatic meat factories in the 1950s. Because of this, the status of pork has declined, and although late twentieth-century cookbooks still value the meat, they never fail to stress that it is particularly common among the working classes. Today, Belgium has 6.2 million pigs (over 90 percent of them are in Flanders), slaughters about 10 million pigs per year, and widely exports fresh and processed pork throughout the world. The Flemish pig, which is believed to go back to Celtic times but has been improved through crossbreeding with foreign types, is the most common, alongside a Yorkshire and German breed. In the 1950s, the Piétrain pig (named after a small village in Brabant) was seen as providing the "ideal" pork, for it contains little fat, which responded to consumers' preferences. Pork consumption is similar in Wallonia and Flanders, but it is about 30 percent lower in Brussels.

Fresh pork has a special place in cookbooks. Late nineteenth-century recipe collections often started by describing the edible parts of the pig (loin, chops, ham, etc.) before giving numerous recipes. Among these were and are *côtelette* (pork chop), *gebraad* or *rôti* (roast), and ground meat. Each requires a particular part of the pig, and the butcher (or an instructive label on the package in the supermarket) can assist shoppers in their selection. If the consumption of pure pork has slightly diminished in recent years, that of ground meat has grown. Often, ground pork is sold mixed with ground veal or beef. Meatballs and hamburgers were always popular but have recently gained in popularity (some claim this is caused by the less visible connection between the animal and the food). The composition of Belgian ground meat differs from that found in surrounding countries: two sorts of meat are mixed, and it contains fat and spices.

Beef and Veal

In the last quarter of the nineteenth century, beef had obtained a special status: some believed it possessed medicinal traits, others praised the energy that it produced (demonstrated by English laborers' high work productivity), but, above all, beef had become the meat of the rich. Not only the high price testified to this, but also the many mentions in menus and cookbooks around 1900. Cooks could prepare beef in manifold, varied, and refined ways, apparently much more than was the case with pork. Popular were *bœuf à la mode* (beef wrapped in bacon, marinaded for 24 hours in herbs, spices, white wine, and vinegar), *filet de bœuf à la financière* (fillet of beef with a sauce of truffles, mushrooms, and Madeira wine), roastbeef, rumpsteak (written in one word, and sometimes transformed into *rosbief* and *rumsteak*), and filet mignon (grilled beef wrapped in butter and bread). In the 1920s tournedos and entrecôte became fashionable. The long-standing English tradition of eating beef appears in the names of some of these Belgian preparations. In the 1960s, *beefsteak* became the number-one favorite of the Belgians, who forgot about lesser parts of the animal (such as *langue de bœuf*, beef tongue that was prepared with Madeira sauce and became a classic of bourgeois cuisine). They relished a nice half pound of tender steak (rare or medium), with *pommes frites*, mayonnaise, and a little lettuce. More traditional ways of preparing beef, such as stew with beer (*stoverij* in Dutch, *carbonnades à la flamande* in French) and *choesels à la bruxelloise* (a stew of beef pancreas, kidneys, and tail, with mutton), were almost abandoned; these have been recently rediscovered in fancy brasseries. Each preparation requires a distinct part of the animal (chef's apprentices are supposed to learn these names by heart). Thus, *culotte* (rump), *tête d'aloyau* (loin), and *cuisse* (ham) are best for *bœuf à la mode*, while *flanchet* (groin) is used for preparing *bœuf roulé*, and *spiering* (lower flank) is used for *carbonnades à la flamande*.

The upgrading of beef around 1900 may be linked to improved breeding. As with pigs, local cattle breeds have been crossed with foreign ones (for example, the Durham shorthorn).[13] Moreover, farmers specialized in cattle breeding and, as in England, started to raise animals only to be slaughtered for meat (and not for pulling plows or giving milk), which improved quality and flavor but also increased prices. In this search for sophistication, veal takes a special position. Around 1850, veal cost about 1 franc per kilo, which was somewhat less than pork, but 50 years later the price of veal had more than doubled, exceeding by 40 percent the price of pork. Cookbooks enthusiastically acclaimed the qualities of veal, sometimes linking veal to Brussels: "There are few cities where one may find veal of such quality as in Brussels. The meat is white, succulent, and the fat of immaculate whiteness."[14] According to them, the meat is light, digestible, and nourishing, and all parts make exquisite dishes. *Blanquette de veau* (*kalfsblanket* in Dutch, or veal stew) was highly esteemed around 1900 and was regularly served at fancy social occasions. The dish made its way into bourgeois and later into popular cuisine, and today it is served in school and factory cafeterias, and it can be bought in glass jars in supermarkets. Veal is very popular in Wallonia and Brussels, but far less so in Flanders (where households spend one-third less on it than in the other regions).

Veal Stew (*kalfsblanket* or *blanquette de veau*)

1 pound veal (chest or shoulder)

1 carrot

1 onion *piqué*

bouquet garni (thyme, parsley, and bay leaf)

nutmeg, salt, and pepper

2 egg yolks

1 tablespoon butter

2 tablespoons flour

1 tablespoon lemon juice

Cut the meat in pieces, put it in a pot, cover with cold water, and put onto the flame. Add the carrot, the onion *piqué* (slice an onion in half; lay two bay leaves on the flat side and spike them with whole cloves), and the bouquet garni, and cook gently on moderate heat until the meat is tender (coming loose from the bones). Remove the meat from the pan, and keep warm. Prepare the sauce: Take some of the hot water, add the butter and the flour, and stir well, adding the egg yolks to bind the sauce. Add nutmeg and just a little lemon juice. Serve with mushrooms and small onions. Veal meatballs go well with the *blanquette* but are not necessary. Before serving, garnish with finely chopped parsley. Plain potatoes or rice may accompany the dish.

Poultry

The high consumption of poultry in Belgium is very recent (as in the whole of Europe). All 40-year-old Belgians will recall roasted chicken as a special treat in their youth, as a regular Sunday dish in their twenties, and as common cafeteria food in their thirties. Steeply rising per capita consumption of chicken reflects this trend: 8.8 pounds per year in the 1950s, 17.6 pounds in the 1960s, 30.8 pounds in the 1980s, and 44 pounds today.[15] Prior to World War I, poultry had an ambiguous image in Belgium. In the city and the manor, this food was served to the rich and famous; in the countryside, farmers now and then put an old chicken in the pan, although they viewed the meat as not very nourishing or tasty. Often, the birds were roasted. In fancy milieus, a wide variety of preparations were possible, with poultry served as a first course as well as main dish.

Around the big cities, particularly in the Brussels region, poultry farms were set up, supplying the expanding demand of restaurants and bourgeois kitchens. Some of these farms specialized in eggs, others in meat. The latter tried to increase production by selecting and crossbreeding, applying fast-feeding techniques (feeding the chicken buckwheat and buttermilk to obtain white meat) and fast-breeding techniques (heating systems with running hot water or heat lamps). In the 1950s, these farms expanded and mechanized, which led to immensely increasing output and cheaper meat but, according to many consumers, also to loss of flavor. Up until then, the *Mechelse koekoek* (*coucou de Malines*) was reputed for its meat, which was particularly famous in Brussels (where its name became *poulet de Bruxelles*). However, the new breeding method in battery cages introduced foreign breeds that have higher productivity than the Belgian sorts (requiring less feed and growing faster).

In the 1970s, Belgium housed 43 million chickens, but today this number has dropped by half, and a large quantity of chicken is imported from France. Because of criticism about the loss of flavor, many of the 1,200 chicken farmers in Belgium have reorganized their means of production, reinstalling, for example, free-range farms or breeding organic animals (in this, legislation has helped: in the 1980s a minimum space per animal was imposed). Since the 1990s, supermarkets have offered a wide range of poultry: precut, only the breast or the wings, the whole bird, organic, corn-fed, free-range, and so on. Today, chicken consumption in Flanders is similar to that in the Brussels area but about 30 percent higher than in Wallonia.

Game

Other fowls and birds are consumed too, but to a far lesser extent than chicken. Mention should be made of turkey (*dinde* in French and *kalkoen* in Flemish), which was quite exotic around 1900 and only appeared during fancy occasions in rich households (for example, *dindonneau braisé sauce aux huîtres*, or braised turkey with oyster sauce). Rapid commercialization in the 1980s led to the common availability of turkey fillets in supermarkets (and whole birds around Christmas). Duck, goose, guinea fowl, quail, and peacock are to be found as well, particularly in the game season (fall). Amazingly, Jean De Gouy's cookbook (1926 edition; it was first published in 1900) opens the section on game with a recipe for bear meat (mentioning dryly that "this meat is not widespread"). During the hunting season many appreciate the meat of deer, roe, wild boar, or pheasant. Game used to be the meat of the rich (actually hunted by them in their lands and woods), but nowadays it is fairly popular among wider social layers during the end-of-the-year feasts. Public hunting is strictly regulated, and most game originates from special breeding places in the Ardennes. Game poaching used to be important, and still today one may read now and then about the catching of a poacher.

Rabbit and hare deserve a special mention. Rabbits were kept both in the city and the countryside and often made a special treat for poorer people in the past. The meat of hares and wild rabbits has more flavor, but that was the privilege of the rich people. Nineteenth-century cookbooks mention recipes for preparing rabbit and hare, which are rather exclusive. For example, Cauderlier's *Het spaarzame keukenboek* (The economical kitchen book; 1907) gives a recipe for *Haas op zijn Vlaamsch gebraden* (*lièvre rôti à la flamande*, or Flemish-style roasted hare), with lots of butter, cream, and vinegar, ending by stating, "This is a rather expensive preparation, but one that leads to an extremely flavorful hare."[16] Wild rabbit is prepared differently from the domestic kind. The former needs to marinate for at least a day in a mixture of spices and vinegar (or wine). Quite popular is the preparation of rabbit with beer, served with plums.

Rabbit with Plums (*konijn met pruimen* or *lapin aux prunes*)

One rabbit (about 2 1/2 pounds)

1 bottle of dark beer (1 1/2 cups)

1 slice of bread

1/2 pound dried plums (about 2 cups)

5 shallots

1 tablespoon butter

prepared mustard

thyme, bay leaf, pepper, and salt

Cut the rabbit into large pieces and fry in butter until the meat is brown; sprinkle with some salt and pepper. Then, chop the shallots and add them. After 10 minutes, put in the beer, thyme, and bay leaf; spread the mustard on the bread and add to the meat. Simmer for at least 25 minutes on a very moderate flame, then add the plums. Cook for another 15 minutes. Serve with floury potatoes. (Older recipes are more complex: much more butter is used, and the animal's blood and liver are used for the sauce, which presupposes the availability of both ingredients.)

FISH

Belgian culinary authors appreciate the fact that Belgium, although a small country, has woods, mountains, plains, and sea, which provide all possible vegetable and animal foods. The 40-mile-long coast has three important fishing ports, Ostend, Nieuwpoort, and Zeebrugge, which bring in about 19,000 tons of fish every year. The most important fish varieties are cod, plaice, and sole, next to crustaceans. Belgians go fishing in the North Sea but also in the Atlantic Ocean and the Baltic Sea. In the 1960s much more fish was caught (around 50,000 tons), but out of concern for the environment and fair competition, the European Union has imposed fishing limits (which fishermen hotly dispute). Consumers may purchase many more sorts of fish and crustaceans that are imported in large quantities. Today, the most popular fresh fish and crustaceans are cod, salmon, mussels, and North Sea (grey) shrimp, which together account for about 50 percent of an average Belgian household's total expenditure on fresh seafood (the rest being divided between half a dozen different sorts among which sole is important). In addition to fresh fish, consumers purchase frozen fish (cod and fish sticks are very popular), canned fish (especially sardines and tuna), salted, dried, and smoked fish (turbot, salmon, and herring), and ready-made fish dishes that are increasingly becoming fashionable (fish salads and especially dishes that combine fish with sauce and vegetables). The latter dishes are much more popular in Flanders than in other parts of Belgium. The same goes for mussels, with double the consumption in Flanders than in Brussels and Wallonia. Counting all seafood together, Flemish and Brussels households spend about 240 euros per year on seafood, whereas Walloon families spend 20 percent less.

Mussels with Herbs (*mosselen in fijne kruiden* or *moules aux fines herbes*)

1 pound very fresh mussels

1 onion

2 celery stalks, sliced

parsley

2 tablespoons butter

pepper and salt

Wash the mussels with plenty of water, then put them into a pot with 2 teaspoons of the butter, the onion, the sliced celery, and two cups of water; add some pepper. Cook on high heat, shaking regularly. Once the mussels open, put them into a colander, but reserve the cooking liquid (remove the empty shells). Add the remaining butter to the cooking liquid, heat well while stirring, and add the parsley and some pepper. Put the mussels back in, warm on a low flame, and serve at once. Adding some white wine or a couple of tomatoes with a tad of garlic to the sauce may vary this simple but tasty dish. In any case, *pommes frites* should accompany the mussels.

The average seafood consumption in Belgium used to be low. In the nineteenth century it reached about 6.6 pounds per person per year, but there were important regional differences, with much higher consumption in large cities than in small towns or in the countryside, where fish was almost unknown. Urban working-class families ate mussels on Fridays. Small vessels used waterways between Zeeland (the Netherlands) and Flemish cities, selling the mussels directly at the quaysides of Ghent, Brussels, Liège, and Antwerp. Late nineteenth-century cookery books warn about the very "laborious" digestion of mussels. De Gouy preferred fresh fish, which is "abundant, cheap, nutritious, and therefore of inestimable value."[17] He listed the kinds that were eaten in Belgium in the 1920s, not distinguishing between sea fish and freshwater fish, indicating characteristics, prices, and ways of preparation. He started with the "king of fish," namely, turbot, then presented brill, halibut, plaice (including its salted variant, *scholle*), sole, ray, salmon ("excellent meat and very nutritious," p. 280), trout, sturgeon, cod ("an excellent fish of moderate price," p. 285), haddock, whiting, herring ("this little sea fish that is eaten so commonly has been known for a long time. From the eleventh century measures were taken to limit the fishing of herring; its salting started in the fourteenth century," p. 288), carp, pike, and so on. Next come the crustaceans, where special mention is made of crayfish, North Sea shrimp, oysters, mussels, and lobster. Eels are listed too, including the well-liked *anguilles au vert* (*paling in 't groen*, or eels with a sauce of six herbs in which garden sorrel is dominant). The then-pricey types (turbot, lobster, and sole) are still the most expensive today, but cheap kinds have been upgraded, and only fish heads and tails (used for soup or sauce) are cheap. The common mussels, eels, herring, or cod have become expensive as well. In 1999, the price of cod equaled that of the luxury fish sole, in a total reversal of traditional hierarchies, which made it into the newspapers.[18] Together with the belief that fish is less nourishing than meat, the high price of fresh fish nowadays has made it a foodstuff chiefly for well-off people. This high price is also connected to the fact that consumers may buy expensive fish fillets (fully cleaned, and often without fish bones), whereas they used to get a whole fish or a big piece of it, which has bones, skin, and other unsavory parts.

VEGETABLES

The vegetable is the third element of the Belgians' typical plate. Cookbooks from the late nineteenth and early twentieth centuries include many recipes for vegetables. Today these are considered *traditional* side dishes.[19] Spinach, endive, *witloof* (*chicons* in French, or Belgian endive), red, green, and white cabbages, cauliflower, carrots, beans, peas, leeks, *scorzonera* (black salsify), and celery appeared in most cookbooks around 1900. These vegetables had been known for a long time, but, as with fruit, industrialization and commercialization of agriculture had made them cheaper, which was especially beneficial to the middle classes, who followed the rich's long-established preference for very young vegetables (*primeurs*). De Gouy's 1925 recipe book mentions beans, peas, carrots, leeks, cauliflowers, and others, but prepared in a different way from the one presented in popular cookery books. He stresses, for example, that most vegetables should be cooked only briefly and served in a plain way in order not to lose their taste and nutritional value.[20] De Gouy pays a great deal of attention to more sophisticated vegetables, such as asparagus, tomatoes, artichokes, eggplant, beets, mushrooms, hop shoots, lettuce, and truffles. Some of these already appeared in more ordinary cookbooks, although in a very marginal role. Today's cookbooks do mention these and other vegetables, with growing attention to foreign vegetables (daikon radish, zucchini, pimentos, and broccoli), "forgotten" vegetables (such as fennel and parsnip), and "authentic" vegetables (such as cauliflower and Brussels sprouts). In Belgium most of these old and new vegetables are produced in open fields and, increasingly, in greenhouses.

Fresh vegetables make up the bulk of Belgian vegetable purchases, with canned and frozen products lagging far behind. Sales of organic vegetables increased steeply in the 1990s, but growth has stopped since the year 2000. Regional differences are clear: today inhabitants of Flanders and Brussels spend 15 percent more on vegetables than do Walloons. Social differences are even more marked, with the lowest-income groups spending almost three times less on vegetables than the highest-income category. Richer people tend to buy washed, highly selected, chopped, and packaged lettuce, cauliflower, broccoli, carrots, and cabbage, or a seasonal "wok mix," which are sold at a higher price.

Belgian (or Brussels) endives have a nice story that may be read in many books and Web sites.[21] Around 1840, chicory producers near Brussels needed to store chicory, the cheap product that was used as a coffee substitute, because its price was very low. They put it in rows in a dark cellar and covered it with some soil for protection against the cold. When picking up the chicory, they discovered to their surprise that white flowers (like tulips) had grown out of the chicory. They tasted these and were struck by the delicate, sweet-bitter flavor. The white leaves gave the name to this new product, *witloof* (literally, white leaf). In French-speaking Belgium, this vegetable received the old name of *chicons*, which existed since the 1650s and referred to the word *chicorée*. When farmers could not sell the chicory roots, they cultivated the leaves for their own consumption and, most likely out of hunger, ate the leaves as a salad (for these were the years of starvation). But soon cooks started to appreciate *witloof* as a fine ingredient in fancy dishes (a highly sought-after good, the price of *witloof* rose significantly as a derivate of chicory that could be sold without difficulty). When a big Parisian trader discovered this vegetable in the late 1870s, it became known all over the world as Belgian (or Brussels) endives because, once cooked, *witloof* resembles endives. The story of this discovery may be read on the official Web site of the Belgian government. A Jan Lammers fled his farm during the revolutionary days of September 1830, and on his return found the white flowers on the chicory roots.[22] So, the "white gold," as some like to label *witloof*, was born out of the Belgian revolution, which makes it a genuine Belgian product. Still, this vegetable was mentioned as *uytspruytsels van chicoray wortels* (sprouts from chicory roots) in a popular Dutch cookbook, *De verstandige kock of sorghvuldige huyshoudster* (The sensible cook or the careful housekeeper), that had been published in Amsterdam in 1669, as well as in other Dutch and Flemish agricultural treatises.[23] Back then, however, it had not been commercialized, and, even more importantly, only individual leaves of the chicory roots were harvested and not the whole flower.

It took quite some time before *witloof* found its way into the more popular cuisine. In the nineteenth century only the richer people consumed this vegetable. The 1907 edition of Cauderlier's *Keukenboek*, for example, mentions endives but no *chicons* or *witloof*, and only *suikerij*, which is the nineteenth-century name for chicory, was briefly used, saying that it is prepared in the same way as endives. De Gouy does mention "Chicorée witloof" (he did not use *chicon*, which was unknown in France), presenting two methods of preparation (boiled in water and served with a white sauce or, in gourmet fashion, steamed with butter). Interwar cookbooks, addressing a large public, mention the now very popular *witloof* with ham, as well as the use of fresh *witloof* in salads. Today, *witloof* is produced in the region east of Brussels, occupying about 7,980 acres, which is slightly less than 10 years ago. Much of this produce is exported throughout the world. In August 2008, *witloof* was added to the European Union's Protected Designation of Origin list.[24]

Rolls of Belgian Endives with Ham and Cheese (*gegratineerd witloof met hesp or chicons gratinés au jambon*)

4 pieces of fresh *witloof*

4 slices of ham

1/2 pound shredded Gouda or Gruyère

butter

1 tablespoon flour

some pepper, nutmeg, and salt

fine bread crumbs

1 cup cream

Cut large *witloof* pieces in half lengthwise, but leave smaller pieces whole. Steam the vegetable with some butter for about 20 minutes on low heat, and add some pepper and salt. When they are almost done (a fork should not pierce the vegetable easily), remove them from the heat and leave to dry. Then, roll the *witloof* in the ham slices, and put these in an ovenproof dish. Prepare the roux: Melt butter in a pan over moderate heat, add some flour, and stir well. Add the cream, then most of the cheese, while stirring. Add pepper, salt, and nutmeg, and pour the sauce over the rolls. Top with bread crumbs and some cheese, and place in the oven at 390°F or 200°C for about 20 minutes. Serve with mashed potatoes.

It is impossible not to mention Brussels sprouts, although *spruitjes* or *choux de Bruxelles* are not popular in Belgium. In 1925 De Gouy noted that sprouts are a particular variant of young cabbages that would lose any taste or nutritious value when growing further. They are at their best when they reach the size of a nut. De Gouy stresses that sprouts should not be overcooked. After being cleaned ("get rid of the yellowish leaves, and wash abundantly," p. 349), they need to be blanched and rinsed again; then, they should be sautéed in butter with some nutmeg. Cauderlier's *Keukenboek* only mentioned that *spruiten* (literally, offspring) should be cooked thoroughly in salted water, braised with lots of butter and some salt and pepper, and finally bound with white sauce. In 1979 Clément labeled Brussels sprouts as *mignon* (cute), emphasizing that they are the aristocrats among the wide range of the *Brassica oleracea* and accompany pork nicely.[25] He added that they make an excellent *stoemp* (a mix of mashed potatoes with vegetables) with onions, lard, and potatoes.

Together with other types of cabbages, sprouts emerged in the Mediterranean region and were probably introduced into northwestern Europe by the Romans in the fifth century. In the thirteenth century they were grown in the southern Netherlands, where they became quite popular two centuries later. *Spruiten* were mentioned in a cookbook of 1587. They spread from this area over the rest of Europe, which is how they got their name. By the nineteenth century the bourgeoisie appreciated one or two Brussels sprouts in a *pièce montée* (decorative construction) of vegetables. The miniature cabbages were consumed by all social classes in the twentieth century but disliked by many because of the very distinct smell when they are being cooked. Nowadays, *spruitjesgeur* (smell of sprouts) means a boardinghouse smell. Some nutritionists try to improve sprouts' image by stressing the high content of vitamins A, B1, and C and of potassium, magnesium, and phosphorus. "Sprouts keep you in shape," states the Web site of Flandria, the Flemish institution that promotes vegetables and fruit. Seed-producing firms, however, wish to get rid of the sprouts' boring taste and image by making them sweeter and thus attractive to children. Genuine gourmets reject this, of course.

Cauliflower (*bloemkool* in Dutch, *chou-fleur* in French) is part of the same family as Brussels sprouts and very closely related to broccoli. It has been found in the Low Countries since the Middle Ages, probably coming from Italy. It disappeared, however, in most of southern Europe, but its cultivation remained in some parts of western Europe. In 1925 De Gouy mentions it only briefly together with broccoli. Both vegetables may be prepared in the same way (au gratin, with white sauce and cheese). The chef adds one other recipe (*chou-fleur à la dauphine*, in which the vegetable is covered in Parmesan cheese and then fried). A similar low interest in cauliflower is apparent in Cauderlier's cookbook of 1907. This chef gave the same recipe for preparing cauliflower as De Gouy did, pointing out that the cheese should be half Gruyère and half Parmesan. The mention of Parmesan cheese in both recipe books testifies to the rather elite aspect of the dish (in those days, Parmesan cheese was truly expensive).

Cauliflower appeared on the tables of the richer people. Its production was time-consuming (bedding out of seedlings, protecting against the cold and the sun, weeding, etc.) and the harvesting a very delicate and always uncertain matter, which made this vegetable a costly product.

In the last quarter of the nineteenth century, villages between the towns of Leuven and Mechelen specialized in cauliflower production. Together with some regions in France, Germany, and the Netherlands, they long remained the only production centers in Europe. The output rose, but prices dropped only moderately. As was the case with *witloof* and Brussels sprouts, the middle classes started to enjoy cauliflower in the 1890s. The De Paeuws' 1931 recipe book shows this growing interest: in addition to cauliflower au gratin (not with Parmesan cheese, but with Gruyère), they mention serving cauliflower with butter sauce ("brown" butter and nutmeg) and white sauce (made of butter, flour, salt, pepper, and milk or cream). Also, cauliflower may be served cold, "with mayonnaise, grey shrimp, parsley and tarragon, and adorned with chopped ham,"[26] which again indicates the elite character of this vegetable. The 1972 edition of *Ons kookboek* (Our cookbook), edited by the Women Farmers' Association since the 1920s, mentions six recipes using cauliflower: a soup (cauliflower soup with cheese), a cold starter ("Greek cauliflower" with mayonnaise, ham, tomatoes, lettuce, and hard-boiled eggs), and four hot dishes (among which, of course, is cauliflower au gratin, but also stuffed cauliflower, which combines the vegetable with ground meat).

Stuffed Cauliflower (*gevulde bloemkool* or *chou-fleur farci*)

1 pound ground meat (mix of beef and pork)

1 cauliflower

1 egg yolk

salt, nutmeg, pepper, parsley, and garlic

oil (or butter)

1/2 tablespoon of cream

flour

Clean the cauliflower and cut it into pieces, keeping only the white flowerets. Put these in a pan with water and boil for about 10 minutes (the vegetable should not become soft). In the meantime, mix the ground meat well with the egg yolk, adding salt, pepper, nutmeg, and chopped garlic. Take the cauliflower out of the pan (reserve the cooking water), and drain well. Then, take an ovenproof dish and build a "tower" (with a large base and a small top), using the ground meat to hold the cauliflower in place. Sprinkle some oil (or butter) on top of the tower, and put in the oven (390°F or 200°C, 25 to 30 minutes). To prepare the sauce, make a roux (put some butter or oil in a pan on a low fire, add the same quantity of flour and stir frequently, add some water, but leave on a moderate fire), then add the cream, pepper, and enough salt, and stir well. Before serving, decorate the tower with freshly chopped parsley. Serve with plain potatoes.

Nowadays, cauliflower production is declining in Belgium. In the early 1990s, about 95,700 tons were sold for direct consumption, which today has dropped to 20,000 tons. However, cauliflower is increasingly produced for agribusiness and for ready-made dishes. Consumption in Flanders is higher than in Wallonia and especially Brussels.

BEER AND OTHER BEVERAGES

Since ancient times, beer has been drunk with meals, and Belgium is known as a beer country (according to some, *the* beer country). There are indeed dozens of brewers and hundreds of beers in Belgium, together with

A souvenir shop near the Brussels Grand'Place, 2008, that sells about 250 sorts of Belgian beers. About 800 different varieties of beers are brewed in Belgium. Courtesy of the author.

many beer museums and beer restaurants (where most dishes are prepared with beer, and carefully selected beers are served instead of wine). Tim Webb's Good Beer Guide to Belgium (2008) presents 120 breweries, 800 different types of beer, and 500 specialist beer cafés. Thousands of Belgians consider themselves genuine beer connoisseurs. Belgian beer's high quality is internationally recognized, which is, of course, amply stressed in the Belgian press. In particular, the yearly Top 100 Beers in the World contest is extensively covered.[27] In 2008, 1.4 million people rated 76,000 beers from 8,000 brewers worldwide: fifteen Belgian beers made the top 100, six of them are in the top 20, and two of them in the top 5 (Westvleteren Abt 12 is number 2 in 2008 but was number 1 in 2005, and De Struise Black Albert is ranked 4). In the list of the top 100 brewers, there are 13 Belgian breweries, with De Struise (in the tiny village of Woesten, West Flanders) as number 1. Belgian beers have been popular in the United States in recent years. The Manhattan pub Hop Devil, for example, sells dozens of Belgian beers, as well as Belgian-style beers that are increasingly brewed in the United States. New Yorkers gladly spend up to $55 on one bottle of Westvleteren. Since 2006, New York has a yearly "Ultimate Belgian Tasting" festival, where Duvel, Chimay, Kwak, Leffe, Stella, Rodenbach and other specialty beers are served.[28]

Brewers' international success contrasts with the continually declining beer consumption in Belgium over the last century: consumption reached 57 gallons per capita per year around 1900 but is only 23 gallons now. The most dramatic fall occurred in the first half of the twentieth century (31 gallons per person were consumed in 1950), and despite a slight increase in the 1970s (to 34 gallons per person), the decline is gradual but seemingly inevitable since 1980, occurring equally in Flanders, Wallonia, and Brussels. The two World Wars and the depression of the 1930s may explain the rapid fall in the first half of the twentieth century, while the fast-growing consumption of mineral water, soft drinks, and wine explains the steady decline since the 1950s.

Between 1965 and 2005, consumption of mineral water and soft drinks grew by 4 1/2 times (to reach 65 gallons today), and that of wine doubled (to 6.2 gallons per person per year). Belgium produces some wine (in the Brabantine region of Hageland, which was formally recognized in 1997 as the northernmost wine-producing region of Europe), reviving an old tradition that was completely lost for centuries. The country imports most of its wines from France, although Italian, Spanish, Australian, South African, and Californian wines are sold too. In the nineteenth century, many small, local producers of fruit juices, sparkling water, and carbonated and noncarbonated soft drinks existed, but fierce competition with big international brands largely led to their disappearance in the 1960s. Some managed to survive, though, doing quite well. Very successful were the producers of bottled water; the oldest and best-known brand is probably Spa. Production of bottled water started in the little village of Spa near Liège as early as 1583. The rich and famous of Europe loved to spend some time in chic Spa. When visiting the small town in 1717, the Russian Czar Peter the Great was cured from stomachache after drinking Spa's water.

Since the Middle Ages, brewers could be found in almost every village of the Low Countries, generally producing two types of beer: *kleinbier* (little beer) and *middelbier* (middle beer). Beer was much safer to drink than water from wells or rivers (bottled water being far too expensive), and its alcohol content was usually low. There were types with 9% alcohol content, just like today's better beers, but these were very expensive and therefore only drunk at special occasions or by the elite. Brewers in the bigger cities were particularly successful. The Antwerp brewers, for example, produced 3,434,000 gallons of beer in the 1540s, but 8,717,700 gallons 20 years later, which implies genuine commercialization and professionalism.[29] Also, they exported beer to France, England, and Germany. Some of these breweries evolved into big companies, sometimes merging with other brewers, to become strong players on the national and international markets, rapidly integrating new techniques, such as the pilsner (or lager) beer of the late 1860s or marketing innovations of the 1890s. Inbev, today one of the world leaders in the sector, evolved out of a modest brewer, Den Horen, established in 1366 in Leuven, where later Artois settled (which is the actual founder of Inbev and produces Stella Artois, one of the most widespread beers in Belgium today). Many of the small, local brewers hardly changed and managed to survive all innovations of the nineteenth century. Thus, in 1900 there were still 3,220 breweries that were spread all over Belgium, which means that every village had at least one brewer. The first half of the twentieth century, however, was disastrous for small brewers, and by 1950 only 660 brewers remained; many smaller ones had vanished. Today, some 120 brewers are left, of which most are part of big companies, but some are still independent. Belgian brewers produce much more beer today than a couple of decades ago. The fact that Belgians drink less beer is compensated for by the rapidly increasing exports: between the year 2000 and today, exports of beer rose by no less than 85 percent, mainly to France, the Netherlands, Germany, England, and the United States.

Of all the beer consumed in Belgium, about 70 percent is plain pilsner beer, the most common brands being Jupiler, Maes, and Stella. This beer contains between 4.5 and 5.2 percent alcohol. Then come the renowned abbey beers (Trappist), the specialty beers (regional varieties), the fruit beers (such as *kriek*), and a group composed of various types (table beer, alcohol-free beer, *witbier* or "white beer"). Table beer (Piedbœuf, for example) used to be the most popular drink up to the 1960s, with a low alcohol content (0.8 to 2.5 percent), and was perceived to be a healthy beverage. In 1906, for example, home economics teacher Louisa Mathieu wrote about the daily beer, "It is a healthy, pleasant and digestive drink, very nourishing. Beer suits children, convalescents and delicate persons. Excessive beer drinking may lead to obesity."[30]

Belgian beer's richness appears fully when considering the long list of various types. One book lists 751 beers alphabetically, giving information on the fermentation, style, ingredients, alcohol content, color, way of serving, temperature, and flavor, plus a photo of each beer bottle and the accompanying glass for drinking it. The book starts with Aardmonnik (8 percent alcohol content, brewery De Struise, pilsner, with a "complex, earthly aroma, with a wine-like elegance") and ends with Zinnebir (6 percent alcohol, brewery De Ranke, golden blond, "character beer with taste evolution. Round and hoppy. Malty and full at the start, pleasantly bitter, long-lasting aftertaste").[31] Some beers are missing, though, like the common lager or the renowned Westvleteren. Abbey beers are not just a name: some of them are actually brewed in abbeys, such as the beers of Achel, Affligem, Bornem, Chimay, Orval, Rochefort, and Westvleteren, and have the label of "recognized abbey beer," referring explicitly to a religious institution. Most of these abbeys brewed beer since the Middle Ages but stopped because of social and political upheavals. Some of them resumed brewing by the middle of the nineteenth century, applying the then-modern techniques. Alongside these beers, many abbey-style beers are produced, but without a link (nor payment) to the monks; therefore, these are not recognized as genuine abbey beers. In 2006 Geuze, Kriek, Faro, and Lambiek have obtained the official European Union label of Traditional Specialty Guaranteed.

SNACKS

Not long ago the *vieruurtje*, or the 4 P.M. snack, was popular, but nowadays this tradition has almost vanished. Nonetheless, people do eat a lot of snacks, among which are waffles, potato chips, cookies, candy bars, and chocolate. Dieticians try to persuade children and adults to eat fruit or yogurt, but they are not very successful. Chocolate is particularly liked and comes in many forms and varieties. The 1.4-oz chocolate bar is a classic. In addition to plain milk chocolate and dark *(fondant)* chocolate bars,

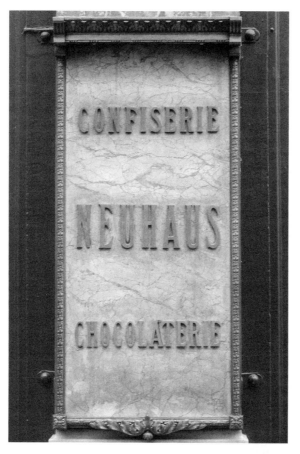

The marble sign of the Brussels chocolate manufac‐
turer Neuhaus, Galerie de la Reine, established in
1857. In 1912 the filled chocolate bonbon, or the pra‐
line, was invented here. Courtesy of the author.

there is an enormous selection: praline, white, extra dark, with nuts, with
fillings (cream, banana, strawberry, cherry, and more), and so on. Each
brand has its own specialties. Côte d'Or, for example, developed "Dessert
58" for the 1958 Brussels World's fair, which is still produced nowadays.
Alongside chocolate bars, bigger portions are sold (units of 3.5, 4.4, 7.7,
and 14 ounces), with many flavors and varied composition. Pralines, or
small filled chocolate bonbons, are particularly popular. A box of pralines
(4.4 or 8.75 ounces) used to be the classic present that people offered when
invited for dinner at a friend's home. In the 1990s small, independent arti‐
sans renewed the manufacture of pralines by adding surprising flavors and

ingredients, changing the shape and content (unexpected textures), and selling them at a high price: they upgraded the product and started a fresh commercial enterprise. One of them, Pierre Marcolini, designs a collection of chocolates for the season, as famous couturiers do. In fancy cafés and restaurants a praline by Marcolini accompanies the espresso, and in everyday cafés a simple but tasty *Mignonette* (a bit of chocolate that comes in four flavors) is offered with the coffee. Chocolate in Belgium is a matter of daily consumption as well as for special occasions. It is everywhere: in shops, advertisements, people's minds, and definitely households' cupboards.

A Belgian leaflet invokes five reasons for the success of Belgian chocolate; its title is "Why Belgian Chocolate Is the Best in the World."[32]

Leonidas has manufactured "fine Belgian chocolates" since the 1910s. U.S. citizen Leonidas Kestekides attended the World's fairs in Brussels (1910) and Ghent (1913) and soon thereafter established three shops in Belgium. Today the firm has hundreds of shops throughout the world. Courtesy of the author.

First, the cocoa beans are of excellent quality and are processed in optimal conditions. Second, the roasting and breaking are done very carefully, and, third, all other ingredients are of top quality. Fourth, small and large producers combine long-established tradition with daring innovation, and, finally, Belgian chocolate has to have at least 35 percent cocoa, although most Belgian chocolate actually contains 43 percent or more. Other countries allow less than 10 percent.

Foreign visitors appreciate Belgian chocolate, and, in general, most countries associate Belgium with first-rate chocolate.[33] Many Belgian producers export to other countries or have a shop in chic districts. Marcolini, for example, has boutiques in France, Japan, Kuwait, the United Kingdom, and the United States. The 87 Belgian chocolatiers produce 479,000 tons of chocolate annually, of which 76 percent is exported.[34] Half is sent to France, the Netherlands, Germany, and Luxembourg, and the rest to all corners of the globe. This makes little Belgium the second biggest exporter of chocolate in Europe, after Germany. There are two sorts of exported product: the final product (bars, pralines, etc.) and liquid chocolate that may be used for further production. Belgians are big consumers of chocolate, at almost 22 pounds per person per year; in this, they come second to British consumers and are close to Germans. Flemings and Walloons spend the same amount of money on chocolate products, leaving the inhabitants of Brussels behind them (who spend 15 percent less). Differences between income groups are significant, with people at the lower end spending about 3.5 times less on chocolate than those with higher incomes. Still, all Belgians consume more chocolate today than in 1995 (when Belgium, at 15 pounds per person per year, came fifth after Switzerland, the United Kingdom, Norway, and Germany).

Belgians' general love for chocolate is fairly recent.[35] It used to be a luxury import product that was extremely expensive. In the seventeenth century cocoa became a fashionable drink. Cocoa was dissolved in hot water, sugar (another costly ingredient) was added, and this mix was poured into milk and served hot. People of more modest origin tasted chocolate when a pharmacist deemed it necessary to cure a particular illness. Some of these pharmacists started to produce chocolate cookies (a mixture of cocoa, sugar, and spices like vanilla or cinnamon) that could be used to prepare the hot drink or eaten as such. Later, they introduced new, cost-saving technology (for example, for breaking cocoa shells or mixing cocoa butter). These were not Belgians, though. Belgian *confiseurs* (pastry cooks) and chocolatiers bought machines abroad (invented or installed by Fry and Cadbury in England, or Lindt in Switzerland), and some foreigners came to Brussels to set up businesses. For example, in 1857, Frédéric Neuhaus left Switzerland for Brussels, where he started a chocolate shop (his grandson is considered to have invented pralines in 1912). Around 1880, Belgian chocolate producers met with fierce foreign competition, and they reacted by radically modernizing their production process and marketing strategies. As a consequence, the price of Belgian chocolate dropped considerably, and Belgians started to sell chocolate all over Europe. Some of the big producers of today go back to these years, such as Côte d'Or (now part of Kraft Foods, Inc.), Jacques, and Callebaut (today both Barry Callebaut).

When the prices of cocoa and sugar continued to decline around 1890, the middle classes began to increasingly consume chocolate. For working-class people, however, chocolate remained a true festive treat that appeared in children's dream around the time of Saint Nicolas and Christmas. This changed in the Belle Epoque, a period of fast-rising wages and almost universal employment. Ongoing decreases in prices, nonstop publicity, and the image of chocolate as healthy, enriching, and exotic turned this delicacy into a massively consumed good around 1910. An indication of its general acceptance is the fact that between 1919 and 1939 the price of chocolate was part of the official cost-of-living index, together with 55 prices of other basic goods and services. Working-class households were particularly fond of chocolate and made up arrears with regard to other social groups very quickly. To be sure, this was due to falling prices, but also to the swiftly changing image of the foodstuff (from a fancy tidbit to a healthy necessity), its widespread availability (vending machines, for example, appeared in the 1920s), and its nutritive content, which was stressed by medical doctors until the late 1930s. Belgian recipe books mirror this chocolate mania in a moderate way, though. Most cookbooks from around 1900 mention chocolate as a drink and give only one or two dessert recipes. The nutritive qualities are always emphasized. In the course of the twentieth century, many more recipes are given, such as *chocoladesorbet*, *mousse au chocolat*, chocolate truffles, and chocolate cake. Today, chocolate desserts are served in many households and are on every menu, with specialties such as *dame blanche* (vanilla ice cream topped with fresh hot dark chocolate and whipped cream) and chocolate mousse.

CHEESE AND PROCESSED MEATS

A cold meal is eaten in the evening that consists of bread, cheese, and processed meats, accompanied by beer or coffee. Popular cheeses are white cheese (*plattekaas* in Flemish, literally, flat cheese, or *fromage*

The cheese display at the restaurant L' Alban Chambon (Brussels Metropole Hotel), with an assortment of Belgian and French cheeses. Courtesy of the author.

blanc in French), plain Gouda-type cheese, and soft cheeses. In 2005 Belgians spent about 250 euros per household on cheese. Some of the soft cheeses smell particularly strong, even stink, such as the traditional Brussels cheese, which some refer to as *stinkende kaas* or, in the local dialect, *ettekees* (literally, hard cheese, because of the hard crust).

However, processed meats are even more popular. In 2005 the average Belgian household spent 450 euros per year on charcuterie, which represents a 40 percent increase compared to the 1970s. Yet, this growth is more moderate than that of total expenditures on food; moreover, spending on charcuterie evolved in a very different way in Flanders, Wallonia, and Brussels. Since the 1970s, Flemings have spent more on processed meats than have other Belgians, although the Walloons made up arrears, especially in the 1990s. Bruxellois lag behind, and today they spend about 40 percent less on processed meats than Flemings or Walloons. Social differences are even bigger than regional differences, though, with the lower-income groups spending 3.6 times less on charcuterie than the higher-income categories.

The regional disparity cannot be linked to income differences alone, and preference should be invoked. In this respect a sweeping change occurred. Around 1900, people in Brussels consumed more charcuterie than the Flemings and Walloons, with the working classes in particular appreciating simple products like dried sausages, *kipkap* (minced, seasoned meat that is eaten cold on bread, often with mustard), and *pâté de foie* (liver paste). In the course of the 1960s Flemings and Walloons started to consume more sophisticated and costly sorts of processed meats, such as salami and salted and smoked ham, thus disregarding the more traditional, cheaper products that were popular in Brussels around 1900. However, nowadays this type of coarse food, with a reputation for authenticity, has been upgraded. The present-day products contain more flavors and sorts of meat, are far better regulated, and are definitely more expensive. They can be found in supermarkets, *traiteurs* (caterers' shops), and butcher's shops that offer a large variety of local hams, salamis, pâtés, sausages, meat salads, and terrines. The sector is doing well, with a gradual growth of production and export since 1995 (95 percent goes to the European Union, especially to France, Germany, and Italy). Streekproducten.be (a Web site that presents local Flemish products) gives a long list of traditional processed meats, among which are *Antwerpse witte pensen* (Antwerp blond pudding), which was first produced in 1900 and consists of lean pork, bread, milk, eggs, nutmeg, and coriander; *Veurnese boerenpaté* (farmer's paste from Veurne), made of pork and especially liver, with onion, spices, and a lot of salt; and *Boulogne*, a salami produced in East Flanders, already mentioned in a cookbook of 1752 (two recipes are given: one with beef and pork, which is salted and smoked, the other with pork, pepper and salt, blood, and white wine, which is dried and briefly smoked).[36]

Processed meats have a very long history. In the pre-Roman period, parts of the pig were used to prepare sausages, while organs (liver, heart, and kidneys) were used in pastries. Meats of whatever sort were salted and, later, pickled (the meat needed to be put in water before being prepared). Other techniques, such as smoking and drying, were used too. Many older cookbooks provided recipes for homemade charcuterie, such as *boudin de sang aux fines herbes* (blood sausage with fine herbs) or *boudin de Liège* (sausage from Liège; made of pork, bread sopped in milk, and green herbs). Cauderlier's *Keukenboek* took two pages to explain the pickling of ham, which required 40 quarts of water, at least 110 pounds of salt, and 1.1 pound of saltpeter; he indicates the precise number of days needed for the process. This cookbook also gave recipes for preparing *tête pressée* (*geperste kop* in Dutch, chopped meat from the pig's head), *fromage d'Italie* (pork liver), and *lard à piquer* (*lardeerspek*, or larded bacon). Cauderlier was an expert in preparing processed meats, for he had published a whole volume on this art.[37] Very famous today is the *Jambon d'Ardenne*; its name and mode of production are legally protected in Belgium since 1974 and in the European Union since 1996 (under the label of Protected Geographical Indicator). The latter is also the case for *pâté gaumais*, or paté from the Gaume region in the province of Luxembourg. Responding to a deterioration in the quality and a series of scandals around 1990, meat producers and the government launched the quality label *Meesterlyck–Magistral* (Masterly) in 1992, which is granted to products that meet high standards of hygiene, taste, and substance. *Coburg ham*, *Filet de Saxe* (smoked ham), and bacon were added to the select list of products in 2003.[38]

LIQUOR

A nightcap may conclude the day. A tiny glass of *jenever* (*genièvre*, or gin) is perfect. This drink (the alcohol content is 18–54 percent, but most commonly 30–38 percent) goes back to the Middle Ages, when it was distilled from grain, juniper berries, and spices and mostly used as a medicine. Today, large and small producers can be found in Flanders, Brussels, and Wallonia (where the drink is called *pèkèt*), making traditional brands such as Blauwe Druif (1918, 30% alcohol), Elixir d'Anvers (1863, 37% alcohol), or Töpfergeist (1836, 38% alcohol). Today, fruit gins are popular, particularly ones with lemon such as Wortegemsen (24% alcohol).[39] The consumption of *jenever* fell significantly in the course of the twentieth century because of the rising popularity of wine and the quaint image of *jenever*. However, in the 1980s this changed: *jenever* and *pèkèt* were rediscovered as authentic, healthy drinks (presumably good for digestion and sleeping), new types were launched (such as ones with fruit, which attracted younger and female consumers), and huge campaigns promoted a new, trendy image. The official European Union protection of *jenever* (produced only in Belgium, the Netherlands, and northern France) in November 2007 testifies to this new success. Another sign of the new popularity of *jenever* is its frequent consumption at public celebrations of whatever kind. For example, during Ghent's public New Year's Eve reception in January 2008, which was organized on a public square in the city center and attended by about 7,200 people, *jenever* and hot cocoa were served. Another sign of the recent success is the yearly organization of the *Jeneverfeest* in Hasselt (Limburg), one of the old production centers where a *Jenevermuseum* was established in 1987.

The new enthusiasm for *jenever* not only contrasts with the disinterest up to the 1980s but also with the public authorities' radical crusade against alcohol consumption in the past. Production of *jenever* was sometimes forbidden, for example, in the early seventeenth century (to redirect grain toward millers and bakers), or severely regulated, as throughout the nineteenth century. Around 1890, regular increases in taxes and legislation concerning public drunkenness and sales of alcohol had managed to reverse the growing alcohol consumption (which rose from 1.7 gallons per person per year in the 1830s to 2.2 gallons in the 1870s, then fell to 0.4 gallons in the 1930s). Huge anti-alcohol campaigns by physicians, priests, women's associations, the army, and civil servants, which were aimed at the lower classes' consumption of gin, which had become cheaper, helped reduce consumption. In 1918 a law temporarily prohibited production, trade, and consumption of *jenever* and *pèkèt*, but its final version in 1919 only limited production and especially consumption.

NOTES

1. This is nicely illustrated by numerous books that have recently appeared in Belgium, upgrading ancient or banal foods, ingredients, and drinks; see, for example, Eric Boschman and Nathalie Derny, *Le goût des Belges* (Brussels: Racine, 2006).

2. All information on recent agricultural statistics is taken from the official Belgian statistical portal, http://www.statbel.fgov.be/figures/d52_nl.asp#1 (accessed May 4, 2008).

3. This linguistic difference between the Dutch *gewonnen brood* and the French *pain perdu* is remarkable; I have no explanation.

4. See Eddie Niesten, Jan Raymaekers, and Yves Segers, *Vrijwaar u van namaaksels! De Belgische zuivel in de voorbije twee eeuwen* (Leuven, Belgium: CAG, 2002).

5. Delhaize Supermarket Web site, http://www.delhaize.be/food/thetaste/butter/_fr/index.asp (accessed April 6, 2008). *Beurre d'Ardenne* has the European Union certificate of Protected Designation of Origin (see the official Web site, http://ec.europa.eu/agriculture/qual/en/be_en.htm). Official European labels (carrying the acronyms PGI, [Protected Geographical Indication], PDO, [Protected Designation of Origin], and TSG, [Traditional Speciality Guaranteed]) have been granted to several Belgian products.

6. Jacques Collen, *Stroop, een parel van ons culinair erfgoed* (Antwerp: ASG, 2007).

7. Eddie Niesten and Yves Segers, *Smaken van het land: Groenten en fruit vroeger en nu* (Leuven, Belgium: Davidsfonds, 2007).

8. Eddie Niesten and Ovide Standaert, *Patatfooi: De gouden geschiedenis van een bescheiden knol* (Leuven, Belgium: CAG, 2001), 45.

9. Chris Vandenbroeke, "La culture de la pomme de terre en Belgique (XVIIe–XIXe siècles)," *Flaran* 12 (1990): 115–129; Yves Segers, *Economische groei en levensstandaard: Particuliere consumptie en voedselverbruik in België, 1800–1913* (Leuven: Universitaire Pers, 2003), 259.

10. The United Nations chose the year 2008 as the International Year of the Potato, stressing the nutritive qualities and low cost of the tuber in the war against hunger; see International Year of the Potato—Web site, http://www. potato2008.org/en/potato/factsheets.html (accessed April 7, 2008).

11. See U.S. Census 2000, http://allcountries.org/uscensus/1370_per_capita_ consumption_of_meat_and.html (accessed April 5, 2008).

12. Segers, *Economische groei en levensstandaard*, 358–359. See also Eddie Niesten, Jan Raymaekers, and Yves Segers, *Lekker dier!? Dierlijke productie en consumptie in de 19e en 20e eeuw* (Leuven, Belgium: CAG, 2003), 100–121.

13. Niesten, Raymaekers, and Segers, *Lekker dier*, 125–147.

14. Jean De Gouy, *La cuisine et la pâtisserie bourgeoises à la portée de tous* (Brussels: Office de Publicité, 1925), 166.

15. Niesten, Raymaekers, and Segers, *Lekker dier*, 178 and 64–97.

16. Cauderlier, *Het spaarzame keukenboek* (Ghent: Hoste, 1907), 277.

17. De Gouy, *La cuisine*, 269.

18. "Kabeljauw wordt even duur als tong" [Cod is getting as expensive as sole], *De Standaard*, December 18, 1999.

19. I have compared information on vegetables in *Ons kookboek* (Leuven, Belgium: KVLV, 1999) with Cauderlier, *Spaarzame keukenboek*; Louisa Mathieu, *Notions d'économie domestique* (Verviers, Belgium: Hermann, 1906); and Jane De Paeuw and Leo De Paeuw, *De moderne huishouding* (Brussels: Office de Publicité, 1931).

20. De Gouy, *La cuisine*, 325.

21. I refer to Gaston Clément, *Cuisine et folklore de Bruxelles et Brabant* (Brussels: Le Sphinx, 1997), 1361.

22. *Witloof* or Belgian endives: Belgium's white gold, http://www.belgium.be/ eportal/application?languageParameter=en&pageid=contentPage&docId=6998 (accessed May 2, 2008, but inaccessible today).

23. The 1669 recipe book is presented (with an English version) at Kookhistorie (Cook History), http://www.kookhistorie.nl (accessed May 4, 2008). See also Jozef Schildermans, Hilde Sels, and Marleen Willebrands, *Lieve schat, wat vind je lekker? Het Koocboec van Antonius Magirus (1612) en de Italiaanse keuken van de renaissance* (Leuven, Belgium: Davidsfonds, 2007), 69–70.

24. "Brussels witloof erkend" [Brussels endives recognized], *De Standaard*, August 7, 2008, p. 9. Another seven products were also proposed for official European Union recognition (e.g., North Sea grey shrimp, and Lokerse horse meat sausage).

25. Clément, *Cuisine et folklore*, 1363.

26. De Paeuw and De Paeuw, *De moderne huishouding*, 267.

27. Best Beers in the World, http://www.ratebeer.com (accessed May 7, 2008); "West Vlaamse Struise brouwers zijn 's werelds beste" [West-Flemish Struise Brewery is the best in the world], *De Morgen*, February 9, 2008, 7.

28. "Amerikanen storten zich massaal op Belgische pils en speciaalbieren" (Americans pounce en mass on Belgian pilsner and special beers), *De Tijd*, December 14, 2007, 32. See also "More or Less Pale But All Belgian," *New York Times*, August 22, 2007.

29. Raymond Van Uytven, *Geschiedenis van de dorst: Twintig eeuwen drinken in de Lage Landen* (Leuven, Belgium: Davidsfonds, 2007), 73–97.

30. Mathieu, *Notions d'économie domestique*, 241.

31. Hilde Deweer, *All Belgian Beers* (Oostkamp, Belgium: Stichting Kunstboek, 2007), 14, 1516.

32. Jacques Mercier, *Le chocolat belge et les pralines: Le guide* (Tournai, Belgium: Casterman, 1996), 49.

33. For example, "Masters of Chocolate Look Abroad and See Something Even Richer," *New York Times*, January 30, 2006.

34. For data, see the Royal Belgian Association of Biscuit, Chocolate, Pralines and Confectionary Industries, http://www.choprabisco.be/engels/choprabisco_frameset.htm (accessed May 9, 2008).

35. Peter Scholliers, "From Elite Consumption to Mass Consumption: The Case of Chocolate in Belgium," in *Food Technology, Science and Marketing: European Diet in the Twentieth Century*, ed. Adel Den Hartog (East Linton: Tuckwell Press, 1995), 127–138.

36. VLAM-Streekproducten (Flemish Organization for Regional Products), http://www.streekproduct.be/ (accessed May 10, 2008).

37. Philippe Cauderlier, *Le livre de la fine et de la grosse charcuterie* (Ghent: Hoste, 1877).

38. Meesterlyck (or Magistral in French) offering a "quality label for fine charcuterie," http://www.meesterlyck.be (accessed May 10, 2008), contains the criteria, the recognized producers, the protected foods, and a brief history.

39. Stefaan Van Laere, *Jenever, van korrel tot borrel* (Leuven, Belgium: Davidsfonds, 2005); Eric Van Schoonenberghe, ed., *Jenever in de Lage Landen* (Bruges: Stichting Kunstboek, 1996).

3

Cooking

The way Belgians obtain and prepare food is constantly changing, depending on such factors as agriculture, imports, manufacturing, retailing, and kitchen technology. Some claim these changes have accelerated in recent years due to globalization. Proponents of globalization argue that more products are available throughout the year, and identical foodstuffs will be accessible all over the globe. Because of its truly international character, Belgium will quickly pick up new trends and serve as a region for market testing, where new products are introduced before they are launched onto a wider market. Hence, Belgian foodways would be particularly sensitive to international changes. This may be true, but if recent changes such as ready-to-eat lettuce in small, plastic packages (implying complicated harvesting, selecting, cleaning, packing, marketing, and transporting) seem noteworthy, in fact, many more innovations with broad consequences have occurred since the middle of the nineteenth century. This chapter focuses on three components that directly affect food culture in Belgium: the food supply, kitchen equipment, and cooking skills.

FOOD SHOPPING

Today, most Belgians buy food in supermarkets of various types, where they make 94 percent of total food purchases, with the remaining 6 percent of sales coming from traditional ("corner") shops, markets, and farmers.[1] In this, Belgium is far from exceptional. Small, independent shops are responsible for the same tiny share of food sales in the Netherlands or France. Not long ago, the individually owned food shop in Belgium was the most common retailer, with 75 percent of total food sales in 1972. The number of shops reached 34,900 in 1972, but 10 years later this had dropped to half that number, and in 2006 only 5,600 shops remained. Although the decline has slowed, their number is still decreasing. These data point not only to a radically transformed retail landscape but also to bankruptcy or loss of capital.

Up until the 1850s grocers used to be limited to dry, easily stocked products like spices, sugar, or coffee that arrived mostly from wholesalers in the direct vicinity. Such goods were known as *koloniale waren* (*denrées coloniales,* or colonial goods). These generally bore no brand name and were stocked in big sacks or wooden boxes that arrived straight from manufacturers or tradespeople. The largest number of grocers was found in the old town center, where particular streets and squares emerged as important commercial hubs. Many small shops sold luxury foods, such as foie gras, Beluga caviar, or the best Bordeaux wines, meant for a rich clientele. The shopkeeper weighed the goods, using balances that were regularly inspected by the city police.

Potato sellers at the open market in Brussels, 1930s. This form of retailing still occurs. Courtesy of the AMSAB-Institute of Social History, Ghent.

In the last quarter of the nineteenth century, many of these shops started selling then-new products such as wrapped chocolate bars, candy, or cookies, as well as large quantities of different kinds of canned foods (sardines, beef, peas, or prunes). Shopkeepers with particular business sense installed cooling systems and started selling dairy products, poultry, and cured meats. These changes transformed the appearance of shops, which generally became bigger, more organized, and hygienic. Also, advertisements appeared because big firms and importers provided goods that were sold all over the country and abroad. National brands, such as Marie Thumas (canned vegetables), Côte d'Or (chocolate), and Soubry (dry pasta), or international ones, such as Cadbury (chocolate) or Del Monte (canned fruit), became familiar.

Moreover, the character of retailing altered in the first half of the twentieth century in that some food shops became highly specialized, focusing on a fancy market (mostly these stayed in the expensive commercial centers), whereas others oriented toward a more humble clientele (often appearing in suburbs). Many of the latter disappeared after 1950 (with the closing of a stunning 400 shops per year between 1996 and 2007), although in the 1970s some shops, particularly in cities, were taken over by immigrants, who sold foreign ingredients and foods alongside products known to Belgians. If at first Belgians hesitated to visit such grocers, some of them discovered the unfamiliar foods and low prices in the 1980s. Many of the shops that specialized before 1950 managed to expand and are doing well today. Rob: The Gourmets' Market (Brussels) is a good example: today this shop offers a refined, cosmopolite, and wealthy public exclusive wines, dairy, seafood, meats, vegetables, fruit, and bakery products, coming in from all over the world daily. The corner shop practice of granting credit to regular customers, whether rich or poor, ended in the late 1950s.

Two new types of small food stores emerged in the 1980s and developed further in the 1990s: the night shop and the small food shop that is part of a larger company. The former is open between 7:30 P.M. and 6:30 A.M. and sells alcohol, tobacco, and some basic foods such as bread, dry pasta, margarine, and, increasingly, convenience foods. Today, many towns wish to limit the number of these shops and their hours of operation because of noise and competition with day shops. The other new type is part of a big chain of stores and often found together with a gas station. It sells fresh fruit, vegetables, meat, dairy products, ready-made dishes, and drinks (as well as candy, newspapers, and tobacco) and stays open until 9:30 P.M. or later. Depending on the social-geographic environment, these shops may offer a sophisticated selection, and their supply amply covers the requirements for a tasty and trendy meal (although not the cheapest one).

Around 1900, small, independent stores started selling bread, meat, and fresh food, which used to be sold by bakers and butchers and in public markets. The public markets go back to the early Middle Ages. Although at that time markets appeared to be a spontaneous event where peasants coming from the countryside offered their produce directly to city dwellers, in fact municipalities strictly regulated markets in terms of supply (number of merchants), timing (start and ending), hygiene (clean water), quality (freshness), and price (weekly maximum price for basic products). Municipal police regulated markets tightly, for these were the places where social unrest often started when the prices were deemed too high and merchants were stridently accused of fraud or indecent profit making. Bigger towns had markets on specific days (for example, vegetables and fruit on Monday, poultry and eggs on Wednesday, fish on Friday) and in specific streets or squares. Big cities had and still have daily vegetable and fruit markets. Street names testify to this, such as Butter Street or Poultry Market. These street names are still to be found in most Belgian towns, and some of them have retained aspects of their centuries-old trade. The surroundings of Brussels' Sint-Katelijneplein (Place Sainte-Catherine), for example, which used to be accessible for vessels bringing in fresh fish, are still renowned for the many seafood restaurants and fishmongers.

When towns grew in terms of inhabitants, political rights, and status, they built market halls. The Ghent Vleeshuis (Meat House), for example, opened in 1251. The wooden construction was replaced in the early fifteenth century by a stone building that still exists.[2] In the nineteenth century, many towns and villages erected market halls that responded to the hygienic requirements of the day (in particular, with cool cellars with iceboxes to store the food). Many of these buildings have vanished or are no longer used as food markets. Nowadays, the chaotic aspect of public markets is still present. Stallholders try to entice the public by low prices, particular foods (such as fresh honey, roasted chicken, or organic produce), and their appearance or chatter. Often, customers have a preference for a vendor, which may be totally irrational but implies a bond of trust between vendor (who may also be the producer) and customer. Every village or town district in Belgium has a weekly food market.[3] The vast Zuidmarkt (Marché du Midi, near the Brussels South railroad station) is famous for its Mediterranean atmosphere; Belgians love to spend Sunday morning there, buying foreign spices and ingredients.

Vendors are continually on the move. They may go to markets throughout Belgium, but they may also ask the municipality's permission to sell food individually in specific streets and squares. This is the world of the street vendors with only a few pounds of fruit or vegetables, pushing around their goods on a handcart. Up to the late nineteenth century, there were many such vendors, who often had a bad reputation for selling low-quality food to mostly poor people. Also, many unauthorized street vendors, offering only a couple of eggs or apples, strolled the streets. Today, street vendors account for only a very minor part of total food sales in Belgium. They appear in the winter selling roasted sweet chestnuts or hot dogs, or in the summer selling ice cream. Still, they have played a crucial role in the diffusion of (new) foods in urban and rural areas. When vendors started to use little vans to drive around, they transported bakery products, fresh fish, or spices (which are all "city foods") to people in rural and remote areas, who had little access to these foods previously. Nowadays, these vans are sophisticated and highly specialized (for example, selling on-the-spot roasted chicken).

Corner shops started to sell bakery products (cookies) and processed meats (salami, pâté, ham, etc.) in the 1880s. It took, however, many more years before grocers sold bread and fresh meat. Bread was and is, of course, baked and sold by bakers. Together with the millers, they played a central role in a town's life since the Middle Ages. The elegant houses their guilds built on the Grand'Place in Brussels, for example, illustrate the economic, political, and cultural power of millers and bakers. With the economic expansion and the end of guild regulations around 1800, the number of bakers started to grow significantly, often overtaking the growth of the number of inhabitants. Contemporaries often saw this as a reason for high bread prices. In fact, bread prices started to fall significantly beginning in the 1880s thanks to rising imports of cheap grain. This was the period when small, individual bakers had to compete with emerging bread factories that used automatic ovens and supplied the cheaply produced bread to various vending points. Productivity and sales increased, which lowered production costs and pushed up profits. This competition forced many small bakers to quit their trade or to specialize, initiating a much more sophisticated and varied supply that included plain *viennoiseries* (little pastries like croissants), cookies, and ice cream. It was only in the late 1980s that bread factories sensed this change in consumers' demand and began to produce *viennoiseries* and quality bread of very diverse types (like the artisan's baguette or whole-grain wheat-rye farmer's bread). Since the 1880s, the number of bakers has been declining, despite the fact that Belgians highly appreciate the *warme bakker* (hot baker), as opposed to factory products. Too often, bakers wishing to retire cannot easily find younger bakers to carry on their business. In the village of Damme (near Bruges), a bakery had been established in 1897, which was continued by children and grandchildren. It survived the advent of *Expobrood* and bread improvers (enzymes to act on yeast and gluten, to speed up the bread production) in the 1960s and 1970s, and specialized in coarse *boerenbrood* (*pain de campagne*, or farmer's bread) and apple pie. Yet, the bakery had to close in 2004, because of lack of a new baker.[4] Belgium had 6,592 traditional bakers in 1998 but only 5,339 in 2005. However, in spring 2007 newspapers announced and cheered the fact that, for the first time in a long while, the number of *warme bakkers* in Flanders was again on the rise. The number of artisan-bakers in Wallonia, however, is tending to decrease further.[5]

Butchers offer a similar story to bakers. The number of individual butchers has gradually declined since the 1970s but at a higher speed since 1990. "A butcher is a fine job!" claimed an advertisement in February 2008 in order to attract badly needed (male or female) workers. Today, individual butchers account for about 35 percent of total sales of cured and fresh meat (beef, veal, pork, horsemeat, mutton, goat, and game, but no poultry), with the supermarkets taking 40 percent and other stores (hypermarkets, discount stores, and markets) the remaining 25 percent. This is considered an achievement, although newspapers frequently report the closing of a butcher's shop due to low profits, problems with finding new personnel or a successor, and harsh labor conditions. Up to the 1980s, however, starting a butcher's shop in Belgium was the right thing to do, because the ever-growing meat consumption ensured good profits. In all Belgian villages, towns, and cities the number of butchers rose significantly, often at a faster pace than grocers and bakeries.

Until the eighteenth century, slaughterers and butchers were one and the same, which not only led to nuisance (smell and noise) but also to bloody scenes in streets where the general public comes. In most towns in the course of the nineteenth century, the slaughtering of animals was transferred to slaughterhouses that could be regulated more easily. Butchers kept their shops in the vicinity of the slaughterhouse. One of these, the Anderlecht *abattoir*, dates from 1890. It has a superb glass-in-iron roof that spans 10,750 square feet, about 50 stalls for butchers and *charcutiers*, and 26,900 square feet of refrigerated cellars.

As with bakeries, Belgians deplore the current loss of butchers, their know-how, and, consequently, the variety in tastes and types of meat preparation. A nostalgic viewpoint may be read on the blog at Senioren net.be (the Senior Web site), where people express clear opinions about present-day meat (as compared to the rich flavor in the 1950s and 1960s). One example, related to the preparation of *blanquette de veau* (ragout of veal with mushrooms and cream): "First we need to consider the ingredients, because one of the reasons why nowadays blanquette does not taste as good as in earlier times, is the quality of the meat."[6] Due to increasing competition with supermarkets, butchers have tended to specialize,

Road to modernity: The cooperative retailer COOP in Liège in the 1950s. Note the counter with a cooling system. Courtesy of the AMSAB-Institute of Social History, Ghent.

diversify, and offer other products than meat. These may include wine, cheese, sandwiches, fruit, and vegetables. This specialization and diversification appears via the list of products of a butcher in the village of Tielt (in the province of East Flanders). In 1984 Slagerij José had started as a traditional butcher: along with fresh meat he produced cured meats (charcuterie) such as ham, pâté, and salami. In 1992, the shop expanded to include freshly made dishes such as meat stews or *koninginnehapje* (literally, queen's tidbit, called *bouchée à la reine* or *vol au vent* in French, and consisting of chicken pieces in cream sauce with mushrooms, presented in pastry), and in 2002 fruit and vegetables were added. Today, the core business is still fresh and cured meats, but ready-made dishes, dairy products, poultry, wine, vegetables, and other foods are sold, which makes this shop a little supermarket that specializes in fresh meat. One of this butcher's advertisements reads, "Homemade salami. The taste of yesteryear. You have to savor it!"[7] Such reference to "old-fashioned" taste and traditional ways of processing meat has become quite common in the European meat business. It is a reaction against factory products that represent safe and correct, but standardized food. Belgian butchers strive to produce flavorful, characteristic, and healthy meats to secure their business. They may apply quality labels. Today, Flemish, Walloon, Belgian, and European authorities grant quality labels to producers who meet specific requirements for processing, ingredients, and origin (see Chapter 2). Local hams, salamis, pâtés, sausages, meat salads, *boudins* (cured sausages), and terrines carry names such as Filet d'Anvers, Ficelle d'Ath, or Jambon d'Ardenne.

Numerous competitors have challenged these centuries-old forms of grocers, public markets, bakeries, and butcher's shops. Supermarkets have become the most important retailers today, but they were not the first challengers. Beginning in 1850, workers set up stores, aiming to sell safe food at a fair price and fair weight. In Ghent, the socialist cooperative Vooruit (Forwards) started baking bread in the cellar of a pub in 1880. After a few years, this turned out to be extremely successful. By 1900 thousands of bread loaves were sold daily (home delivery was possible), and this activity soon formed the core of a store that sold not only food but also garments, coal, and medicine. Moreover, its success allowed the financing of a newspaper, a sick fund, socialist propaganda, a library, and many more activities. Gradually, Vooruit opened new shops throughout Flanders, which inspired the cooperative movement in western Europe and brought cheap, good bread and urban foods (like canned pineapple) to remote villages. In the 1960s, however, sales started to drop because of growing competition from supermarkets and the outdated image of cooperative stores; today nothing is left of the once-proud cooperative stores (activities have been reoriented toward insurance, health care, and expertise in social economics).

Another challenger appearing and vanishing in the second half of the nineteenth century was the company store. Company stores bought large quantities of basic goods (like sugar, coffee, flour, or bacon), which were sold to the company's workers. Often, workers were forced to buy in these shops; this was prohibited in 1887, which meant the shops' end. Also in the 1880s, another challenger to traditional corner shops appeared, the chain store *(maison à succursales)*. A central storehouse provides shops throughout the country with foods at a fixed price, is able to use nationwide advertisements, and aims to present a recognizable image. In 1867 Delhaize started on a moderate scale with a central depot and some shops in the province of Hainault.[8] Around 1870, it moved to Brussels, and in 1910 Delhaize possessed no fewer than 670 shops all over Belgium. This retailer wished to control the whole food chain (import, manufacturing, marketing, and selling) of chocolate, cookies, coffee, and similar products, trying to keep prices down, offering a widening variety of products, and applying modern retailing techniques. In the 1950s, Delhaize owned about 750 shops and had 1,500 franchise stores, thus being present in remote villages. This chain store participated with large stalls in World's fairs in Europe and America, as well as in the Voedingssalon—Salon de l'Alimentation (Hall of Food), an exposition that has been organized each year in Brussels since 1924 and that attracts thousands of professional and lay visitors.

In an attempt to modernize Belgian retailing, Delhaize introduced the concept of the supermarket in Belgium in 1957. Two Delhaize managers had visited the United States in 1919, which led to some modernization of the Belgian stores around 1930. In October 1957 managers again visited the United States, which directly led to the opening of a supermarket in Brussels only two months later: a copy of an American supermarket. Innovations in Belgium were numerous and radical: self-service that implies prepackaged fresh foods, the shopping cart, constantly refilled shelves, direct payment (no longer credit), and the central cash point. Posters and advertisements showed customers how to shop in this new environment. Because of the immediate and immense success, Delhaize started closing its chain stores and erecting supermarkets in suburbs, with more selling

The next step on the road to modernity: The modernized butcher's section of the cooperative in Liège in the 1960s. Courtesy of the AMSAB-Institute of Social History, Ghent.

Another step on the road to modernity: An updated corner shop, with counter and cooling systems. Courtesy of the AMSAB-Institute of Social History, Ghent.

space and car parking. In 1958 the Antwerp-based Grand Bazar opened Super GB and, in 1961, Superbazar, the first hypermarket in Belgium. Belgian companies (e.g., Colruyt) and foreign companies (e.g., ALDI) later appeared. In 1960 supermarkets accounted for a mere 1.5 percent of total retail sales. Ten years later this had reached 9 percent, but the 1970s saw the hard-hitting breakthrough of supermarkets in Belgium. Today, a dense net of supermarkets of various sizes covers Belgium. The country has 75 hypermarkets (stores with more than 27,000 square feet), 688 big supermarkets (between 10,000 and 27,000 square feet), 1,644 small supermarkets (between 4,000 and 10,000 square feet), and 1,947 so-called superettes (of less then 4,000 square feet).[9]

Within these shops important shifts have occurred since the 1980s. Hypermarkets' share in total food sales grew (from 46 to 53 percent between 1985 and 2006), but that of the so-called hard discounters (such as ALDI and Lidl, which sell their own brands at low prices, and Colruyt, which sells various brands) rose very sharply (from 5 to 14 percent between 1985 and 2006).[10] Especially the very deep discounters (ALDI and Lidl) were successful. Average supermarkets' share in food sales remained fairly stable, whereas superettes lost in importance. Regional differences within Belgium appear as well. In Brussels, corner shops, night shops, and superettes account for almost 80 percent of all food shops, which is more than in Flanders and Wallonia. The number of hard discounters, however, is lowest in Brussels. Average-sized supermarkets (Delhaize, Super GB) are important in Flanders and Wallonia, but less so in Brussels. Put into the European context, Belgium is a country of average-sized supermarkets, similar to the Netherlands, but unlike France or the United Kingdom, which are countries of the hypermarket.

Within Belgian supermarkets the supply differs, but all sell food: the bigger the supermarket, the more choice and variety. Apart from their size and supply, the hierarchy between brands of supermarkets is equally important, with Delhaize having a classy reputation and ALDI a more grassroots one (not only in terms of price, but also with regard to variety and quality). Since 1957 all supermarkets supply very diverse foods, including bread, fresh meat, vegetables, spices, dry goods, fruit, fish, and beverages (beer, soda, wine, and liquor), mostly alongside nonfood products.

Crucially, because of their scale and international network, supermarkets are the places of food innovation. Through purchases in supermarkets many people experienced for the first time frozen products (vegetables and fish, later ice cream and pizza), convenience foods (a wide and still-growing selection of ready-to-heat dishes), foreign spices (fresh cilantro, chili pepper, or ginger), unfamiliar fish varieties (scampi, fresh tuna) or meats (*merguez*, a spicy north African sausage made with lamb), organic and health foods (all light products), beverages (Californian wine, fruit beers), new vegetables and fruit (eggplant, broccoli, mangoes), and other items. Huge advertising campaigns via free leaflets and, nowadays, Internet sites accompany this ever-expanding supply of innovative food, explaining to the uninformed clientele how, when, and why to prepare these new foods. A chronology applies. Exotic products appeared in cookbooks and on culinary television shows in the 1970s, but occupied only little space on supermarkets' shelves. They were expensive, and moreover people had difficulty integrating them into their daily cuisine. This changed drastically in the 1990s, when the prices of fresh cilantro, avocados, or dried noodles dropped, and people were sufficiently familiarized with these foods to be able to integrate them into daily cooking. Supermarkets' growth forced other retailers to specialize and upgrade their supply, leading to an ever-increasing sophistication of the food supply.[11] Supermarkets, of course, react to this upgrading process by using market research and anticipating customers' wishes. Today, two trends appear: health (focusing on fresh) and convenience (focusing on easy-to-prepare foods). Both are not always reconcilable.

Shoppers have changed. Today, more men go shopping than in the 1980s (although this is still primarily a female activity: per week women spend about double the time shopping that men do). Shoppers have adapted not only to the supermarket cart and, recently, to self scanning but also to the colossal and hugely varied supply (more than half of the customers have a little shopping list to which they rarely stick), the prepackaged foods, the complex labeling, and the shopping hours (supermarkets' hours run generally from 8:30 or 9:00 A.M. to 8:00 P.M., but they remain open until 9:00 P.M. on Friday and are open on Saturday but so far closed on Sunday). Packaging and labeling are of great importance because, alongside the publicity on television, in magazines, and in leaflets, the wrapping paper *is* an advertisement: color, style, text, and images are intended to seduce the shopper much more than to inform her or him. Present-day marketing experts claim that this is a matter not only of selling but also of creating an ambiance and, especially, a bond between retailer and customer. In Belgium, the latter has succeeded. In a 1998 investigation of the confidence

The breakthrough of kitchen appliances in the 1960s: A sales room for refrigerators. Courtesy of the AMSAB-Institute of Social History, Ghent.

Belgians have in food retailers, supermarkets scored better than small grocers and markets (but worse than farmers, where only a handful of people shop).[12] Still, compared to the European Union average, Belgians' trust in supermarkets is lower (the European Union average is 47 percent as against 39 percent in Belgium). Overall, Belgian consumers have gained a reputation for being demanding in terms of quality and freshness.

KITCHENS

Like other people, Belgians appreciate new technology and convenience in the kitchen and food preparation. The massive success of convenience food illustrates this. A recent survey shows that 78 percent of Belgians regularly buy ready-made food, that ready-made (fresh or frozen) pizza is extremely popular during the weekend, that buyers of convenience food are primarily young families with little children living in Flanders, and that they appreciate the taste, the speed and ease, the variety, and the fact that most ready-made dishes have become cheaper. However, most consumers think convenience food is too sweet, salty, and fatty, quite expensive, not very healthy, and of average quality.[13] This inquiry concludes that ready-made dishes are a makeshift solution. Total sales of convenience food rise year after year at an increasing pace. The Belgian market for fresh food is equally expanding, although more slowly. The recent supply of "forgotten" but now-trendy vegetables in supermarkets, like parsnips or fresh prepackaged spinach, is telling. Despite the boom of ready-made food, people remain attached to traditional ways of cooking: microwave ovens are added to today's kitchens, but they have not replaced familiar stovetops.

The rapid growth of ready-to-heat dishes goes along with new technological devices that have become very familiar in many European and Belgian kitchens. Microwaves embody this. Still, food preparation has been changing for a long time. Vegetables in cans and jars, for example, have facilitated cooking since the late nineteenth century. A major breakthrough appeared in the 1960s with the refrigerator, which may be seen as the forerunner of all electric kitchen appliances. In 1951 a survey among four social categories revealed that only 6 percent of working-class families possessed a refrigerator, versus 9 percent of families of white-collar employees, 30 percent of managers' families, and 34 percent of liberal professionals (lawyers, doctors, architects and the like). Asked about their ambition with regard to electric household appliances, all households said they would like to buy a refrigerator much more than anything else but that the price was too high.[14]

Working-class families were particularly interested in possessing household appliances, which social observers explained by the fact that in the late 1940s the Belgian government had launched a special program to reequip workers' houses and that workers had adopted a radically new mentality vis-à-vis machines "that mechanize household work."[15] In other words, they were ready, and in the 1960s working-class families started to buy electric household appliances. In 1970, 87 percent of working-class households in the Liège area, for example, possessed a refrigerator.[16] To be sure, the price had gone down (and wages had increased), but there were more reasons that made it worthwhile to own a refrigerator. Belgian publicity of the 1930s lists the reasons: refrigerators were safe, comfortable, luxurious, and modern. "Safe" refers to health and hygiene, two major concerns of the early twentieth century in most towns, "comfort" is linked to having all food within reach of the busy cook who does not need to run to the cellar or another cool room, "luxurious" refers to cool food (ice cream) and drinks (champagne), and "modern"—the characteristic that is most emphasized—describes sprucing up outdated kitchens and, hence, cooks. The images used in these advertisements show a slim, stylishly dressed young woman in high spirits. The 1951 study stressed all these elements that make up the dreams of modern consumers, mentioning that people imitated their friends who already had a shiny white refrigerator. At present, almost all Belgian households own a refrigerator (which may have a tap for cool water and produce crushed ice).

Today's refrigerators are bigger than those of the 1960s, and they mostly have a separate and rather large freezer on top. Around 1980, most people kept fish and ice cream (bought in the freezer section of the supermarket) in their freezer, as well as meat and vegetables that they themselves had frozen. The former was mainly done by white-collar workers and self-employed people, the latter by working-class families who saw freezing as a means of saving money.[17] Home freezers, therefore, present a peculiar form of technology diffusion: contrary to most electrical devices, the freezer was first and foremost popular among rural families. The monthly review of the Women Farmers' Association, *Bij de Haard* (At the hearth) wrote in 1960, "How fast time passes! A couple of months ago a Belgian freezer was launched at a low price, and now hundreds and indeed thousands of our members own a home freezer and enjoy its use: healthier, cheaper and fresh products."[18] The review also emphasized the cost savings, the constant availability of ice, the possibility to keep meat for months, and the solution for "emergency slaughtering" (when an animal needed to be urgently butchered and stocked). Working-class households were rather reluctant to buy a freezer in the early 1970s but started to do so in the late 1970s, when freezer prices fell, while it appeared that frozen fish and vegetables were often cheaper and handier than the fresh product. Today, freezers are more widespread in Flanders and Wallonia (70 and 64 percent, respectively) than in Brussels (32 percent). This may be explained by the availability of space: Brussels has many more apartments, which in general are smaller than houses. Moreover, apartments rarely have a cellar, which is traditionally used to store food.

Belgium is a country of homeowners: 76 percent possess their dwelling. Along with the house often comes the possession of a garden. People who do not have a garden may rent one. Peas, tomatoes, or beans are grown in many gardens, then cleaned and put in the home freezer. Until the 1970s, these products were preserved in jars, after sterilizing them, which was a time-consuming activity. Quite popular are the small parcels of land called *volkstuintje* ("people's little garden"), which are tilled by thousands of women and (mostly) men in urban wastelands and working-class districts that were built between 1890 and 1950. Since the 1890s gardener organizations have existed with traditional goals, such as frugality and industriousness, aimed at healthy and cheap food, sound leisure time, and values such as self-respect and family. The most important organization, the Ligue du Coin de Terre et du Foyer (League of the Land Parcel and the Home), was launched in 1899 and has 38,000 members today (it used to have more than 100,000 members during the two World Wars, when the produce from the small bits of land helped many people survive).[19] Nowadays, mostly retired people devote time to growing vegetables and, particularly, socializing with fellow gardeners.

A totally different form of garden socializing is having a barbecue. In the 1970s a few simple barbecue sets were a genuine curiosity in the neighborhood. This started to change rapidly in the 1990s, with a real breakthrough around the year 2000, which is illustrated by the fact that the money spent on barbecue grills tripled between 2001 and 2003. Nice summers have, no doubt, spurred this fast growth. Walloons particularly love cooking in the open air, but people in densely populated Brussels also spend time and money on barbecuing. Like elsewhere, Belgian men love to prepare food on the barbecue. Nowadays, sophisticated barbecue grills, or rather fully equipped outdoor kitchens, have replaced the simple models of the 1970s, while specialized cookbooks and Web sites are devoted to barbecuing. Two more signs of the importance of barbecuing are that Belgium has a yearly barbecue championship and that an (all-male) Belgian team won the fifth world barbecue championship in Jamaica in 2003, beating out teams from 37 other nations. In the summer of that year, Delhaize supermarkets announced that the sales of barbecue meat (sausages of

A bourgeois kitchen, late nineteenth century. Note
the vast cookstove and ovens. This type of stove was
used throughout the nineteenth and twentieth centuries. From *Le Bien Social*, 1898.

various colors, burgers of different sizes and flavors, or marinated chicken)
overtook the sales of traditional meat.

If the refrigerator and freezer represented kitchen modernity in the 1970s,
the microwave oven stood for modernity in the 1990s. Just like the fridge
and the freezer, the microwave is part of a long line of industrial processing,
up-to-date retailing, and more new kitchen technology. Microwaves arrived
in Belgium in the 1980s. After a brief period during which newspapers,
magazines, and television chefs had to explain the advantages—heating
the food within minutes, while not burning the wrapping—microwaves
were quickly integrated into Belgian kitchens after 1985.

Before the arrival of microwaves and refrigerators, all cooking was done in a very traditional way. Around 1880, poor people cooked in an iron pot on legs, heated with wood or coal, unless they used a plain open fireplace where a pot could hang, which limited the cooking to one-pot dishes (hence, the popular *hutsepot* or *hochepot*, a vegetable stew with some meat). Richer families had a *fourneau* (a square stove with two ovens and four burners) of various sizes. It remained the archetype for stoves until today (although they now use gas or electricity instead of coal). A new type of cooking appliance appeared in these years, the so-called *Leuvense stoof* (Leuven stove). This was a vertical stove with a large heating plate on top and a large oven, supported by a fire pot that burned coal or wood. This type was particularly popular in the countryside and was used up to the 1970s. Still, nowadays, some cooks would claim that the *Leuvense stoof* produces the best possible pancakes. In the 1910s and late 1920s, new cookstoves using gas and electricity appeared. Most household books were very enthusiastic about them because they were clean and easy, and

A working-class kitchen in 1956, Ghent. The cookstove consists of two small burners, and there is no oven. A sink has a tap that provides cold water. Courtesy of the AMSAB-Institute of Social History, Ghent.

Modernization, efficiency, and technology in the cafeteria kitchen: The kitchen of the children's holiday resort Kindervreugde (Children's joy), in the seaside town of Nieuwpoort, 1950s. Courtesy of the AMSAB-Institute of Social History, Ghent.

they allowed a finetuning of the heat. Around 1960, 36 percent of Belgian households used coal; gas (provided by communes) came second (35 percent), and propane gas (in containers) third (24 percent). The 1960s brought a revolution in cooking equipment: the use of coal vanished within the decade. At 3 percent, electric stoves were totally marginal in 1960. In 1970, however, 12 percent of cookstoves were electric.[20] In 1995 half of the Belgians used an electric stove, and today almost two-thirds cook with electric stoves and ovens.

The steady decline in the price of microwave ovens in the 1990s helped their swift diffusion. By 1995 half of Belgian households owned a microwave, and 80 percent owned one by 2005. Microwaves are standard equipment in new kitchens, holiday resort rooms, and students' rooms. This success is remarkable, since a short but vehement controversy accompanied the introduction of microwaves around 1985. Many chefs opposed their use because they feared loss of quality and taste. Today, some cooks still refuse to use the microwave oven, although most chefs use it without restraint, cooking schools teach its use in gastronomic cuisine, and most cookbooks and culinary Web sites advise how to use it (and not just for heating water for tea).

Ghent Stew (*Gentse hutsepot* or *hochepot gantois*)

about 1/2 pound beef bones or meat for broth

1/2 pound lamb (shoulder)

1/2 pound beef (brisket)

3.5 oz bacon (desalted and cut into small pieces)

1 smoked sausage or about 3 oz ("cervelat")

1 green cabbage

3 medium-sized carrots

3 medium-sized turnips

2 onions

2 cups broth

bouquet garni (parsley, thyme, and bay leaf)

salt and pepper

Start by making the broth (4 cups water, 1/2 pound beef bones or meat, and salt and pepper; cook for two hours). Cut the lamb and beef into square pieces, put in a casserole dish, and add the broth and the bacon. Cook on medium heat for half an hour. Meanwhile, cut the carrots and turnips in big, regular pieces and quarter the cabbage. Take two medium-sized onions, chop them, and heat in some butter, and prepare the bouquet garni. Add the vegetables and spices to the meat, and simmer on low heat for at least half an hour. A smoked sausage may be added.

Other kitchen appliances, like dishwashers, electric knives, multifunctional mixers (called *robots*), blenders, or fruit juicers, have appeared. The latest hype was launched in 2001 with a huge publicity campaign: the home espresso machine (or rather, the Senseo, for in Belgium this brand name designates the object). The campaign appeared to be largely unnecessary: the public was very keen on the possibility of making strong, fashionable, and tasty coffee at home (like that which it had become acquainted with in Italy and, later, in Belgian cafés and bars). The fact that the coffee pads (little packets of coffee that are ready to be put in the machine) are expensive has not stopped the swift diffusion of these machines (since then, the English word *pad* has become part of the everyday vocabulary in Belgium). The manufacturers expected sales of about 150,000 Senseos in the first year, but they sold 350,000. Many people not only wished to own electric household tools but also thought they were the perfect gift. As the price of these devices has dropped, and most women's magazines and television programs applaud them, Belgians keep on buying hand blenders, microwave ovens, espresso machines, and electric can openers. High-income groups take the lead, but since the 1970s there are few social differences in this respect. Young families (with two incomes and two children) spend more money than elderly people on these gadgets. However, the boom in household equipment is over: in 1975 its share in total family spending was two times higher than in 2005. Some cooks prefer wooden spoons and old-fashioned pans.

Convenience foods and kitchen technology have greatly affected the time spent on cooking. In 1966 women spent about 85 minutes per day cooking, but by 1999 this had dropped by almost half, to 49 minutes. Convenience foods and kitchen devices freed women from a centuries-old burden. Figures for men are 4 and 11 minutes, respectively.[21] Somewhere in the 1980s, Belgian men discovered food preparation (not just the barbecue). Not only do they cook, but they also set the table, clean up, and do the dishes (which takes them 10 minutes per day versus 29 minutes for women). Moreover, some men do more kitchen work than others: those with high incomes and between 45 and 65 years of age are the most active in the kitchen. But feeding the family is certainly still a woman's task. Significantly, women spend less time on Sundays (39 minutes), whereas men's kitchen activity does not diminish during the weekend.

The time women spent cooking is linked to income class and age. The higher the income, the less time women spent on cooking: 58 minutes for the lowest incomes and 41 minutes for the highest incomes, or a significant gap of 30 percent. This resembles the situation in 1966, when working-class housewives needed about 20 percent more time for cooking than did wives of doctors, managers, or lawyers. The survey-takers explained this difference by the presence of full-time or part-time help in the better-off households. In the 1999 data, it also appears that the older the women are, the more time they use for cooking: 11 minutes for women younger than 24 years, 47 minutes for the cohort between 25 and 43 years, 57 minutes for women between 44 and 65 years, and 68 minutes for women above 65. Connecting age to income, it thus appears that relatively poor and elderly women spend the most time preparing food. The time for cooking is certainly linked to the availability of cooking devices in the kitchen, although elderly people may in general have a more traditional way of cooking, implying homemade mayonnaise or soup with fresh tomatoes. The declining cooking time in Belgium is reported in newspapers. Recently, two opposite views have emerged: one says that the loss in culinary heritage is enormous, but the other claims that Belgians will retain sufficient cooking skills for the next decades.[22]

COOKING SKILLS

A newspaper article of 2003 alarmingly quoted the administrator of Ter Duinen, the renowned cooking school on the Flemish coast: "Our culinary culture is no longer passed on to the next generation. In the past, young girls learned the skill by helping their mother in preparing food. Now this happens too rarely."[23] The administrator referred to the ancient way of diffusion of cooking skills: by watching and practicing (with, of course, trial and error). This was and is the way people learned to cook professionally and privately.

Home Cooking

Most women learned cooking skills from their mothers by watching and imitating. This, however, does not mean that they follow exactly the recipes and the ways of doing: most interpret, modify, and innovate. A French study revealed changes over time in the relationship between mothers and daughters with regard to cooking. In the 1960s, daughters did conform less to their mothers' cooking methods than daughters in the late 1990s. In the 1960s, cooking like mom was seen as old-fashioned and submissive, hence the wish to innovate, modernize, and experiment in the kitchen with time-saving techniques, unfamiliar recipes, and bizarre ingredients. In the 1990s, however, women reacted to industrialization and globalization of the food business by revalorizing their mothers' ways of doing.[24] It is likely that this change in attitude may be found in Belgium too, judging by the way cookbooks, publicity, chefs, and television programs in the last 10 years consider traditional home cooking with great respect. In fact, during the meeting of the jury for the 2006 Flemish Culture Prizes (Section: Taste), it was suggested that a tribute be paid to "mother" as the most important figure in passing on culinary know-how.[25]

Since mothers and daughters take less time for cooking, daughters have to learn the skills elsewhere. Until the 1960s, many girls younger than 12 received some household skills lessons in primary schools (boys would be trained in woodworking). Household education, including basic cooking, started in a few schools in the 1870s, aiming at the formation of future mothers who would create a cozy environment that would keep husbands away from pubs and provide a home for the children.[26] This teaching was meant for working-class girls. The *gâteau du dimanche* (Sunday cake) did play a role in this: husbands and children would be rewarded for good behavior during the week through the mother's baking. Home-economics

Depiction of a male cook, 1909. From *Le Bien Social*,
1909.

education expanded in two ways up to 1940, involving children of the
middle classes as well: first, separate classes appeared in basic schools, and,
second, distinct household schools were erected. The latter offered not
only lessons in cooking but also in cleaning, knitting, and adequate income management. Thousands of young girls attended these classes. In
many training books in schools up to the 1940s, it was stressed that cooking should be done with thrift and concern for nutritive value but also,
and crucially, with attention to taste, diversity, and appetite. Hence, the
large section devoted to sauces in one schoolbook, written in 1912, stated
that a modest meal, even the most faint, can taste excellent thanks to the
sauce. Also, this book published many recipes for cake and other desserts.
In the 1930s, most Belgian households could make these recipes, thanks
to better kitchen equipment. Of course, it is impossible to know the effect
of this teaching, but the fact that thousands of girls were trained in this
way cannot help but have led to a carryover to daily cooking. Household
classes in general education for girls up to 12 years of age ended in the

1960s, and, so far, no one has requested that this training be reinstituted. Alongside formal cooking education for girls, other forms with big influence appeared: the training of adult women in the countryside and the towns. Often, this was done via "traveling classes." Attention was paid to the making of butter and cheese, the preservation of vegetables and meats, and, of course, cooking. All this contributed highly to the ideal of the perfect housewife, a person who was hardly referred to before 1880, but who peaked in discourse and practice between 1930 and 1970.

The perfect housewife, particularly the middle-class housewife, used cookbooks. Cookbooks in Belgium go back a very long time, with the *Notabel boecxken van cokeryen* (A notable little book of cooking; Brussels, 1512) as one of the oldest printed European cookbooks, meant for the kitchens of the upper classes. Until the early nineteenth century, however,

Dominique Michou, chef of the restaurant L'Alban Chambon, Brussels Metropole Hotel, 2007. Courtesy of the author.

the more successful ones were French such as Menon's *La cuisinière bour-geoise* (The bourgeois female cook) (1746). The first Belgian cookbook refers to Menon and other French authors. In 1861 Philippe Cauderlier (1812–1887) wrote *Het spaarzame keukenboek/L'économie culinaire* (The economical kitchen book), which was extremely successful and appeared in several revised print runs up to the 1920s. It was a mixture of French haute cuisine and regional Flemish, Brussels, and Walloon recipes. Jean De Gouy's *La cuisine et la pâtisserie bourgeoises en Belgique et à l'étranger* (The bourgeois kitchen and pastry making in Belgium and abroad) (Brus-sels, 1895) and *La cuisine et la patisserie bourgeoises à la portée de tous* (The bourgeois kitchen and pastry making for all) (Brussels, 1900) challenged Cauderlier's supremacy and became *the* cookbooks of the interwar years, although Paul Bouillard's *La gourmandise à bon marché* (Gastronomy at low cost) (Paris, 1925) and Gaston Clément's *La bonne cuisine ménagère* (The good home cooking) (Brussels, 1935) were widely diffused too. Moreover, De Gouy, Bouillard, and Clément were not only authors and chefs (Bouil-lard was the owner of the celebrated restaurant Filet de Sole in Brussels); they had also entered the public arena as culinary journalists. In contrast to nineteenth-century cookbooks, which were written for use by servants, the books of the twentieth century were aimed at the housewife (wage-earning cooks became too expensive for many bourgeois families). Hence, these books are more varied, they welcome time-saving techniques, and they present cooking as an opportunity to acquire status and show affection.

Clément's cookbook remained influential until the 1960s, when a myr-iad of cookbooks appeared. Most of these were labeled Belgian, but later Flemish (1970s), Walloon (1980s), and Brussels (1990s) cookbooks were published as well, alongside innumerable best-selling translations into Dutch and French of writings by television chefs such as Jamie Oliver or Nigella Lawson, and recipe books for Italian or Chinese cuisine. Today, most world cuisines are represented on booksellers' shelves, next to cook-books for beginners, health devotees, kids, clumsy men, dieters, students, fast-food lovers, gourmets, sportsmen, and aficionados of tapas. Belgian chefs, becoming semistars and appearing on television and in magazines, often write best-selling cookbooks. In many Belgian bookstores the gas-tronomy section is one of the largest. In addition to cookbooks, housewives may find recipes, ideas, and ingredients in richly illustrated magazines, (al-most) daily television programs, and numerous Web sites of very diverse nature, quality, and purpose. Since the early 1950s, some newspapers have paid attention to cooking, but nowadays all papers in the country have weekly columns on cooking, recipes, restaurants, food innovations, chefs, and other culinary topics.

A relatively new form of diffusion is the very popular cooking classes for adults. Again, cooking classes are not new, but they boomed in the 1990s. Cooking classes for adults, and increasingly for children, are organized by enthusiastic amateurs as well as by renowned cooks. For example, chef Yves Mattagne of the Sea Grill Restaurant in Brussels, worth two stars in the Michelin guide, has a cooking workshop (designated by the word *atelier* to underline the practical aspect) and offers day and evening lessons in basic cooking, garnishing, dessert, wine, and cigars.[27] There are dozens of similar classes all over the country. Moreover, well-established cooking schools also offer training to amateurs. Newspapers conclude that this is a new phenomenon in Belgium, which attracts men in particular, who seem to enjoy themselves a lot and, more than female pupils, pay great attention to marinating, braising, or frying.[28]

Professional Cooking

In 1908 the Union Syndicale des Hôteliers, Restaurateurs et Cafetiers de Bruxelles (Association of owners of hotels, restaurants and cafés in Brussels), opened a cooking school that turned out to be a failure, because of the indifference of restaurant owners, chefs, cooks, and waiters. In the late 1930s a few schools opened. Only in the 1950s, when further training in management and nutrition was needed, did cooking schools appear all over the country; today, Belgium has about 35 *écoles hôtelières* (cooking schools). This swift development is also connected with the transfer of training costs from restaurants to state-supported schools. Boys and girls between 12 and 18 years old are trained as cooks, pastry chefs, waiters, or butchers and may receive one year of further training (in *cuisine gastronomique*, for example). In general, the Belgian cooking schools have an excellent reputation. Via contests, such as the Junior Cook of Belgium (since 1971), the Most Tasty Class (2002, for pupils of Flemish cooking schools), and the Prix Prosper Montagné (1952, for all cooks), the schools aim to maintain high standards. Pupils of these schools often win international prizes. Also, they are invited to provide the catering for special occasions, such as the wedding of Prince Laurent (son of king Albert II) with Miss Cooms in 2003. A final indication of their good reputation is the fact that the Flemish and Brussels cooking schools have been nominated for the 2007 Cultural Prizes (Category: Taste) by the Flemish government. The jury argued that "cooking schools combine tradition with the use of local ingredients and cuisine. They, thus, both conserve and diffuse the classic and regional cooking. They also pay attention to innovation and new trends."[29]

However, today cooking schools have trouble finding sufficient and motivated pupils, while some restaurant owners criticize the outdated program and the lack of practical training, claiming basic skills and knowledge about the ingredients' structure and taste are going by the wayside. Cleaning and cutting fresh fish is no longer taught in all schools. Hence, restaurants are forced to buy cleaned and cut fish, which means a decline in experiments, innovation, and know-how.[30] Nowadays, fish fillets are often cheaper than the whole fish (saving time is crucial in professional cuisines), and more and more restaurants no longer need all traditional cooking skills. Still, many of today's great chefs in Belgium have studied in cooking schools, like Guy Van Cauteren (Ostend), Roland Debuyst

Cooks at Comme chez Soi, place Rouppe, Brussels, 2006. This restaurant has been in business since the 1920s. For decades it has been considered one of the best of Belgium, receiving Michelin stars and great appreciation from many culinary journalists and gourmets. Courtesy of the author.

(Leuven), and Ferdy Debecker (Anderlecht), who own their own businesses, have won international prizes, and are acclaimed by various restaurant guides.

Some famous Belgian chefs, however, have not been trained in professional schools. For example, Pierre Wynants was kicked out of a cooking school and started to work (washing dishes) in his father's restaurant. Later, when young Wynants had taken over the kitchen, culinary guides recognized this place, Comme chez Soi, as one of the finest in Europe. In the past, cooks were trained on the spot, often starting with the lowest jobs, like dishwashing and potato peeling. Very gradually, young boys or girls would start to do other tasks, like helping with roasting the meat or steaming the vegetables. Later, they were allowed to help with sauces and desserts. The cleverest apprentices would use this time to observe and learn. After a while, some would get little tasks and start cooking. As many of today's great chefs testify, this was often accompanied by rude verbal and physical treatment. Apprentices were hardly paid, worked day and night, and often slept on the kitchen floor. After being with a chef for a year or so, apprentices would try to go and work elsewhere in order to have new experiences and improve their skills. Little by little, they acquired sufficient skills to become a professional cook after about six years of training in several kitchens. Once a professional, the striving for improvement continues via working in renowned restaurants or with famous private houses (which include the Belgian royals). Every chef gladly enumerates the places where he or she has worked, as a kind of certificate list. Female cooks are often employed by private families (male cooks more readily enter restaurants). Improving skill means higher status and pay. The final goal of most cooks is to become a chef or, even better, a restaurant owner.

Cooks travel from one place to another, often crossing the Belgian border, and for many Belgians this certainly includes time in France. Wynants, for example, worked in Le Grand Véfour and Tour d'Argent (both in Paris) in the early 1960s. By so doing, he continued a centuries-old cooks' training practice. Throughout the existence of restaurants in Europe and Belgium (see chapter 5), the grand hotels in big cities and important tourist resorts attracted an international staff of cooks and waiters. Belgian cities, particularly Brussels and Ostend, became part of an international labor market for kitchen staff (mostly men, though), with Belgians going abroad and foreigners coming to Belgium. For example, in the Rue de la Fourche, a genuine gourmet street in the old center of Brussels, no less than 68 percent of restaurant staff was foreign in the 1890s, with the majority coming from France. This implied a regularly functioning labor market. Even today, particular cafés are known as "employment places" for job-seeking cooks and waiters. Top chefs and ambitious younger cooks would not go there, for they rely on their own networks. In order to set wage standards, wage-earning cooks set up unions (such as the Société Philanthropique de Secours Mutuels des Cuisiniers de la Ville de Bruxelles [the Philanthropic Association for Mutual Aid of Cooks of the City of Brussels]), which began in 1869). Later, the city's administration installed the Bourse de Travail to bring together employers and employees. Today, Belgian hotel, café, and restaurant personnel may join three different unions that group thousands of members. Restaurant owners have associated as well in order to negotiate work conditions and pay.

Restaurant owners and chefs have also founded associations to promote gastronomy and protect culinary traditions. For example, in 1980 Meesterkoks van België/Maîtres cuisiniers de Belgique (Master Chefs of Belgium) was set up, which assembles top Belgian chefs who wish to promote Belgian haute cuisine in and outside the country. Thus, during one week in September, for a low price (35 euros, all inclusive) young people under 23 may eat in top restaurants. The aim of Meesterkoks is to tell about the view of Belgian chefs nowadays: "As artisans of the taste and in full respect of produce of the land, we wish to share, in this period of generalized *malbouffe,* our love of our trade with our customers, for there is no better place than a good table for linking happiness to conviviality."[31] Also, Belgian chef Romeyer played a crucial role in launching Euro-Toques International (1986), for the "defense of European culinary heritage," with about 120 Belgian members today.

Every two years since 1987, the Bocuse d'Or is organized in Lyons, France, an event that is labeled the "Olympic games of cooking." Gold, silver, and bronze medals are granted to chefs from several (mostly European) countries. The ambiance around the arena, where cooks prepare and present the food to the international jury of eminent chefs, is comparable to that of an English soccer game or the carnival in Rio de Janeiro. Belgian chefs have never won the first prize, but they have won the second and the third prize several times.[32] With their six awards over 20 years, they come second after France (eight medals) and are on par with Norway (also six medals). However, Belgium's last medal was obtained in 1999. Does this imply a decline of Belgian cuisine in the 2000s? It rather means that the traditional way of cooking is taught at cooking schools and applied in restaurants where the latest fashions, like the so-called molecular cuisine à la Ferràn Adrià, are not fully integrated.

Retailing, kitchen technology, and cooking skills have changed radically in Belgium, as in all of Europe, over the past decades. Most of these changes continue long-term developments, although at an escalating speed. This appears in all three components, and taking these together it is obvious that cooking and food culture in Belgium have changed greatly since the early 1970s. Whether one considers where and what Belgians buy, which tools are utilized to prepare the food, and where know-how comes from, the changes are deep, radical, and lasting. This process is ongoing. But despite these huge changes that may upset some observers, culinary heritage is not likely to disappear because of the immense flow of information in books, magazines, television, and the Internet; the many classes for amateurs; the many associations; and the overall interest in *good* food.

NOTES

1. Annual report of AC Nielsen, *Voedingsuniversum* (Brussels: Nielsen, 2007), 24–25. This American company appeared in Belgium in 1954, providing retailing expertise.

2. In 1884, a new hall was built; the old one was renovated in 1912 and still exists. It was reopened in 2002 as a center for promoting regional food and drink; see Het Groot Vleeshuis (The Great Meat Hall), http://www.grootvleeshuis.be (accessed February 3, 2008).

3. A list of daily and weekly public markets, for food and nonfood items, may be found at Opebare Markten (Public Markets), http://www.openbare-markten. be (accessed August 4, 2008).

4. "Sluiten met pijn in het hart" [Closing down with pain in the heart], *Het Nieuwsblad* Regionaal, September 18, 2004, 15. Another famous example is the closing of century-old patisserie Bloch in the main commercial street in Ghent in March 2008.

5. "Warme bakker maakt come back" [Hot baker makes comeback], *De Morgen*, February 24, 2007, 2.

6. Keukenweetjes [Cuisine know-how], http://blog.seniorennet.be/ keukenweetjes/archief.php?ID=207 (accessed February 4, 2008).

7. See the Web site of Slagerij José in Tielt, http://www.slagerijjose.be (accessed February 4, 2008).

8. Emmanuel Collet, ed., *Delhaize "De Leeuw." Kruideniers sinds 1867* (Brussels: Delhaize Group, 2003). See also the history pages at Delhaize's Web Site, http://www.delhaizegroup.com/divclassdg_MenuText_RedTHEGROUPdiv/ History/tabid/86/language/en-US/Default.aspx (accessed August 4, 2008).

9. *De handel in 2006 in cijfers* [2006 trade in numbers] (Brussels: Fedis, 2007); see also the site of the Belgian retailing association, http://www.fedis.be (accessed August 4, 2008).

10. Annual report of AC Nielsen, *Voedingsuniversum*, 16ff.

11. *Upgrading* refers to the permanent search for profit in the food industry, which leads to the launching of new foodstuffs of an ever more refined nature,

thus replacing the simpler ones. Peter Scholliers, "Novelty and Tradition: The New Landscape for Gastronomy," in *Food, the History of Taste*, ed. Paul Freedman (London: Thames & Hudson, 2007), 332–357.

12. *Consumers in Europe: Facts and Figures* (Luxemburg: European Community, 2001), 64.

13. *De bereide gerechten* [Ready-made dishes] (Brussels: OIVO, 2006); see also the Web site of the Centre de Recherche et d'Information des Organisations de Consommation (Research and Information Center for Consumer Organizations), http://www.oivo.be/FR/doc/dcdc/alimentation/document-1745.html (accessed March 12, 2008).

14. Guillaume Jacquemyns, *L'équipement ménager* (Brussels: INSOC, 1951), 17, 24.

15. Guillaume Jacquemyns, *Les budgets familiaux d'ouvriers et d'employés 1947–1948* (Brussels: INSOC, 1949), 32.

16. Roland Renard, *Budgets et conditions de vie des familles en milieu urbain* (Liège: Vaillant-Carmanne, 1973), 77.

17. *Koopgewoonten, gedragingen en opinies van verbruikers in België* [Buying habits, behavior, and views of consumers in Belgium] (Brussels: BCD, 1979).

18. *Bij de Haard*, March 1960, 32.

19. Yves Segers and Leen van Molle, eds., *Volkstuinen: Een geschiedenis* [People's gardens: A history] (Leuven, Belgium: Davidsfonds, 2007).

20. *Volkstelling: 31 December 1970* (Brussels: National Institute Statistics, 1973), 105.

21. Claude Javeau, *Les vingt-quatre heures du Belge* (Brussels: ULB, 1970) and Ignace Glorieux, Kim Coppens, Suzanne Koelet, Maarten Moens and Jessie Vandeweyer. *Vlaanderen in uren en minuten* (Brussels: VUBPress, 2002).

22. Belgen besteden minder tijd aan zelf bereiden van eten [Belgians take less time for cooking], *Het Volk*, February 7, 2003, 2.

23. Huisvrouw staat nog maar acht minuten in keuken [Housewife stays no longer than eight minutes in the kitchen], *Het Volk*, October 8, 2003, 9.

24. Jean-Pierre Poulain, *Sociologies de l'alimentation* (Paris: PUF, 2003), 40–41.

25. Because of the difficulty in finding "the" mother, it was decided to grant the prize to *Ons kookboek*, a recipe book that allegedly is passed on from mother to daughter.

26. See Peter Scholliers, "Vreugde heerst aan de dis: Essay over de huisvrouw en de voeding van arbeiders in de politieke economie van België (1840–1940)," *Jaarboek voor Vrouwengeschiedenis* 19 (1999): 73–97.

27. L'Atelier Yves Mattagne, http://www.atelieryvesmattagne.com (accessed February 16, 2008).

28. "Gezellig samen leren koken" [Cozily learning to cook together], *De Tijd*, December 3, 2004, 17.

29. The schools did not win the prize, however (see Cultuurprijzen Vlaanderen, http://www.cultuurprijzen.be [accessed February 17, 2008]).

30. "Goede koks worden schaars" [Good chefs become rare], *Het Laatste Nieuws*, November 7, 2007, 8.

31. *Malbouffe* ("bad gobbling") appeared in France to designate fast food and standardized or manipulated food; see Meesterkoks van België, http://www.meesterkoks.be (accessed February 17, 2008).

32. See Académie des lauréats Bocuse d'or, http://www.academie-bocusedor.com/EN/pages/chef.php?type=pays&pays=BE; and Concours mondial de la cuisine, http://www.bocusedor.com/2007/EN/concours/palmares.php (accessed February 16, 2008). Gert Jan Raven, a Dutchman who has worked in Belgium since the early 1980s and whom the Bocuse d'Or prizewinners' academy considers a Belgian, won the 1991 bronze medal.

4

Typical Meals

Although Belgians have begun eating out much more often in the last 25 years, most meals are still eaten at home. On an average workday, 67 percent of Belgians eat at home (slightly more women than men), 18 percent have a meal at work or in school, and the remaining 15 percent eat "elsewhere" (slightly more men than women).[1]

Since the late nineteenth century, cookbooks and school manuals have presented a three-meal pattern as traditional and optimal: breakfast (*petit-déjeuner* or *ontbijt*), lunch (*dîner* or *middagmaal*), and dinner (*souper* or *avondmaal*). Four to five hours between each meal are recommended, which implies breakfast around 7:30 A.M., lunch around noon, and dinner at 6 P.M. Eating between these meals is discouraged because "it kills the appetite and wears out the intestines," as was noted in a schoolbook of 1931.[2] Rigid eating times were highly promoted as enhancing digestion and thus promoting good health. Other practical guidelines regarding meals are given: chew sufficiently in order to mix the food with saliva, eat varied foodstuffs to improve the appetite, and provide a pleasant environment ("A nicely laid table and a gentle conversation improve digestion," states the aforementioned 1931 manual). Such views are repeated in cookbooks, school manuals, and women's magazines throughout the twentieth century and until the present. For example, in its 1972 edition *Ons kookboek* (Our cookbook), edited by the Women Farmers' Association,[3] mentions breakfast in the morning, a hot meal at noon, and a cold evening meal around 6 P.M. Throughout the entire twentieth century this meal pattern was strongly promoted by this cookbook, adding the usual recommendations with regard to variety, cleanliness, and coziness.[4] Today, Gezondheid.be (the "Health Web pages for Flanders") still fervently recommends three meals a day if one wishes to remain healthy (although two tiny in-between snacks are permitted).[5] It remains open for discussion to what extent this ideal three-meal pattern with a hot lunch was ever applied in practice.

Taking a long-term view, it seems that this pattern had existed generally within the middle classes for a long time but that it became the model from the moment the upper classes adopted it. Until the early eighteenth century, richer people tended to eat only twice a day: the *déjeuner* around 10 A.M. and the *souper* around 4 P.M., with meals lasting a couple of hours and containing a wide variety of dishes. When it became fashionable to eat later in the evening (after 8:30 P.M.), the need was felt to have a *premier* or *petit déjeuner* in the morning (with the hot drinks that appeared in the late seventeenth century, that is, coffee, tea, and especially hot cocoa), thus adopting three meals a day. At the court of the unfortunate Empress Charlotte in the 1870s and 1880s,[6] three meals were served: *premier déjeuner* at 11 A.M., *second déjeuner* around 1:30 P.M., and *dîner* at 6:30 P.M. Some of her menus mention extras such as "un consommé, sandwich au poulet" (a light soup, and a chicken sandwich) at 4 P.M. and, for the same day, "une aile de poulet" (a chicken wing) at 8 P.M. At the court of the Belgian king and queen in the 1880s, ordinary days had three meals with a strict timing: *déjeuner* early in the morning (mostly around 8:30 A.M.), *luncheon* at 12:30, and *dîner* at 6:30 P.M. For the (quite recurrent) festive occasions, lunch and dinner were generally at 1 P.M. and 8 P.M., respectively. The middle classes ate somewhat earlier, which was linked to business hours. They preferred a strict eating schedule with breakfast before 8 A.M., lunch at noon, and dinner at 6 P.M. sharp. Poorer people generally ate four meals per day, with a first meal around 7:30 A.M., a second meal around noon, a third meal at about 4 P.M., and the last meal around 7:30 P.M. Mill regulations of the early nineteenth century indicate the duration of eating breaks: half an hour in the morning, one hour at noon (which allowed most workers to go home), and half an hour at 4 P.M., with the workday starting at 5:30 A.M. and ending at 8 P.M. With the shortening of the workday in the late nineteenth century, breaks also grew shorter. This prevented workers from going home at noon, thus establishing the habit of eating a cold meal at the workplace, which was common until the 1960s, when firms started providing hot meals in cafeterias (see Chapter 5). Yet, despite undoubtedly huge social and geographical differences in actual meal patterns, Belgians, like most western Europeans, adopted in the second half of the twentieth century the ideal of three meals with a hot meal at noon.

Recently, a large study on food intake was conducted, resulting in the National Food and Health Plan that was presented in December 2005.[7] This plan's recommendations evoke the fears and warnings of the early twentieth century and advocate the family meal as the norm. Especially children were put at risk, it seems, because of the far-too-impulsive and irregular eating pattern (in terms of mealtimes, snacking, number of meals, lack of breakfast, disappearance of the family meal, and success of "individual" food consumption). Such findings seem to confirm a widespread belief that the traditional three-meal pattern, which is believed to actually exist, is currently threatened. Newspapers, magazines, and television mirror and contribute to this belief by referring to the "atomization" (or demolition) of the meal pattern, and "grazing" or "snacking" instead of regular and planned eating. For example, in 2004 the popular Flemish newspaper *Het Laatste Nieuws* wrote that ever more people just have a cup of coffee in the morning, a sandwich while seated at the office desk at noon, and a microwave TV-dinner in the evening, with family members coming in at different times and eating whatever and whenever they wish (busy as they are with sports, meetings, school, work, and friends). The article adds that "Within twenty years we all will eat when driving or walking," which will be too bad because eating together at regular times prevents obesity, deters children from using alcohol, drugs, or tobacco, contributes to better school results, and adds to the general well-being, conviviality, and coherence of the community.[8]

TEMPORAL, SOCIAL, AND SPATIAL MEAL SHIFTS

This question of the alleged atomization of the traditional Belgian meal pattern has been studied thoroughly, which allows assessment of the present-day typical meal pattern, as well as questioning the consequences with regard to family life, the role of the housewife, and matters of health.[9] A comparison between 1966, 1999, and 2004 may be made. In 1966, during the week the average number of meals per day was 3.18 to be precise, meaning that a snack was often eaten around 4 P.M.; in 1999 and 2004 the numbers were 2.83 and 2.26 meals per day, respectively, meaning not only that the 4 P.M. snack had disappeared but also that often a meal was skipped, which occurred more frequently in 2004 than in 1999. If, in 1966 and 1999, 50 percent of the Belgians consumed three meals a day, this number fell in 2004 to 45 percent, while people having only two meals a day rose from 24 percent in 1999 to 32 percent in 2004. On the weekend, the number of meals tended to decrease even more. On Sunday, only 35 percent of Belgians ate three meals in 2004, whereas this number still reached 52 percent in 1999. Moreover, an increasing number of people do not eat proper meals at all on Saturday or Sunday (about 6 percent). Judging by these data, the three-meal pattern is waning. This coincides with a shift in eating times in that people have breakfast, lunch, and dinner later in the day. In 1966, 20 percent of the people had eaten breakfast before 8 A.M., but in 1999 only 12 percent had done so; 45 percent were having lunch at 12 P.M. in 1966, but only 30 percent did so in 1999. Moreover, the time used for meals is slowly shrinking. On weekdays in 1966, an average of one hour and 40 minutes was used for eating the three meals, which dropped to one hour and 20 minutes in 2004, or 20 percent less. On Sundays, more time was taken for eating, but this too was declining (from one hour and 53 minutes in 1966 to one hour and 33 minutes in 2004, or 17 percent less).

Along with changes in mealtimes, Belgians' habits related to eating with other people have also changed. In 2004 it was noted that they tended to eat alone much more than before. This is particularly the case in the morning and the evening. Moreover, the family meal, which was common in 1966, only applied to a quarter of the people in 1999. Nowadays, people eat lunch with colleagues or fellow students much more than in the 1960s. Still, during weekdays and the weekend, household members (when not living alone) gather for the evening meal: in 2004, 81 percent shared a family dinner. Finally, where Belgians eat has changed too during the last decades: they tend to eat at home less nowadays than in the 1960s, which is more marked during weekends than during weekdays. Still, the home remains the most popular place for eating even though eating at restaurants, bars, friends' homes, and "elsewhere" has grown in popularity. Thus, if the 1966 meal pattern reflects the traditional and ideal model, it is clear that changes since then have challenged this model. However, although the trends are less marked, a three-meal pattern still applies nowadays, with breakfast, lunch, and dinner eaten somewhat later than in the 1960s and people skipping meals more than before. Eating is much more flexible than it used to be in terms of time, place, and company. This flexibility has many causes, among which are family composition (many more singles), the type of occupation (the spread of the "service" society), and convenience foods in various forms (with frozen meals for microwave ovens as the most radical form).

MEALS' CHANGING CONTENT

Household spending for in-home eating, according to official, large-scale household budget studies, reveals general changes in the typical

Menu board of Aux Arcades, a restaurant in the Brussels Rue des Bouchers, promoting typical Belgian dishes (once inside the restaurant, the choice of dishes and the prices may totally change). Most of these dishes are referred to as "traditional home cooking." Courtesy of the author.

meal. A first but fundamental observation refers to the proportion of total family expenditure spent on food eaten at home, which fell from 17.6 percent in the late 1970s to 12.3 percent in 2006 (no later data are available), whereas housing, communication, and leisure expenses rose significantly. Until the early 1950s, the share of food reached at least 50 percent of total family spending, thus showing the colossal weight of food expenditure for most families in the nineteenth and first half of the twentieth century. The fall from 50 to 12 percent after 1950 demonstrates the fundamental transformation in household expenditures, consumption, and daily life. This radical fall should be linked to income and price developments: earnings grew significantly since the early 1960s, whereas food prices diminished considerably due to productivity increases in agriculture, transport, and food processing. Between 2005 and 2007, however, food's share in household expenses hardly changed, which is explained by increasing food prices. What is more, between July 2006 and December 2007 average food prices in Belgium rose by 7.2 percent, which is more than the general inflation of goods and services, with peaks for potatoes (+53 percent), frozen fish (+20 percent), eggs (+13 percent), and milk (+12 percent). Food prices are increasing worldwide, caused by growing international demand, bad weather conditions in some important producing countries, and skyrocketing energy costs. The current 12 percent of total household expenditures spent on food will probably rise moderately in coming years, which is a radical alteration of familiar trends. This rise in food prices has caused social tension between workers and employers. Up to now, this percentage mirrors the European average (12.8 percent for the 27 European Union countries in 2005).

Within food expenditures, huge shifts appear, reflecting general European changes in food consumption over the past 25 years. Roughly summarized, spending on unprocessed foods, such as milk, meat, or potatoes, diminished, whereas spending on processed foods, such as ice cream, sandwich meats, or potato chips, increased. This contrasts with long-term developments up to the 1960s, when the big change involved ever-growing expenditure on a variety of fresh meat. By examining family spending on clearly discernible items such as ready-made dishes, fresh meat, pasta, or bread, comprehensive conclusions may be drawn with regard to everyday food consumption since the 1970s. Between 1978 and 2005, the amount of money spent on all food rose by 70 percent (in so-called current prices).[10] Much more was spent on fresh fish (+170 percent), cheese (+125 percent), and milk products (+100 percent) but also on couscous and similar products (+290 percent), pasta (+185 percent), fruit (+100 percent), vegetables (+90 percent), and pastry and candy (+90 percent). Amounts spent on some other foods increased less than the average of 70 percent: bread (+50 percent), fine meats (+40 percent), fresh meat (+4 percent), eggs (−20 percent), and butter (−50 percent).

The very modest rise in spending on fresh meat is striking. This actually shows a slow but steady diminishing in consumption of fresh meat over the past three decades, which indeed means a radical break with a long-term tradition that highly valued meat and involved a continual rise in meat consumption. In general, fresh meat has always had a high status. Rich people bought large quantities of beef, pork, or veal, whereas poor people purchased offal at the lowest price and enjoyed eating bacon or cold meats whenever they could afford it. The middle classes' consumption lay between both extremes. Around 1950, all households spent an average of 1.3 percent of total family expenditures on fresh meat; this almost tripled to reach 3.8 percent in 1978, which illustrates meat's high status up until that time. However, mainly due to several food crises in the 1980s as well as to price movements of other products and services, the share of meat in total family expenditures started to decline to reach 1.3 percent again today. The fall of meat, in terms of consumption, status, and expenditure, may be linked to yet another phenomenon: health concerns and slim body ideals, to which the rapid reduction in butter consumption between 1978 and 2005 also testifies (see Chapter 7).

Foodstuffs that have become hugely popular are desserts (increase of 120 percent), ready-made meats (+140 percent), spices and sauces (+255 percent), prepared fish (+420 percent), and convenience foods (+430 percent). All are foodstuffs that, heated or not, may be consumed readily, thus causing a substantial gain in preparation time (see Chapter 3). Recently, some great Belgian chefs started collaborating with supermarkets to produce luxury convenience foods. For example, in 2005 Pierre Wynants, chef at an exclusive Brussels restaurant, created recipes for Hot Cuisine, a producer of processed foods that would be sold exclusively by Delhaize supermarkets. In 2006, this retailer sold 21 million ready-made meals.[11]

The annually conducted household budget inquiries reveal many social and geographical differences. On average food expenditures in Belgium rose by 70 percent between 1978 and 2005, but this reached 80 percent in Flanders, 64 percent in Wallonia, and 62 percent in Brussels. The spending on particular foodstuffs shows a similar growth in the three regions with regard to convenience foods, desserts, ready-made fish and meat, and bread, but quite a different one with regard to fresh meat, fruit, and vegetables. The amount spent on fresh meat actually fell by 19 and 1 percent in Brussels and Wallonia, respectively, whereas in Flanders it rose by 12 percent. Flanders stands out with regard to money spent on fruit and vegetables, leaving Brussels and especially Wallonia behind. It seems that consumers in Flanders are more sensitive to health concerns than in Brussels or Wallonia (taking fresh fruit and vegetable consumption as a reliable proxy for health concerns). This, by the way, corresponds with the faster decline in the number of regular smokers in Flanders compared to Wallonia and Brussels.

Rather than being seen as linguistic or geographical characteristics, such differences should be seen within social divergences of income, family composition, or age. In particular, income disparities may explain divergent spending on food. Thus, in 2005 the lowest-income groups spent 3,820 euros on food per household, but the highest a comfortable 6,040 euros, or 3.2 times more. Compared to a decade earlier, this gap had widened (the difference was 2.7 times in 1995), which indicates growing inequality. Looking at particular foodstuffs it is possible to discover some of the underlying differences between poor and rich households with regard to food consumption. Between 1995 and 2005 well-off families spent much more money on fresh fish, cheese, fresh fruit, and fresh vegetables than poorer households did. It seems that freshness is particularly important to higher-income groups. This may be linked to health concerns that are more present among higher-income groups. Especially expenditure on fish diverged during the 1990s, with the richer households spending 230 euros in 2005 (an increase of 65 percent vis-à-vis 1995), against the poorer families' spending of only 49 euros in 2005 (a *decrease* of 15 percent).

Expenditure on convenience foods and desserts, in contrast, converged, although richer families still bought more of these products than the low-income families. Looking at more details about food expenditure, it appears that most culinary innovations in food habits are linked to income. Thus, in 2005 high-income groups spent much more money on organic food than low-income groups, as well as on ready-made fish dishes, pasta, or couscous. This is not a recent phenomenon: in 1995 richer people spent much more money than the low-income groups on *brochettes* (pieces of meat to put on skewers) and other barbecue meats, salmon, or so-called gourmet meat (a fonduelike preparation), which all became quite fashionable in the 1990s. With regard to traditional foods, such as potatoes, margarine, sugar, and mussels, richer households do not spend more money than poor families. All in all, changes in food consumption in Belgium seem to reflect adequately the broader European developments that testify to ongoing internationalization, productivity rises, and food-quality upgrading.[12] These have led to radically changed "typical meals" in terms of composition and content in the last 25 years.

BREAKFAST

In 1966 most people ate breakfast between 6:30 and 9:00 A.M., but in 2004 this was delayed, with breakfast times ranging from 7:30 to 10:00 A.M.

The average time spent eating in the morning was 16 minutes in 1966 but only 13 minutes in 2004 and 11 minutes in 2007.[13] In both 2004 and 2007, breakfast time was five minutes longer on Sundays than on week-days. More important, the number of breakfast skippers (on weekdays) rose dramatically from 23 percent in 1966 to 45 percent in 2004, as a result of changing sleeping habits (people tend to stay up later and sleep longer in the morning, which affects the digestive process and leads to having no feeling of hunger in the morning), together with the morning rush hour with horrendous traffic jams. In a 2007 study, only 22 percent of interviewees claimed to be regular breakfast eaters, and only 18 percent said that breakfast was a daily family routine.[14]

The decline in breakfast as a regular family meal worries nutritionists. An Internet site states: "Breakfast offers the chance for the family to be together, and it is THE meal of the day!"[15] Children in particular seem to neglect breakfast, preferring snacks that are bought and eaten on the way to school. This is not only more expensive, but also generally unhealthy since candy bars, cookies, waffles, and the like contain lots of fat and sugar. Children skipping breakfast, however, goes way back. In 1894, the Brussels municipality already organized an inquiry into breakfast habits of the city's schoolchildren, which showed that one-fifth got through the morning without eating (and often had no midday meal either). Some 18 percent of the children were distinctly undernourished. Poverty caused this situation, which led in the 1920s to initiatives to provide the children with milk at school.

Skipping breakfast does not affect only children, of course. Today's nutritionists emphasize the need for having breakfast for young and old. Present-day recommendations emphasize a light and varied breakfast that should be consumed in a relaxed setting ("Better to set the alarm clock a quarter of an hour earlier, and to enjoy that nice breakfast!").[16] The Web site Gezondheid.be (which calls itself Flanders' Health Web site) translates nutritional knowledge into comprehensible and applicable con-cepts.[17] It states, "A healthy breakfast contains multiple carbohydrates and is fat-poor. Moreover, it provides fiber, vitamins, and minerals. It is this combination that allows us to get through the day in a good mood and with full concentration." Not having breakfast leads inevitably to an energy dip in the morning, which entails snacking and, in turn, loss of appetite at noon. Converting this general advice into specific food items, the Web site suggests eating whole wheat bread and drinking a glass of milk or eating a container of yogurt. Jam, cheese, or ham—but all in little portions—may be eaten as well. With some fresh fruit, this makes the perfect breakfast. One should avoid fillings that are too sweet.

That so many Web sites, cookbooks, and magazines nowadays stress the need for a decent breakfast, that the time taken for breakfast has shrunk, and that almost half of the Belgians do not eat breakfast anymore shows the generally poor status of this meal in Belgium. Actually, today's most common breakfasts may be divided into two types: the traditional and the American. The former consists of a cup of not-very-strong coffee (mostly with milk and sugar), together with some buttered bread with strawberry jam (see Chapter 2). It is primarily popular in Flanders. The latter breakfast includes cornflakes, rice crispies and cocoa crispies, or pop-tarts, with (canned) orange juice. Walloons seem to enjoy this breakfast more than Flemings. Nevertheless, there are occasions when Flemings, Walloons, and Bruxellois (the inhabitants from Brussels) do put effort and time into a nice, varied, and tasty breakfast. Testifying to this are the many shoppers on Sunday mornings in the country's towns and villages who buy croissants, *pistolets* (a little round crusty bread), *couques suisses* (a long, freshly made, sweet pastry), and other *viennoiseries* (other little sweet breads) at a bakery, taking these home to eat with freshly made coffee. Also, some firms specialize in delivering ready-made breakfasts (admittedly, to offices rather than homes), consisting of croissants hot from the oven, coffee or tea, jams, fresh orange juice, champagne, and flowers (which costs 20 euros per person and is delivered at home, in the office, a meadow or a park).

The Christian Sick Fund's Recommendations for a Diverse and Appealing Breakfast, January 2008

Day 1: Muesli or cornflakes with slices of banana; milk or yogurt.

Day 2: Two to four slices of whole-wheat bread with cheese (Gouda-type) or ham; cup of cocoa or milk; an apple to finish.

Day 3: Two to four slices of bread with scrambled eggs; one cup of coffee or tea; container of yogurt with pineapple slices.

Day 4: Two to four slices of bread with fresh cheese (slightly sweetened); slices of banana or strawberries; cup of tea.

Day 5: Apple heated in the microwave oven, eaten with some slices of bread; glass of (butter)milk.

Day 6: French toast (*gewonnen brood* in Dutch, *pain perdu* in French[18]); glass of milk and a glass of freshly squeezed fruit juice.

Day 7: Two to four slices of bread, cheese (Gouda), slices of tomato, radish, and cucumber; cup of coffee or tea; slightly sweetened yogurt.

Nutritionists' emphasis on light, varied, and healthy breakfasts is rather recent and reflects the growing importance of health concerns in the last couple of decades. Prior to World War II, breakfast was mentioned but hardly valued, and up until the 1950s most cookbooks emphasized sufficient quantity. A slight change occurred in the 1970s, followed by radical transformations only in the late 1980s. This slow change may be illustrated by recommendations in numerous cookbooks. In a book that was published in 1931, the authors mentioned the familiar three meals, stressing that the hot meal (preferably at 12 P.M. but evening was acceptable as well) should provide half of the required nutritional needs, whereas the second meal should cover one-third and breakfast only one-sixth of these needs.[19] When considering the breakfast of children between 12 and 16 years old, though, the authors recommended, "the child should eat as many slices of bread with fruit jam as he wishes. If he does not like having a big glass of milk, some coffee with lots of milk and sugar is advised. Do not allow soaking the bread in the coffee. A plate of oat groats with buttermilk is excellent too."[20] This emphasis on milk, sugar, and sufficient quantity (certainly for children) should be understood in the context of the generally poor nutrition of the interwar years.

The cookbook *Ik kan koken* (1951) testifies to the upgrading of breakfast compared to the prewar years: it divides the total nutritional needs into the hot meal (50 percent) and both bread-based meals (25 percent each), with breakfast thus supplying a larger portion of nutritional needs than it was supposed to provide in the 1930s. But a qualitative change also appeared. The ideal breakfast consisted of a half pound of bread, 1 1/2 tablespoons butter, 1/2 tablespoon jam, one cup milk, and one apple. As for the types of bread, it is recommended to alternate between whole wheat bread, plain white bread, and rye bread, whereas cheese, apple syrup, or an egg could substitute for fruit jam. Also, fresh vegetables or fruit (slices of cucumber, radish, or pear) may be put onto the bread. Coffee, milk, or tea should be served.[21] Today, Jongeren & Voeding (Youngsters and Food), a Web site encouraging young people to eat healthily, for example, recommends that breakfast should supply 25 percent of energy needs, the hot meal 35 percent, and the second bread meal 30 percent (allowing 10 percent of energy intake to come from snacking, which is deemed unavoidable).[22]

The 1972 issue of *Ons kookboek* shows qualitative transformations. It emphasizes the importance of breakfast for young and old, stating that "Not eating in the morning is very bad. Even when dieting, breakfast should be eaten," and concluding straightforwardly, "Breakfast is the most important meal of the entire day."[23] This cookbook suggests two types of breakfast, the ideal and the good one. For both, the beverage should be (hot or cold) milk or another milk product. If coffee is preferred, it is necessary to consume some other dairy product, such as cheese. Brown bread (in Dutch, *bruin brood* and in French, *pain gris*, i.e., whole wheat bread) should be lightly buttered. The *ideal* breakfast includes one egg or 1.75 ounces of meat or cheese, and a piece of fresh fruit. A little bit of jam may be added. The *good* breakfast includes jam, brown sugar, or *chocopasta*, which is a sweet and fat-rich mix of chocolate (8.8 ounces), butter (1 cup and 2 table-spoons), and sweetened condensed milk (one 14-oz. can). *Chocopasta* used to be homemade (recipes can still be found on the Internet), but since the 1950s various commercial brands (the kind with hazelnuts, for example, is very popular) are found in stores. If *chocopasta* is eaten, the bread should not be buttered. No mention is made of quantities. So, if the 1951 cook-book announced innovations that were not commonplace until the 1970s (whole-grain bread, a lot of sweet jams, and some fruit), then radical trans-formations occurred in the 1980s and 1990s with the emphasis on light, varied, and, especially, healthy foods. Such recommendations may be read in present-day cookbooks, Web sites, and women's magazines, thus amply testifying to health concerns (see Chapter 7).

LUNCH

Lunch may be eaten hot or cold. Many Belgians prefer a hot lunch to a cold one, although outdoor activities force people to have a cold lunch in a cafeteria or a sandwich bar. In the following, the lunch is assumed to be hot.

In 1966 half of the Belgians had lunch between noon and 1 P.M., wherever they were.[24] Another 13 percent ate between 1 and 2 P.M. On average, lunch lasted 34 minutes. Hardly anyone ate lunch after 2 P.M. Around 2000, however, only one-third of the Belgians ate a meal between 12 and 1 P.M., while another 13 percent had lunch between 1 and 2 P.M., and some of them left the table just before 2:30 P.M. In general, lunch took only about 25 minutes, or 25 percent less time than in the 1960s. Between 1966 and 2004, thus, lunch has been later and shortened. These data refer to workdays. On the weekend, particularly on Sundays, lunch is longer. In 1966, Sunday lunch took almost 50 minutes (38 percent longer compared to weekdays), but 40 years later lunch lasted only half an hour (20 percent longer than during weekdays). Evidently, busy Sundays limit the lunching time today. Yet, Belgians still tend to linger at the table on Sundays, with some leaving the table at 3:30 P.M., which was very uncommon in the 1960s. The declining importance of the midday meal is accentuated by the new phenomenon that more and more people tend to skip lunch on both workdays and weekends. The noon meal was hardly ever skipped in 1966, and especially during the weekend people had lunch (with barely 4 percent claiming that they did not eat lunch on Sunday, as against 9 percent meal skippers on weekdays). This contrasts highly with the year 2004: during the week no less than 28 percent of people skip lunch, which increases to 32 percent on Sundays. So, eating a proper meal as well as eating together around noon has strongly declined in Belgium: fewer people have lunch, and, if they do eat lunch, they take less time for it.

Causes for the decrease in lunch eating are manifold. The nature of the lunch changed, some people turn down lunch for dieting purposes, and, with regard to weekends, people may brunch. Brunch appeared in the late 1960s as a consequence of striving for innovation and of sleeping in. Traces of "brunch" and "brunching" may be found in trendy cookbooks that deemed it necessary to explain this new concept. Thus, *Fijne hapjes* (Fine Tidbits, 1971), published by the women's magazine *Libelle—Rosita*, writes under the heading "Modern Meals" that between 10:30 A.M. and 1:30 P.M. young people in particular love a *new* meal that is "a combination of elements of both breakfast and lunch, where each may choose of the food according to his or her wishes." This is followed by a long list of bread types, fruit and fruit salads, cheeses, meats, vegetables, and recipes for hot dishes such as meat croquettes, chicken ragout, or fashionable gnocchi *à la Piemontese* (Piemont-style, or gnocchi au gratin).[25]

Linen workers during their lunch break, Flanders, 1950s. Note the bottles of beer on the table. Courtesy of the AMSAB-Institute of Social History, Ghent.

Present-day time budget studies do not reveal intensive brunching in Belgium, though. Alongside this leisurely innovation, the opposite has appeared: many people tend to combine eating at noon with other activities such as cleaning, cooking, and other household work; reading; or watching television. This corresponds to a general trend to link lunch to meetings, lectures, concerts, debates, movies, seminars, and other outdoor activities that erode the significance of the midday meal.

As with breakfast, nutritionists advise people to pay ample attention to lunch and to reinstate it as the freshly prepared family meal that it once was supposed to be. Recommendations about eating lunch mostly concern lunch eaten away from home. An abundance of information on lunch at work or school is available on Belgian Web sites. A new trend has emerged in that lunchboxes brought from home are becoming popular (not just for factory workers or peasants, as it used to be); they save money and time, are lower in calories, and are supposed to be healthier than the food served in cafeterias and sandwich bars.[26] Nowadays, rules or recommendations with regard to the nature of the midday meal have disappeared, except for health concerns. "Don't put too much mayonnaise on sandwiches, try to vary your hot lunch, do not eat *pommes frites* too much, and include vegetables and fruit" are the main recommendations.

Not long ago lunch used to be very different. The ideal of the three-meal pattern implied breakfast, a hot meal at noon, and a cold meal in the evening. The midday meal was supposed to provide about half of the daily required calories. The 1972 issue of *Ons kookboek* emphasized the pre-eminence of lunch over breakfast and dinner and indicated three courses: soup, main dish, and dessert.

Soup is a classic opener, although it may be replaced by a milk-based porridge (for instance, buttermilk soup). The 1972 edition of *Ons kookboek* presents about 60 recipes for ordinary soups made of onion, tomato (with little meatballs), or chervil and for more sophisticated soups like Agnes Sorel cream soup (with mushrooms, chicken pieces, smoked ox tongue, and cream) or *bisque de crevettes* (North Sea shrimp bisque). Other cookbooks, women's magazines, and culinary Web sites offer numerous soup recipes, including the traditional tomato-with-meatballs soup, as well as sophisticated types of soup, such as *tom ya gong* (Thailand) or gazpacho (Spain).[27]

Although the 1972 issue of *Ons kookboek* does not explicitly mention it (seemingly, it was obvious), the main dish in Belgium includes the "golden trio" of potatoes, meat, and vegetables. Nowadays, many Belgians, whether young or old and living in Flanders or Wallonia, still consider a proper meal to consist of potatoes, meat, and vegetables, all put onto one plate and covered with gravy.

Potatoes are crucial. "We can hardly imagine a hot meal without potatoes," stated the monthly magazine of the Women Farmers' Association,
Bij de Haard (At the hearth), in 1952, revealing the prevailing view of
those days.[28] *Ons kookboek* provides some 30 ways of preparing potatoes,
including steaming, frying, boiling, simmering, mashing, and baking.
Older cookbooks of the twentieth century contain about the same number of recipes for serving potatoes, which is a higher number than in cookbooks from the nineteenth century or during World Wars I and II, when
some 10 recipes for potatoes were supplied. Up to the early 1980s, between 3 and 5 percent of all recipes in Belgian cookbooks were for ways of
preparing potatoes. This testifies to the importance of this food in Belgian
history, and it explains why many Belgians still cannot do without potatoes during a hot meal. Around 1850, well-to-do people ate *pommes frites*
or *pommes duchesses* (rolls of mashed potatoes baked in butter) and consumed about 220 pounds of potatoes per person per year, while poor peas-
ant workers ate plain one-pot dishes such as potatoes with onion sauce or
potatoes in skim milk, totaling the quite astounding amount of about 790
pounds of potatoes per person per year. This large amount provided workers with almost 40 percent of their total caloric intake. Potatoes supply
many calories at a low price, and they proved to be an excellent substitute
for bread when this became costly, as during extremely expensive years in
the 1840s and 1850s. In the second half of the nineteenth century physicians saw potatoes as food without much nutritional value that led to a
sluggish, counterproductive temper, and they warned against too high a
consumption. The effect was nil, though. In the 1960s potatoes lost some
of their popularity when meat consumption started to rise significantly
and potatoes were gradually replaced by rice and pasta. At first, rice and
macaroni appeared on the plate next to the meat and the vegetables. It
was only in the 1990s that, for example, pasta dishes were prepared and
served in a less "Belgian" way, that is, on their own. Until the 1980s, *Ons
kookboek* indeed had difficulties in situating foreign elements and dishes
within Belgian eating habits. This refers not only to their place within
Belgian cuisine but also to cooking skills: for example, the 1942 issue of
Ons kookboek recommends cooking pasta for half an hour.[29]

Braised Potatoes *(gestoofde aardappelen or pommes de terre mijotées)*

2.2 pounds potatoes

2 cups of milk

1 onion

3 1/2 tablespoons butter

salt and pepper

nutmeg

bay leaf

Peel, wash, and cube the potatoes. Put a pan on low heat, and add some butter. Braise the onion in the butter, and then add the potato cubes, milk, the remaining butter, and the spices. Leave to simmer half an hour; do not stir. Before serving, a little grated hard cheese may be added.

Vegetables form another part of the hot meal, although many Belgians, particularly those with lower incomes, eat only small portions, out of a feeling of obligation. This feeling is most likely caused by dieticians' great emphasis since the 1930s on the nutritive and digestive value of vegetables. Younger women are particularly sensitive to this opinion and began to eat lots of fresh vegetables, especially crudités or cold mixed salads. Many people's near-aversion to vegetables is by no means explained by a lack of choice, because Belgium produces a great variety of vegetables (including classics such as asparagus and *witloof* (Belgian endives)—see Chapter 2—as well as newer products like zucchini and peppers) and imports a large quantity of some others, like eggplant, lettuce, and broccoli. Belgian cooks highlight this rich variety of tastes, and some have become aficionados, trying to convince youngsters and adults of the irreplaceable qualities of fresh vegetables.

Belgians' ambivalent relationship with the vegetables on their plates is illustrated by the attention paid to vegetable recipes in *Ons kookboek*. Between its 1927 and 1999 issues, the proportion of vegetable recipes fluctuated significantly, but in the long run it hardly changed (starting and ending at 11 percent, with 43 recipes in 1927 and 152 in 1999).[30] The percentage of vegetable recipes had significantly diminished in the 1960s and 1970s to less than 8 percent, when recipes for meat dishes became very important, while the actual number of vegetable recipes fell from 66 in 1959 to 56 in 1964. The moderate consumption of vegetables is another clear sign of Belgians' low interest in vegetables. In the late 1930s Belgians consumed about 77 pounds of vegetables per person per year, whereas this reached almost 150 pounds in the surrounding countries. The Belgian average did gradually rise to about 220 pounds today, but it still is below the level of many European countries (and about 30 percent lower than in the United States). Belgian nutritionists agree that the average intake is about 2.5 times too low.

Perhaps Belgians' low enthusiasm for vegetables should be explained by the fact that plain and overcooked vegetables formed the core of hot meals for most people during many centuries. The season's vegetables were put in one pot that hung above the fire, and only in good times was some meat added. Carrots, cabbages, turnips, beans, or peas, with some water, fat, and (perhaps) herbs, were turned into a substantial soup or *hutsepot* (hotchpotch). Later, from the late eighteenth century onward, potatoes were added, which pushed down consumption of vegetables.[31] Would this way of preparing vegetables have prevented many working-class households from enjoying vegetables up to the present? Ways of preparation in recipe books were generally quite simple, with rather long cooking times recommended until 1950. Carrots with chopped onions, for example, were supposed to be cooked for 30 minutes and cauliflower for 15 minutes, although "the vegetables may be left on the fire for a while longer."[32] Quite popular was the combination of mashed potatoes with carrots, beans, or leeks (*stoemp* in Flemish, *purée* in French), sometimes with cream. Interestingly, the popular *stoemp* has made its way into to-day's fancy restaurants and trendy cookbooks. Despite the growing availability of different kinds of vegetables and the long-term decreasing price (because of massive importation and sharply increasing agricultural productivity), most people stuck to only a handful of vegetables. The Belgian top-three vegetables are tomatoes, carrots, and various types of lettuce, probably because they are prepared throughout the year, with cold and effortless preparations in summer and, in the case of tomatoes and carrots, hot versions in winter.

The central part of the typical Belgian hot midday meal is, without any doubt, meat. As mentioned, meat has always been highly valued by all social classes. Even today, after the weakening of meat's status since about 1980, there are still noticeable differences in family expenditures, with high-income families spending more on meat than low-income households. The lowest-income group spent 273 euros on fresh meat in 1996 and 210 euros in 2005 (thus reducing their consumption by 23 percent over this time period), while the highest-income group spent, respectively, 711 and 748 euros (thus increasing their consumption by 5 percent).

School manuals, recipe collections, cookbooks, women's magazines, and gastronomic Web sites testify to the huge interest in meat. The recently diminished status of meat has not altered this. *Ons kookboek*, for example, contains 55 meat recipes (which make up 14 percent of the total) in its 1927 issue but 281 meat recipes (17 percent of the total) in the 1999 issue. Instead of shrinking, the number of meat recipes thus expanded. Above all, they diversified. Alongside customary meat dishes, such as *sto-verij* (*carbonnades* in French; meat stew) or *blinde vinken* (*oiseaux sans tête* in French; literally, blind finches; see recipe), new meat dishes appeared such as chili con carne, chicken curry, or Calypso pork (prepared with hot chili pepper and grapefruit juice). Causes for this diversification are multiple. The internationalization of cuisine plays an important role. However, the shift within Belgian meat consumption is crucial (Chapter 2). Around 1900, beef and pork were the most popular meats, with pork being widely eaten among working-class and rural families. After World War II, beef and veal became more popular, reaching a peak in the 1970s. Then, poultry took over. This development is adequately reflected in the number of recipes for the various types of meat in *Ons kookboek*. In 1929 there were 7 recipes for preparing poultry, but in 1999 there were 103 (13 and 37 percent, respectively, of the total number of meat recipes). The popular pork fell from 44 percent of recipes in the 1920s to 32 percent in the 1970s and a mere 15 percent in 1999.[33] Primarily, price developments guide these shifts. For example, the arrival of "hen batteries" in the 1960s and the application of efficient processing in mechanized "chicken factories" in the 1970s made the price drop. The once-luxury poultry that only the wealthy ate on festive occasions became a frequent Sunday meal in the 1970s and a common weekday dish in the 1980s.[34] Today, the average Belgian consumes almost 220 pounds of all kinds of meat per year.

Blind Finches *(blinde vinken or oiseaux sans tête)*

1 pound veal

1/2 pound minced pork

3 1/2 tablespoons butter

1 onion

bay leaf, thyme, and nutmeg

salt and pepper

flour

1 tablespoon tomato purée

3 tablespoons Madeira wine

Mix the minced pork thoroughly with some salt, pepper, and nutmeg. Cut four to five thin slices (c. 12 × 7 cm) of the veal, put the minced pork on it, and roll to make cylinder-like shapes. Bind each piece with a thin thread, and brown the meat in a hot pan with butter (2 teaspoons). Dice the onion and put it in the pan, together with the thyme, bay leaf, and some salt and pepper. Add half a cup of water, and simmer for half an hour. Meanwhile, prepare the sauce: Melt the remaining butter, add flour, and stir well, adding some water if the sauce is too thick. Gently pour in the Madeira and add the tomato purée, and leave on low heat for about five minutes. Serve with potato croquettes.

Nutritionists see fish as a healthy alternative to meat. In 2006 the Health Council (a governmental advisory board) proposed that eating fish twice a week, and varying the kinds, would be highly beneficial to counter particular diseases and being overweight. This advice is not new. In her *Notions d'économie domestique* (1906), Louisa Mathieu wrote, "Fish enriches the diet and is healthy, tasty, nutritious and, in most cases, easily digestible." She concluded, "It would be wise to consume more of this precious food. Several sorts are sold at a moderate price, and fish may easily replace the rather expensive meat."[35] Similar advice may be read throughout the twentieth century. Nutritionists today, however, can no longer use the argument of the low price, since fish gradually became more expensive in recent years. The average retail price of fish rose by 20 percent between January 2006 and January 2008, while general inflation barely reached 5 percent. Due to this price increase, most fish varieties have regained a higher status nowadays, which is reflected in the fast-growing gap between expenditures on fish by rich and poor families: the latter spent 57 euros in 1996 but only 49 euros in 2005, whereas the former spent 141 and 232 euros, respectively. In 1996 richer families spent 2.5 times more on fish than poor families, but in 2005 this was 4.7 times, which once more demonstrates rapidly rising food inequality in the last decades. Differences between Brussels, Flanders, and Wallonia in spending on fresh fish have tended to shrink. In 1978 the Brussels households spent 65 euros, which was 35 percent more than in Flanders and 55 percent more than in Wallonia. In 2005, spending on fresh fish in Flanders skyrocketed (an increase of 190 percent), leaving Wallonia (where spending increased 170 percent) and Brussels (where spending rose 110 percent) behind.

Compared with the 1960s the fish supply in supermarkets has expanded greatly, which is mirrored in the wide variety of recipes in today's cookbooks. *Ons kookboek* printed 18 fish recipes in 1937, 46 in 1963, but 161 in 1999, increasing these recipes' proportion of the total from 4 percent before World War II to 10 percent in the 1990s.[36] Popular recipes up to the 1970s used cod, ray, herring, eel, and mussels, whereas nowadays recipes also include salmon, sole, turbot, plaice, trout, wolffish, lobster, and other shellfish. Despite the century-long recommendations to eat more fish, the average Belgians consume barely 22 pounds per year, which places them at the bottom of fish consumption in the European Union. Reasons are manifold, including relatively high prices but also the doubt about the caloric supply as well as health scares with regard to fish's mercury content.

If fish has not succeeded in unsettling the position of meat in Belgium, the modern one-pot dishes may do this. These "exotic dishes" include pasta, pizza, stir-fry, moussaka, quiche, paella, cassoulet, tajine, and the like, which appeared in Belgian homes in the 1970s. Belgians learned about these foreign dishes and ingredients through travel or an ethnic restaurant (see Chapter 5), through reading about foreign cuisines in magazines, newspapers, cookbooks, and Web sites, and through word of mouth, watching television or seeing advertisements, and other signs of internationalization of the diet. Belgians were first exposed to world cuisines in the late nineteenth century, when thousands from all social classes visited World's fairs that offered a taste of world cuisines. Until the late 1950s, however, common cookbooks were extremely reticent about publishing foreign dishes or using foreign ingredients. For example, a *sauce blanche italienne* (Italian white sauce with wine, mushrooms, and herbs) appeared in Mathieu's school manual of 1906, with a little white wine as the only "exotic" element, and a *pikante saus* (hot sauce) was mentioned by the De Paeuw couple in 1931, with "lots of pepper" and, before serving, "the addition of little pieces of pickles."[37] Cookbooks of the 1950s seem to warm up the general public for foreign food. Thus, *Ik kan koken* has a separate chapter "Foreign Cuisine," which contained 13 recipes from the United States (such as oyster cocktail and Waldorf salad), 3 from Germany, 11 from England (such as fried haddock livers and oxtail soup), 10 from France (such as mussels in white wine and savarin), 11 from Italy (such as polenta and risotto), and 27 from Asia (which reflects the fact that this cookbook was also meant for the Netherlands, which has many ties to its former colony, Indonesia).[38] Other cookbooks, though, hardly mentioned a foreign dish.

Propelled by growing international tourism and the arrival of many migrants, the interest in exotic cuisine has truly exploded since the 1960s. In the late 1960s, women's magazines started publishing, with great enthusiasm, articles about (inexpensive) sunny beaches, exotic towns, and unknown foods. They gave recipes in order to prepare for the holiday or to prolong the vacation's memory, and advised where to buy the new ingredients in local or specialized shops and markets. With tourists' discovery of further horizons, the interest in exotic food expanded year after year. This diffusion of foreign dishes was fully at work in *Ons kookboek*, which had long been a stronghold of traditionalism.[39] The 1972 edition bears full witness to the internationalization: for the first time it has a special section with the outdated label *Uitheemse gerechten* (literally, outlandish dishes, showing the clear division between "us" and "them") that included short recipes from 10 foreign countries (France is represented with 13 recipes, Hungary and Asia with 11 each, with the remaining recipes divided between Germany, the Netherlands, Switzerland, Italy [only 3], Spain, Scandinavia, and the United Kingdom). Interestingly, this special section disappeared in the 1980s edition: half of the recipes were incorporated into the traditional sections (soup, starters, main dishes), and the rest were simply cut. Incorporated recipes included, for instance, minestrone, pizza, or paella, which may imply the absorption of these dishes into the daily Belgian diet. In the 1999 edition, the exotic section reappears, because of the consideration of "new" countries. Only this time, not only recipes are given, but each culinary culture is presented, and stress is placed on *authentic* eating. The label "outlandish" has disappeared.

Based on the success of pasta cookbooks and pasta Web sites, and on the increasing amount of money spent by Belgian households on pasta, it seems safe to say that pasta has become a favorite in many Belgian homes. For example, Infotalia.be, a Flemish lifestyle e-magazine, has pages where members may post popular recipes: Belgium leads (with 1,167 recipes), followed by Italy (233 recipes), far before other cuisines (France, 148; Morocco, 75; China, 52; Greece, 40; Spain, 39; etc.).[40] Often, foreign recipes are presented as tasty and, generally, easy to prepare.

The element of simplicity was picked up by the food industry, which understood the time pressures and lack of culinary skills of many people. Since the 1890s, the industry had been producing canned food, but this was initially limited to ingredients (like sardines and corned beef) and soup. In the 1960s, some factories produced canned spaghetti or ravioli, ready to be heated. The frozen vegetables and fish of the 1960s opened the way to the frozen pizza of the 1990s. Today, however, the biggest growth in ready-made food is fresh food. As already mentioned, family spending on convenience foods increased 430 percent between 1978 and 2005, one of the biggest augmentations in spending. Interestingly, all income groups share the interest in fresh convenience foods: if the low-income groups still spend less money on this category of foods than high-income groups, they are catching up little by little to the richer families. Fresh lasagna produced by the supermarket Delhaize was the first big success in this field, but nowadays there is hardly any dish that cannot be bought (in glass, plastic, tin, or paper, at various prices), heated in a microwave oven, and swallowed within a few minutes. Advantages are the rapid and effortless preparation and the individual aspect, which are elements that surely contribute to the disappearance of the classic meal pattern. Drawbacks are the relatively high price, the lack of vegetables, and the rather high caloric content.[41] Thus, the typical Belgian hot meal eaten at home is increasingly prepared in an industrial kitchen and no longer on the family stove.

The same conclusion may also be drawn with regard to the last course of the hot meal, the dessert. The average Belgian household spent about 120 percent more on ready-made desserts in 2005 than in 1978. Today,

the offering of desserts in supermarkets is astonishing, including a gigan-
tic variety of containers of yogurt, ice cream, puddings, sweet rice, and
cheese. As with the ready-made dishes, the gap in spending between low-
and high-income groups has been gradually decreasing in the last 10 years.
This growing interest in dessert, however, is not limited to purchases in
supermarkets, since Belgians love to prepare desserts at home too. The
large section devoted to desserts in magazines, television programs, newspapers, cookbooks, and Web sites testifies to this interest. The e-magazine
Epicurien.be, for example, has special Internet pages with countless dessert recipes.[42] The most popular desserts are cakes and pies, sabayon and
tiramisu, and anything with chocolate. All social classes show huge interest in desserts, but at present the lower-income groups are increasing
their spending faster than households with higher incomes. Undoubtedly,
this is partly a matter of making up historical arrears. Up until the 1920s,
working-class households could hardly afford to buy sweet food because
of the high price. For example, in the nineteenth century chocolate was
solely consumed by better-off families, and only very gradually toward
1900 could working-class households purchase chocolate on special occasions such as Christmas (sweet food has always been connected to festive
occasions, shown by the baking of pastry since the early Middle Ages).
When the price of chocolate dropped in the 1920s, it became part of the
daily consumption of the popular classes.

DINNER

With work and school, where people have a cold noon meal than rather
a hot one, a hot meal in the evening has become common in Belgium
(very few people would be happy with only cold meals during a day).
Therefore, information about the typical meal at noon applies to the hot
meal in the evening. The following, thus, deals with cold evening meals
(as well as applying to cold midday meals). In the 1972 *Ons kookboek* it
is written that "A hot meal in the evening may be had when one hasn't
been able to cook properly at noon. Take care, then, that this hot meal is
easily digestible."[43]

Following the general shift in eating times, Belgians tend to eat dinner
much later nowadays than they used to.[44] In the 1960s, people had dinner
between 5 and 8:30 P.M., with most of them at the table at 6 P.M. In 2004,
the dinner period generally started at 5 P.M. and ended at 10 P.M., which
would have been very unusual 40 years earlier. Also, in accordance with
the general reduction in the time used for eating, the weekday dinner took
less time in 2004 (average of 26 minutes) than in 1966 (31 minutes). On

Sundays, people tend to dine somewhat later and take a few minutes longer. Dinner is skipped more often than lunch, which hardly changed over the past 40 years, although the evening meal is abandoned more and more since the 1960s, with today about one-quarter of Belgians simply skipping this meal during the week and even one-third during the weekend.

Nutritionists do not seem to worry about Belgians skipping dinner. They worry about them eating late, eating TV-dinners, and snacking individually. In many cookbooks, eating late is discouraged because it appears to disturb the digestive process. Going to sleep with a full stomach is bad for digestion and hampers the purification of the body. Moreover, eating late leads to little or no hunger feeling when getting up in the morning, which makes people neglect breakfast and causes snacking around 10 A.M. In addition, some believe that dining late leads to being overweight (which is not true: snacking and nibbling after dining do). Eating while watching television is considered to be very bad, although during the weekend one-quarter of children younger than age 16 watch television during the evening meal. Almost 50 percent of Belgian households often watch television during dinner, and 10 percent make this a habit.[45] Some people link being overweight directly to eating while watching television, although there is little proof for this (on the contrary, the whole family sitting together at the table promotes healthy eating). Finally, individual dining causes some worries that people, especially youngsters, would eat unrestrained and enjoy meals that are too fatty and sweet, thereby causing weight problems.

The specialized media give many recommendations to counter bad habits related to the evening meal: eat together, provide tasty food, take sufficient time, and keep it interesting. With regard to the content of the cold dinner, reference is made to recommendations for breakfast: variation, light, and little or no sweet toppings or fillings. The Web site of the Vlaams Instituut voor Gezondheidspromotie (Flemish Institute for Health Advancement, a private center for advice) contains practical tips for an alternative to the perpetual cheese and ham sandwiches.[46] "Have a different filling! Think about fruit and vegetables with your bread" is the start of a long list of original recipes that include strawberry, banana, or peach slices, apple and rhubarb purée, salads with fruit, braised pears with cinnamon, toasted slices of bread with apple (croque pomme), cottage cheese with canned or fresh pineapple, and classics like salad with tomato and cucumber, but also ("yet to be discovered") cooked broccoli with mushrooms, and cheese with oranges and carrots. "Combine and vary" are the key words, which are followed by daring bread-meal recipes such as whole wheat pistolets with a thin slice of chicken, watercress, and peach, or rye bread with white cheese, steamed broccoli, and mushroom pieces. The "bread tower" is also rather inventive: one slice of whole-grain bread with some lettuce and tomato, on top of that one slice of whole-grain bread with gouda cheese, kiwi, or apple, and again topped with a slice of whole-grain bread. Cut this into three triangles to obtain a fancy sandwich.

These are original combinations, reflecting a genuine concern about health. Up to the late 1970s, such concern was present in cookbooks and women's magazines, although to a far lesser extent. When the 1972 edition of *Ons kookboek* considered the cold evening meal, it suggested various sorts of ham, bacon, pâtés, salami, and meat salads (with mayonnaise). Tomatoes, sour little onions, cucumbers, and fresh lettuce were optional and, particularly, decorative. Equally unconceivable nowadays is the suggestion to make waffles or pancakes (with, of course, fruit jams, whipped cream, *chocopasta*, sugar, or syrup) as an alternative to the meal with bread. Going back further in time, health concerns were limited to the recommendation to consume whole-grain bread.

Since the 1970s it has become more difficult to point to typical meals in terms of content, timing, company, and location than before. With the overall changes within Belgian society (ageing, smaller households, growing inequalities, individualization, rising international flow of people and goods, etc.), differences have increased, making it harder than before 1970 to adhere to common ideologies such as the three-meal pattern with a hot lunch. Belgians take less time to eat at home; more of them skip breakfast, lunch, or dinner; some eat alone; many tend to eat later in the day; and a hot meal may be taken either at noon or in the evening. Still, despite many changes, some very familiar patterns emerge nowadays: most Belgians eat at home, a three-meal pattern is still observed, and a lot of cooking is still done in one's own kitchen. All this may seem quite remarkable in the frame of the fantastic economic, social, and ideological changes of the recent past. Finally, home meals appear to be the daily concern not only of those who prepare the food at home but also of nutritionists, physicians, and social observers, who all comment, judge, and advise about typical meals (as well as about family values, the role of the housewife, obesity, TV-dinners, snacking and grazing, and much more).

NOTES

1. Stephanie Devriese, Inge Huybrechts, Michel Moreau, and Herman Van Oyen., *De Belgische voedselconsumptiepeiling* vol. 1 (Brussels: Instituut Volksgezondheid, 2006), 14.

2. Jane De Paeuw and Leo De Paeuw, *De moderne huishouding* (Brussels: Office de Publicité, 1931), 199.

3. This cookbook has gone through numerous reprints and editions, and today it includes some 1,600 recipes alongside many general observations about health, festive meals and decorum, drinks, customary Flemish cooking, and exotic cuisine. Some 2.3 million copies have been sold, and in 2006 *Ons kookboek* was awarded the newly launched Prize for Gastronomy by the Flemish government, to honor its constant efforts at improving the daily diet.

4. Yves Segers, "Food Recommendations, Tradition and Change in a Flemish Cookbook: Ons Kookboek, 1920–2000," *Appetite* 45.1 (2005): 5.

5. See Gezondheid (Health), http://www.gezondheid.be/index.cfm?fuse action =art&art_id=3431 (accessed January 20, 2008).

6. Princess Charlotte (1840–1927), sister of king Leopold II, married Ferdinand-Maximilian, who became emperor of Mexico in 1864. He was killed in 1867, and she returned to Europe, suffering from mental illness. She lived in castles in the immediate surroundings of Brussels.

7. Results may be seen at Nutria. Belgian Food Consumption Survey, http://www.iph.fgov.be/nutria/NUTRIA.htm (accessed December 2, 2007).

8. "Aan tafel, iedereen" [Everybody, dinner is served], *Het Laatste Nieuws*, November 19, 2004, 11.

9. Inge Mestdag, "Destructuration of the Belgian Meal Pattern? Changes in Temporal, Social and Spatial Aspects of Eating Practices by Means of Time Use Data" (PhD diss., Vrije Universiteit Brussel, 2007). This study is presented in Inge Mestdag, "Disappearance of the Traditional Meal: Temporal, Social and Spatial Destructuration," *Appetite* 45.1 (2005): 62–74.

10. *Budgetenquêtes 1978/9–2005*, see Belgian Federal State, Economics: Downloads, http://statbel.fgov.be/figures/download_nl.asp#hbs (accessed November 30, 2007); "current prices" do not consider inflation. Total family spending grew by 150 percent.

11. "Pierre Wynants: Je moet met je tijd meegaan" [Pierre Wynants: One must be modern], *De Standaard Magazine*, September 24, 2005, 14.

12. Peter Scholliers, "Novelty and Tradition: The New Landscape for Gastronomy," in *Food, the History of Taste*, ed. Paul Freedman (London: Thames & Hudson, 2007), 332–357.

13. Mestdag, "Destructuration of the Belgian Meal Pattern?"; Mestdag, "Disappearance of the Traditional Meal"; N. Rousseau, "Belgisch ontbijt bestudeerd" [Study of the Belgian breakfast], http://www.e-gezondheid.be/nl/tijdschrift_ge zondheid/voeding_en_gezondheid/belgisch_ontbijt_bestudeerd-14848-901-art. htm, December 11, 2007 (accessed January 25, 2008).

14. Rousseau, "Belgisch ontbijt bestudeerd."

15. Rousseau, "Belgisch ontbijt bestudeerd."

16. "Uw gezondheid" [Your health], Christian Sick Fund, http://www.cm.be/nl/100/uwgezondheid/gezondleven/voeding/tijdvoorontbijt.jsp (accessed January 8, 2008).

17. "Tien geode redenen om te ontbijten" (Ten good reasons to have breakfast), Gezondheid.be, http://www.gezondheid.be/index.cfm?fuseaction=art&art_id=1150 (accessed December 2, 2007).

18. Note the difference between the Dutch *gewonnen brood*, meaning "gained bread," and the French *pain perdu*, or "lost bread."

19. De Paeuw and De Paeuw, *De moderne huishouding*, 238.

20. De Paeuw and De Paeuw, *De moderne huishouding*, 245.

21. P. J. Sarels van Rijn, *Ik kan koken* (Antwerp and Leiden: Van Tuyl & Sijthoff's, 1951), 104–105.

22. Jongeren & Voeding, http://www.jongerenenvoeding.be/voeding-gezondemaaltijd.html (accessed January 31, 2008).

23. *Ons kookboek* (1972), 10.

24. Mestdag, "Destructuration of the Belgian Meal Pattern?"; Mestdag, "Disappearance of the Traditional Meal."

25. *Fijne hapjes van Libelle–Rosita* (Antwerp: N.V. Tijdschriften Uitgevers, 1971), 89–90. Nowadays, brunch is common in hotels and restaurants, while organizations use it as a substitute for lunch during annual parties or special occasions.

26. "Een gezond lunchpakket" [A healthy lunchbox], posted on the blog Gezond Vermageren [Losing weight healthily], November 25, 2007, http://www.gezond-vermageren.be (accessed January 25, 2008).

27. See, for example, the collection of 70 soup recipes on Receptjes.be (literally, "little recipes") http://www.receptjes.be/menu_soepen.html (accessed January 26, 2008).

28. "'t Zijn maar aardappelen" [Just potatoes], *Bij de Haard*, May 1952, 130.

29. See Inge Mestdag, "Introducing Italian Cuisine into Flemish Home-Meal Cooking in the Twentieth Century: An Analysis of the Flemish Cooking Bible Ons Kookboek (1927–1999)," *Food & History* 1.1 (2003): 172.

30. Segers, "Food Recommendations," 12.

31. Eddie Niesten and Yves Segers, *De smaken van het land: Groenten en fruit vroeger en nu* (Leuven, Belgium: Davidsfonds, 2007), 15.

32. De Paeuw and De Paeuw, *De moderne huishouding*, 267.

33. Segers, "Food Recommendations," 13.

34. Eddie Niesten, Jan Raymaekers, and Yves Segers, *Lekker dier!? Dierlijke productie en consumptie in de 19e en 20e eeuw* (Leuven, Belgium: CAG, 2003), 85–97.

35. Louisa Mathieu, *Notions d'économie domestique pour les écoles normales d'institutrices* (Verviers, Belgium: A. Hermann, 1906), 195.

36. Segers, "Food Recommendations," 13.

37. Mathieu, *Notions*, 194; De Paeuw and De Paeuw, *De moderne huishouding*, 280.

38. Sarels van Rijn, *Ik kan koken*, 570–591.

39. Segers, "Food Recommendations," 6–7.

40. See Infotalia, the on-line life style magazine, http://www.infotalia.be/nl/gastronomie/ (accessed January 28, 2008).

41. "Ook meesterkoks gaan kant en klaar" [Chefs also go for convenience foods], *Het Volk,* February 7, 2003, 2.

42. See Epicurien ("Bienvenue aux gourmands, gourmets et gastronomes"), http://www.epicurien.be/recettes/desserts-fruits/recette-dessert.asp (accessed January 29, 2008).

43. *Ons kookboek* (1972), 234.

44. Mestdag, "Destructuration of the Belgian Meal Pattern?"; Mestdag, "Disappearance of the Traditional Meal."

45. "Veel ouders trekken zich niets aan van gezonde voeding" [Many parents careless about healthy food], *De Morgen,* August 29, 2007.

46. See VIG, Vlaams Instituut voor Gezondheidspromotie (Flemish Institute for Health Advancement), http://www.vig.be/content.asp?nav=themas_voeding&selnav=206,476 (accessed January 31, 2008).

5

Eating Out

As in most European countries since about 1970, Belgians increasingly eat out. A reliable indicator of this increase is the share of total household expenditures spent on eating out. This reached 1.9 percent in 1961, rising to 3.3 percent in 1978, to attain 5 percent in 1990. Since 1990, this proportion has remained fairly stable, with a modest peak (5.5 percent) in 1995 and low (5.2 percent) in 2004. This percentage equals that of Germany (5.4 percent in 2005) and of the Netherlands (5.1 percent), and nears that of France (6.2 percent), but it is below that of the United Kingdom (11 percent) and the average of the 27 countries of the European Union (9 percent). However, the 1.9 percent of 1961 reflects a very different way of eating out than the recent 5 percent does, with the big change being that since about 1970 many more people eat out for pleasure. Before then, this had been the privilege of richer people, whereas eating out related to work has long been common for many people. This chapter, therefore, differentiates between eating out related to work and eating out for pleasure, exploring the perhaps-artificial distinction between the two.

The 1.7 percent increase between 1978 and today may seem trifling, but it corresponds to a huge amount of money. Moreover, the full significance of this humble rise appears in the context of the shrinking expenditures on home-consumed foods, from 17.6 percent of total family spending in 1978 to 12.2 percent in 2006. This decrease links to a long-term development that started around 1880. Back then, food's share in total family spending reached about 60 percent or more, leaving very little room for other expenditures. Confirming the "first consumption law" of the German statistician Ernst Engel, the proportion of food costs fell considerably according to the rising income in the course of the twentieth century (reaching 50 percent in 1948 and 38 percent in 1961). The modest increase of eating out's proportion of total expenditures, in fact, challenges this century-old law.

Before tackling the distinct worlds of eating out for work and for pleasure, the large social differences with regard to eating out must be emphasized. In 2005, the average Belgian household spent 1,560 euros per year on eating out, with the lowest-income group reaching a mere 560 euros and the highest group a pleasurable 2,730 euros (or 4.8 times more). When dividing households into 10 categories from low to high income, the money spent on eating out increases neatly from one category to another, with, however, a solid rise in the three top sections. The average conceals important regional differences, too. Nowadays, money spent on eating out reaches 5.5 percent of total household expenditure in Flanders but 4.8 percent in Brussels and only 3.5 percent in Wallonia. The advance of Flanders appeared only in the 1990s: in 1978, Brussels (4.6 percent) was in the lead of Flanders (3.9 percent) and Wallonia (3.4 percent). Between 1978 and 2006 expenditure on eating out rose impressively by 40 percent in Flanders but only by 6 percent in Brussels and 4 percent in Wallonia. On the surface this may point to differences that are linked to linguistic borders, but, as with the consumption of fresh fruit and vegetables (Chapter 4), dissimilarities should be interpreted by looking at household composition, age, occupation, income, and level of urbanization. The typical Belgian who eats out frequently lives alone or with a partner, is between 45 and 55 years old, lives in a conurbation, and has a white-collar, well-paid job. Apparently, since the 1970s Flanders houses more of such people than both other regions.

There are crucial differences with regard to the location and style of eating out. In the late 1980s, 27 percent of meals eaten out were eaten in restaurants, 8 percent in snack bars, 57 percent in cafeterias of schools and companies, and 8 percent in other places. Except for meals in school canteens, all forms of eating out have become more popular since the early 1980s, which was particularly the case for meals in snack bars and other places (such as milk bars or fries shacks).[1] These data put the notion of eating out into perspective: most of it is work related. Reasons for eating out are manifold because of the variety of the offerings and significance. However, one general explanation goes beyond Belgium and Europe: many household tasks that have long been taken care of in the home and by the housewife (clothes mending, child rearing, cleaning, hair cutting, etc.) are ever more available on the market. Eating has simply become part of this ongoing, broad commercialization, allowing the diner just to choose, eat, and pay, without needing to deal with shopping, preparing food, or washing up.

WORK-RELATED EATING OUT

Old Habits

For centuries, people working in the fields, thus a majority of the population, ate home-prepared food, either provided by the farm or brought by them or by family members during breaks. Bringing food for the rest of the day meant simple, cold meals that consisted of heaps of coarse bread with lard and some bacon, in addition to plain beer. Nowadays, the habit of eating in the fields and meadows has almost disappeared, with workers taking time to have a meal at home. Yet, the old routine of eating out in the fields has a direct link with today's food culture. Since the 1910s the Women Farmers' Association (Boerinnenbond) has aimed to improve workers' fare by advising about healthy, low-cost, and homegrown food. This association organized cooking lessons, and in 1927 it published *Ons kookboek* (Our cookbook), which appeared in many reprints and became a genuine best seller in Flanders.[2] Nowadays, agricultural laborers' diet is abundant, fresh, and natural (although it is increasingly produced with the help of fertilizers). In the 1990s this type of food was labeled "authentic" and was particularly sought after by city dwellers. In fact, already a century before, well-off city dwellers, with nostalgic rural sentiments, visited Dilbeek, Jezus-Eik, and other rural villages near Brussels to taste the *honest* country fare in pastoral taverns that specialized in *Geuze* or *Kriek* (a sour beer made of Morello cherries and sugar), served to accompany big loaves of coarse bread with cottage cheese and radishes. Today, the sightseer can still taste this straightforward countryperson's fare.

Laborers in workshops and modern factories had to provide their own food and beverages. In some cases, employers supplied very plain beer but no food. Up to the middle of the nineteenth century the organization of work allowed most laborers to go home at noon, until the work schedule became too strict, forcing laborers to bring their food in the morning. Those who could afford it would buy some charcuterie (fine cold meats) to go along with the bread they brought from home. Laborers in Brussels, for example, would buy *pâté de foie* (liver paste), *kipkap* (slightly spiced, raw, minced meat), and *boudin noir* or *blanc* (respectively, a black or gray sausage made of blood and bread). These were salty and fatty foods.

Street Food

Since 1900, white-collar workers have bought a snack at noon to eat in the open air or in common pubs. They eat little, round breads from the butcher (called *pistolets* in the local language, which is neither Flemish or French) with cold meat or cheese, or *couques* from the baker (*koffiekoeken* in Flemish), like *couque Suisse* (Swiss cake), *couque au beurre* (butter cake), croissant, *chausson au pomme* (apple cake), *boule de Berlin* (Berlin cake), and *sandwiches* which are little, oval, soft and light breads.[3] They could also have sea snails (*caracoles*), known in Belgium as *caricollen*. A recipe for them already appeared in *Een notabel boecxken van cokeryen* (A little

A female street vendor in Brussels in the 1950s sells *caracoles,* or little snails that have been boiled in a vegetable broth. These snails are particularly appreciated during fancy fairs (*kermis*). Courtesy of the AMSAB-Institute of Social History, Ghent.

notable book of cooking), which was printed in Brussels around 1515. In some districts of Brussels *caricollen* are available daily, but they are particularly popular during the *kermis*, a fair with a great variety of food stalls and children's amusements. *Caricollen* are boiled in a strong bouillon with celery, spreading a typical sealike aroma. They are served in a small bowl.

However, by far the most popular street snack during all seasons in Belgium are *pommes frites* (known throughout the world as *French* fries). They appeared at fairs or in busy commercial streets in the 1840s as a genuine treat and could be enjoyed only sporadically by most people because of their high price. In the last quarter of the nineteenth century *frites* could be bought in the vicinity of every railroad station, commercial center, large industrial plant, or sports event, as is still the case today. They are eaten by hundreds of hungry men and women commuting between home and work. Around 1900, there were multiple forms of selling fries in the street, the most simple being a pot with boiling beef grease over a little coal fire, put on a pushcart, while a more advanced form would be selling fries from a window of a private house. In terms of culinary heritage, however, the selling of fries from a shack is undoubtedly the most important. Fries shacks are only to be found in Belgium and some parts of northern France, although recently replicas may be seen in the Netherlands, Germany, and even the United States. *Shack* is the translation of the Flemish *kot*, indicating the often-humble condition of a small wooden construction of about three by three meters (about 120 square feet), mostly standing apart from other buildings, with a large window on one side where the fries are sold, and spreading the typical smell of hot grease. Some sheds are larger and provide a few tables and stools in a somewhat separate space. In Belgium, these places are called *frietkot* or *friture* (the French *friterie* appearing only very recently). Customers can buy a *cornet de frites* (*pak frieten* in Flemish, that is, a paper cone with fries) with salt and mayonnaise and eat standing up in front of the shed, which usually offers rudimentary shelter from rain and wind. They use their fingers to eat, even if some meat, such as meatballs or sausages, is consumed. Fries from a shack provide a lot of calories, are relatively cheap, and take only a few minutes to be consumed. In the first half of the twentieth century such places had spread widely in all towns and villages of Belgium, which makes *friet/frites* thoroughly Belgian.

Of course, one now may buy fries in fast-food outlets all over the world, but these are not hand-cut, fried in beef grease, salted, and served in a little paper cone with (often homemade) mayonnaise. Even if fries shacks may be found in northern France, Dutch towns, and New York City, they are often labeled as Belgian or Flemish. No one, except a few French

Depiction of a poor male street vendor selling chestnuts in Brussels, 1910s. These vendors still appear in
fall and winter. From *Le Bien Social*, 1912.

people, would claim that fries are French and not Belgian (there is no
frites culture south of Paris). Today, fries shacks are quite noticeable in the
Belgian landscape, with about 5,000 *fritures* all over the country (meaning
that *every* town and village at least has one *friture*). However, because of
strong competition from other forms of fast-food outlets, the traditional
fries shack is under pressure. Moreover, out of aesthetic motives, city architects wish to get rid of fries shacks in the historical centers of Belgian
towns, which leads to gripping debates in Belgian newspapers about culinary heritage in opposition to landscape heritage. So far, the Belgian fries

culture has resisted well, and nowadays there are Web sites that elect the top-10 best *fritures* in Belgium and that proudly depict the history of this truly Belgian foodstuff. Also, there is support to legally preserve typical fries shacks. Slightly worrying, perhaps, is the fact that there is a *Frietmuseum* (Fries Museum), indicating the looming disappearance of a genuine culinary phenomenon.

The Belgian *frites* culture is not only a matter of location, appearance, and habits but above all one of food. *Fritures* offer various portions of fries and a myriad of cold sauces (mayonnaise, tartar sauce, pickles, béarnaise sauce, curry sauce, etc.), which form the basis of any fries shack's menu. They also sell meats (meatballs, various sausages, chicken chunks, hamburgers), fish ("fish fingers," fried fish), sandwiches, and sodas. Since the mid- to late 1990s, influenced by food internationalization, *saté* (or satay, diced meat on bamboo skewers), tacos, *merguez* (little spicy lamb sausages), and pitas are now and then also available. Quite popular is the combination of good old *frites* with pita, which provides a solid meal for about 7 euros, soda included: unbeatable in terms of the price-to-calories ratio. New "ethnic" eateries have appeared in villages and towns, specializing in *kebab* (roasted beef, chicken, or lamb put between Arab-style bread with spicy sauces), *durum* (pancake-like bread with lots of vegetables and meat), or sushi, and open virtually 24 hours a day. Often, they too sell *frites*.

Recipe for *Pommes Frites*

Peel large potatoes, wash them, cut into slices, and then into sticks. Soak in water for about 10 minutes, then dry them well. Fry the potato sticks in hot grease (about 300°F) in small portions. First, cook until the sticks are semidone and glossy (about 5 minutes). Remove from grease and let them cool for a while. Meanwhile, heat the grease until blue steam appears (about 350°F). Just before serving, fry the *frites* for the second time for about 3 minutes. When they have a golden color and are crunchy, they are done. Serve with salt.

Cheap Eating Places

Going way back in time, people who needed to travel for their job or artisans, students, artists, or merchants could eat meals in cheap places like estaminets (inns, but called cafés in the twentieth century) and *auberges* or *cabarets* (pubs, a somewhat better place than the former). Travelers could drink the local beer and choose between a few basic dishes, prepared by the publican or his wife, such as hard-boiled eggs, various soups, mashed potatoes with vegetables (called *stoemp*) and a sausage, or bread with cheese or cold meats from the butcher or *tripier* (the *charcutier*, specializing in cured meats), all at reasonable prices. Most ordinary cafés still sell such cheap food, as for example the Brussels A la mort subite (In the Instant Death, named after a beer), specializing in omelets and *tartines* (bread slices) with white farm cheese and radishes. Prior to World War I, workers' cooperatives opened restaurants, as, for example, Vooruit in Ghent, offering soup with bread and a daily dish. The Brussels Maison du Peuple sold *bifsteck-frites, steak-haché,* or *rôti de porc* (respectively, steak with fries, steak tartare, and roasted pork) at low prices to artisans, blue- and white-collar workers, trade agents, and shopping women. Coopera-tive restaurants disappeared in the 1970s.

In the 1920s a new and popular possibility for eating out emerged: the snack bar. It became very trendy in the commercial and administrative districts of Belgian towns from the 1950s onward. A survey among 4,500 Belgians with a full-time job in early 2007 revealed that 66 percent had a sandwich from a snack bar for lunch. The Belgian sandwich bar is a small shop with a large display window, divided into two parts by a coun-ter, selling slices of bread with cheese, meat, or fish salads, and ordinary drinks such as coffee or soda. The snack bar introduced the baguette (*pain*

Children eating ice cream in the street, 1950s. Courtesy of the AMSAB-Institute of Social History, Ghent.

français or *Frans brood*) as the standard sandwich form. Mostly, snack bars do not provide room to sit, except for few high stools in front of the counter, although the bigger ones may have a rather large dining room (often, customers eat their sandwich in an ordinary café or, when the weather is nice, in the open air). Some of these shops were labeled *milk bars*, not just to stress an antialcoholic (and woman-friendly) environment but also to offer milk-based products like milkshakes and ice cream.

Thousands of white-collar workers swarm out of the offices at noon to purchase a simple meal in these bars, having an ever-increasing choice. Au Suisse, for example, established in the old center of Brussels in 1873, sells 80 different sorts of sandwiches among which are *hareng mayonnaise* (herring with mayonnaise), *mousse saumon* (salmon mousse), and *salade d'asperges et jambon* (asparagus and ham salad). Other snack bars sell simple dishes such as *roll mops* (salted herring fillet), *oeuf à la Russe* (hard-boiled egg with cold, chopped vegetables and mayonnaise), *tomate aux crevettes* (fresh tomato with North Sea grey shrimp), *omelette nature* (a plain, lightly seasoned omelet), or *filet américain* (raw minced beef with capers, Worcestershire sauce, pickles, small onions, salt, and pepper, which Belgians call *toast cannibale* when simply put on a slice of freshly toasted bread). Those who could afford it would have *bouchée à la reine* (pastry with a creamy sauce and bits of chicken and mushroom) or *moules-frites*. In the 1960s, *croque monsieur* (a grilled ham-and-cheese sandwich), *croque madame* (the same, with a fried egg on top), and *croque hawaïenne* (a *croque monsieur* with pineapple) appeared and were popular in the 1970s. At present, a baguette—or rather, a small *ciabata*—with Parma ham and mozzarella is available, which is briefly grilled and is called *tosti* (almost all sandwiches may be put in a *tosti*-grill, including those with mayonnaise). Since the 1990s, sandwich bars tend to specialize: some offer only Italian-like or "authentic" sandwiches, but the persistent trend is toward "bio" or "natural" foods. The Exki-chain, for example, wishes to be an alternative to the "eternally same sandwich and burger," stressing in its advertisements freshness, naturalness, and purity, as well as "good nutritional practice and sustainable development." Naturally, prices and quality differ highly between the various sorts of snack bars, the rule being that high sales may guarantee decent products.

The arrival of multinational fast-food chains in the 1970s only added to the choice. McDonald's, for example, arrived in Brussels in 1978 (seven years after the opening of its first European outlet in the Netherlands). According to its worldwide policy, the company picked the vibrant city center to establish its first restaurant: the Place de la Bourse. Nowadays, the company has 57 outlets in Belgium (of which 60 percent are in densely populated Flanders) and serves about 60,000 customers per day. Yet, per million inhabitants, the country has only 6 outlets, versus 43 in the United States, 18 in the United Kingdom, 14 in France, and 12 in the Netherlands. This low diffusion in Belgium may be explained by the fact that a local hamburger chain, Quick Restaurants, operating since 1971, had a solid reputation by the end of the 1970s and has grown considerably since then. The offerings of McDonald's and Quick do not differ much: Quick does not sell a more "Belgian" choice. Adding the sales of the two hamburger chains, it appears that Belgian consumers match the average hamburger consumption of the surrounding countries. Some Belgians, though, really do not like these restaurants: in August 1999, for example, members of the Animal Liberation Front, a United Kingdom–based animal-rights group, set fire to a McDonald's outlet near Antwerp, which was the eighth assault on these restaurants within the year.

Institutional Cafeterias

From about the 1960s it was believed that the housewife tended to lose her grip on the daily food of her husband and children because of the growing practice of eating out, which meant the loss of her status as caring mother, the start of the decay of the family and its values, and the decline of home cooking. Moreover, it was feared that food quality would greatly deteriorate in terms of sanitation, freshness, and variety. Nutritionists warned particularly against the success of the *cornet de frites* that, at a moderate price, not only provided lots of calories but also a huge quantity of fat. Although nothing of the kind happened, initiatives to guarantee adequate food were taken in schools, factories, big offices, and firms, which were the places where the husbands' and children's diet could be monitored to a certain extent. For, after all, the future of the nation depended on the level of sufficiently well-fed workers and schoolchildren.

Before World War I, most preparatory schools in the larger cities provided small children with some additional food, mostly soup. Studies had shown that about a quarter of the children had not eaten at all before arriving at school in the morning. Moreover, they did not bring any food with them. Of the bulk of children, some had had breakfast, and some did bring along a noon meal, but, in general, it was concluded that undernourishment was very common. During World War I, a huge food program targeted schoolchildren and paradoxically led to a radical change in nutrition and health during and immediately after the war's harsh living conditions. After the war, schools continued providing children with additional free food such as milk and soup.

Moreover, many schools established a kitchen to cook hot meals for all children, which became quite common after 1950. As a direct consequence of the harsh living conditions during the Great War, the ministry of education largely pays for this. In 2008, state subsidies allow for the selling of a school meal (soup, hot dish, and dessert) for a very reasonable 3.5 euros. The meals' quality and the price play a role in the competition between school systems, particularly the Catholic network on the one side and the public (state- and town-organized) network on the other. The quality of school meals is continually monitored and frequently studied. "Quality" refers to safe and healthy food, not to taste and variety. Meals must meet sanitation standards for the ingredients and the preparation. Yet, the meals contain too much fat and too few fresh ingredients. Far too few vegetables appear on the children's plates, whereas *frites,* sauces, and meats are served too often, leading to an unbalanced diet.

Beverages cause another problem, because of the increasing consumption of soda, particularly cola. If primary schools provide milk to about 67 percent of the children, this percentage drops to only 39 percent in secondary schools. In the 1970s, Coca-Cola became the most popular drink among Belgian teenagers. By then, this drink had conquered the minds of the young, whereas two decades earlier it had hardly been liked. A well-aimed publicity campaign in Belgian primary schools in the 1960s, with Coca-Cola vans driving onto schools' playgrounds and distributing Coca-Cola products, was one of the means to achieve full penetration into the market. Kids loved it. Nowadays, vending machines with sodas are prohibited in many schools, because of soda's high sugar content, which adds to the overweight issues among youngsters. Particularly girls have started to drink bottled water. School campaigns and prohibitions hardly influence their decision, but the ideal of slimness and health does.

Nutritionists' advice with regard to school meals is gladly accepted by school cooks, which is slowly leading to a change in preparation and presentation of the food: it is more varied with the introduction of foods like pizza and pasta, and healthier with the addition of vegetables, fruit, and yogurt. Due to high costs for personnel and equipment, schools increasingly use external caterers that offer healthy, safe, and varied food, but it is hardly tasty. The lack of taste and imagination is probably one of the reasons why schoolchildren prefer a meal or snack outside school in one of the many snack bars, *kebab* stands, *fritures,* or fast-food eateries, which are found in the vicinity of almost every school. To this, the rising buying power of youngsters and the pressure of a peer group to behave alike should be added. However, today more people are convinced of the need to provide not just healthy but also varied and fresh food in an attractive environment. Hence, chef Frank Fol persuaded Scolarest (part of the international catering enterprise Compass Group), which serves 40,000 meals in Belgian schools daily, to increase the proportion of fresh vegetables and fruit. He also wishes to change children's ideas about fresh vegetables by introducing the so-called Taste Bomb, which consists of vegetables, pieces of fruit, and *légumaise* (an alternative to mayonnaise, it is a cold sauce made of vegetables such as carrots or cucumbers and herbs and spices such as garlic, parsley, and ginger and contains less than 25 percent fat), aiming at a radical change in schoolchildren's food preferences.

Week's Menu in a College Cafeteria, October 2007

Monday

| Menu 1 | Tandoori chicken brochette |
| Menu 2 | Fish fillets with spinach and hollandaise sauce |

Tuesday

| Menu 1 | Steak Archiduc with French beans |
| Menu 2 | Ham rolls with Brussels endives and cheese |

Wednesday

| Menu 1 | Fish sticks with tomato salad and cocktail sauce |
| Menu 2 | Minced meat rolled in a slice of beef with red cabbage |

Thursday
| Menu 1 | Chicken fillet with fine peas |
| Menu 2 | Meatballs in tomato sauce |

Friday

| Menu 1 | Beef stew with apple compote |
| Menu 2 | Nasi goreng |

Boiled potatoes, *frites,* rice, or bread are included; prices vary between 2.60 and 8.00 euros according to the status of the diner (student, employee, or visitor). Everyday offerings include pasta bar, wok menu, light menu, soup, and meat grill.

For most blue-collar workers in Belgium up to the 1970s, lunch consisted of food brought from home. Nowadays this is still a common practice. The work schedule with shifts and breaks does not permit eating at fixed times, and workers generally prefer a hot meal with their family in the evening; hence, in factories, it is difficult to supply meals at precise times, and decent dining space is absent in many factories. Soup and hot and cold drinks are available. Nutritionists have studied the food brought from home. In the 1960s the food was generally too rich, too fatty, and too sweet. The daily caloric need of most workers was easily covered, while the evening meal would add many more calories. Abundant charcuterie (bacon, pâtés, salamis, *tête de veau* [veal with mushrooms and tomato sauce, eaten cold], etc.) and a solid piece of butter were the cause. Moreover, the lunch consisted of white bread (the so-called *pain de ménage* or *huishoudbrood*) whereas brown bread is healthier; hardly any fruit and vegetables; and far too much coffee (with, generally, a lot of sugar). Recent studies show only a slight improvement with regard to lunches brought from home, concluding that workers should eat less meat, butter, and jam but more dairy products and fruit.

Some big factories, like automobile plants with thousands of workers, did supply hot meals in cafeterias that were constructed in the 1950s. Nutritionists hoped to be able to influence the quality and health of those meals directly through the cooking and indirectly via nutritional advice (the four-leaf clover[4] and, later, the food pyramid were posted on the wall in many cafeterias; see Chapter 7). According to studies, they seem to have succeeded. In the early 1960s there was hardly any difference between homemade and cafeteria lunches in terms of fat, calories, sugar, and so on. Recently, however, the content of the homemade lunch had hardly changed, whereas the cafeteria food had become lighter, less sweetened, and more varied. Yet, the cafeteria food could be improved, in particular, by reducing the frequency and quantity of *pommes frites*. Some workers eat these every day. Such studies reveal a marked difference between the lunches of male and female workers. The latter consume far less fatty food, calories, coffee, and sugar and much more fruit, water, and whole wheat bread. In the course of the 1990s male workers adopted this lighter diet, although very reluctantly.

Office employees can have lunch at the canteen of their ministry, company, or shop. White-collar workers are much more adventurous and demanding with regard to their cafeteria food than blue-collar workers are. If the latter prefer a three-course menu with a thick soup, a plate bursting with potatoes, meat, sauce, and few vegetables, and a pudding-like dessert, the former expect much more variation and innovation. For them, chicken, fish, and game should be served at a moderate price. Particularly, white-collar employees appreciate the option to choose between two or more dishes, which since the 1980s has included a special menu for dieters as well as vegetarian dishes. Nutritionists warn, however, against too much sophistication and the dominance of taste over health; hence, it is advised to consume more low-fat meat (in the 1960s this was horsemeat, in the 1980s chicken), vegetables, margarine, fruit, whole-grain bread, skim milk, and low-fat cheese.

The employees of the Brussels ministries know which cafeteria in the administrative district serves the best food in terms of diversity, freshness, and taste (the price being fairly equal). As in school cafeterias, special catering companies have recently taken over the meal preparation in many ministries and firms, which generally leads to more varied food and a price increase. Often, caterers no longer provide just the daily special but offer a wide selection from a hot and cold buffet, leaving a large and much appreciated choice to the diners (who are mostly quite satisfied with the catering). The 15,000 employees of the ministries of the Flemish community still have a proper catering service that provides 335,000 meals a year. A *plat du jour* (*dagschotel* in Dutch, the daily special) costs about 4 euros, the ingredients are carefully selected, the preparation is meticulously sanitary, and the offerings are varied and healthy. Since about the mid-1990s, many white-collar workers look forward to their daily cafeteria meal that has become enjoyable and much more than just a way to fill their stomachs. Since early 2008, chef Frank Fol reviews cafeterias in the weekly magazine *Jobat* (The Kitchen Report), granting zero to four stars, pointing out strong and weak points, and giving many suggestions to improve the food, the décor, and the service.

EATING OUT FOR PLEASURE

For centuries, enjoying food has been a privilege for rich people, whereas the common people had only some festive occasions, like after the harvest, to take pleasure from food. The quantity and quality, of course, differ widely according to place, company, and time. Often, celebratory eating is done within the home (and the community), and it is a private event. It will be dealt with in the next chapter. Eating *out* for pleasure is relatively new. Many of the aforementioned eateries offer food also during nonwork occasions. Shoppers, students, theatergoers, or soccer supporters may enjoy a *cornet de frites*, a platter of *caricollen*, a cheeseburger, or a *pistolet* with *kipkap* before, during, or after their activities. In the entertainment districts of Antwerp, Brussels, Ghent, or Liège one may indeed find a wide assortment of food almost 24 hours a day. Quite common when going to a café is the habit of alternating paying for drinks (rarely food, though), meaning that each member of the party pays for the whole group, which entails a mental bookkeeping of who paid when for whom. Undoubtedly, this eating and drinking satisfies a great need and may even taste superb. In these cases, however, the main activity is not eating but shopping, partying, and watching a play or a game.

The same may be said of eating during vacations or business travel. In the course of the eighteenth century it became fashionable for rich people to tour Europe, which, in particular, meant visiting spas or Swiss, German, and Italian regions and cities, making stops in Bruges, Brussels, or the Ardennes. In many tourist resorts, comfortable *Gästehäuser* or *alberghi* (inns) appeared. In the late nineteenth century grand hotels opened, offering first-rate food. Although this food may have been superb, the main objective was traveling and not eating. About two centuries ago, however, a new and specific form of eating out appeared in Europe, which was totally and exclusively oriented toward enjoying the act of eating: the restaurant. This became such an extraordinary event that it is worthwhile to make a special trip to another city or country. The legendary Michelin guide labels this as *vaut le detour* (worth taking the detour). For decades now Belgian restaurants are worth the detour.

To comprehend the present-day culture of the restaurant in Belgium it is necessary to make two brief historical digressions. The first leads to aristocratic dining in the eighteenth and nineteenth centuries, and the second to revolutionary France in the 1790s.

Aristocratic Dining

Many of modern restaurants' characteristics may be found in the aristocratic style of eating with regard to opulence, finesse, etiquette, and design. Like in most European countries, rich people in Belgium have distinguished themselves from others by taking on a specific lifestyle, of which food formed a crucial part. Alongside stunning buildings in towns *(hôtels)* and the countryside *(châteaux)*, frequent artistic and leisurely trips, and expensive clothing, food offered a perfect avenue to display richness, success, and status and thus to demarcate crude and subtle social borders and include or exclude people. But together, those who aspired to belong to higher social circles could try to transgress borders by *using* food: fancy food has always been used to express one's aspirations and hopes.

Wealth, success, and status were demonstrated during soirées, dinners, balls, receptions, luncheons, parties, cocktails, openings, and *thés* (or tea parties), with various types of fine food. These were semiprivate occasions in that guests had to be invited, but local newspapers commented on the guests, the clothing, the speeches, and the food, thus making the private aspect of such occasions somewhat public. Nowadays, some magazines, like *L'éventail*, specialize in reporting on the life of the rich and famous, regularly commenting on, and keenly photographing, the food and the

Chez Léon, established in Brussels in 1893, was re-
named Friture Léon in 2005 to revive old traditions.
The firm has restaurants throughout France and in
Dubai and Abu Dabi. Courtesy of the author.

diners at smart social occasions. Guests' commentaries establish the reputation of rich families, labeling the food as outstanding, trendy, or average.
The successive courts in Brussels played an important role in this. Many
diverse guests were frequently invited, they were served the finest foods,
and they imitated the courts' ways of preparing, arranging, and presenting
the food for their own festive dinners, thus contributing to the diffusion of
fancy food and manners. The dimension of this lavish eating and drinking
is reflected by its tremendously high cost. Private aristocratic eating is, of
course, not unique to Belgium, but the role of the Brussels court is. Sov-
ereigns like Charles de Lorraine (1712–1780), Leopold II (1835–1909),
and the current king Albert II (1934–) appreciate fancy food and thus
propagate the culture of pleasure in fine eating and drinking.

Various elements of aristocratic dining applied to the modern restaurant, such as the elitism, the social dimension of *voir et être vu* (see and be seen), the networking, the codes of behavior for all actors (hosts, guests, cooks, and servants), the decorum and presentation, and, particularly, the joy of eating, all this for a high price. There are two crucial differences between aristocratic eating and restaurant eating, however. First, the former was entirely private, while the latter was public, and, second, ensuing from this public aspect, culinary journalists appeared on the gastronomic scene.

French Influence

With the appearance of the restaurant in the 1780s and its triumph in the 1800s, the aristocratic culture of pleasure became public and accessible to the bourgeoisie. With the advent of the so-called popular restaurant (the brasserie) around 1900, even more people could savor a restaurant meal. In this, France and particularly Paris were at the forefront. Belgians say that when it rains in Paris, it drizzles in Brussels, which appears to be very valid for the diffusion of the restaurant culture in Belgium. Resto.be, a Web site that at present lists 15,730 restaurants in Belgium,[5] testifies to the French influence on Belgian restaurants. No fewer than 4,893 restaurants label themselves as French, with names such as Le Champenois, Le Bistrot de Paris, or Le Paris–Brest, although they may also have Flemish names such as Watermolen (Water Mill) or Begijnhof (Beguinage). Moreover, some classify themselves as Provençal, Corsican, or Savoyard (another 32 restaurants). Comprising 31 percent of all restaurants listed in this database, the French presence in Belgium's restaurant culture exceeds by far other national cuisines, including the Belgian (with 20 percent of the total), the Italian (10 percent), or the Chinese cuisines (3 percent). Another restaurant Web site, Deltaweb.be, lists a total of 4,574 restaurants in Belgium, of which no fewer than 48 percent are categorized as French. French restaurants in various price categories are to be found in Brussels, Flanders, and Wallonia, in small villages and in cities. Top restaurants in terms of price are French (50 percent) and Belgian-French (25 percent), the remaining quarter being divided between purely Belgian, international (or fusion), Italian, and Chinese. This astonishing share must be explained by the influence of French cuisine through three innovative waves in the nineteenth and twentieth centuries. Hence, a second brief historical digression is needed to understand the present restaurant culture in Belgium.

The diffusion of the fancy Parisian restaurant throughout Europe is largely unknown. For Belgium, a key element is the close connection to

France, particularly between Brussels and Paris. Since 1847 a direct train ran between the two cities, carrying businesspeople, tourists, artists, traders, artisans, and students. Today, fast Thalys trains take only one hour and 20 minutes to travel between the two capitals, which seduces Bruxellois to dine in Paris and Parisians to attend an opera performance in Brussels. The coming and going of businesspeople, military, and diplomats in the early nineteenth century, together with the wealth of entrepreneurs that came along with the industrialization of Belgium, led to great interest in luxury eating. Right from its start in the 1800s, this fancy eating was French. The Parisian model appears in the naming of restaurants (e.g., La Maison française) and of the food (e.g., *Dîners parisiens*, or Parisian dinners), as well as the vast presence of French chefs, *commis* (cooks' assistants), waiters, and sommeliers in Belgium. Moreover, many Belgian cooks and waiters toured in France in order to improve their skills. Today, the internationalization of the catering business has gone further with

Eating out in fancy restaurants: L'Alban Chambon in 2007. The room is being prepared to welcome the diners. Courtesy of the author.

personnel arriving in Belgium from all over the world. The labor market is highly segmented, with a top layer of highly qualified, well-paid chefs and a bottom layer of unskilled, poorly paid people who, moreover, often work illegally. Despite the declining proportion of French personnel, many restaurants have no problem classifying themselves as French.

The permanent French influence in Belgian restaurant culture is linked to the second and third French innovative waves, which both have been tagged *nouvelle cuisine*. Around 1900 Auguste Escoffier (1846–1935) renewed the haute cuisine so that it became lighter and more daring for the diners, and more stringently organized for the cooks. The coming of the grand hotels and their magnificent restaurants around 1900, of which the Savoy in London is the most eminent example, widely spread this type of cuisine. Around 1970, Paul Bocuse (1926–) revived the haute cuisine largely along the same lines, reacting against too heavy food (with lots of crème fraîche and gratins) and launching a new way of presentation (colorful square plates, meat on top of the sauce, and surprising combinations and colors). Belgian restaurants eagerly adopted this nouvelle cuisine.

For example, Dominique Michou, chef of L'Alban Chambon (the restaurant of Hôtel Métropole in Brussels, which was built in 1895), serves a genuine French cuisine. Born in Orléans in 1951, he was trained in France (in Paris, Thiezac, Beaugency, and Orléans), worked in the restaurant of the London Hilton, and became chef in the Brussels Hilton in 1977. After service in Strasbourg, Paris, Orléans, and, again, Brussels, he started as *chef des cuisines* (executive chef) in Hôtel Métrolpole when he was 38. He has been working there for 18 years now. During his career he was awarded many prizes, earned Michelin stars, and obtained nice ratings from famous restaurant critics. He made frequent study trips to other countries. Asked about the core of his cuisine, he exclaimed that his cooking is classic French ("C'est l'Escoffier," [It is Escoffier] referring to Escoffier's basic work[6]) with new ingredients and spices, new ways of preparing and serving, and new combinations, that is, a distinctive interpretation of the 1970s nouvelle cuisine. Asked about Belgian products or ways of doing, he said that he rarely uses these and sticks to French cuisine. Another great chef, Pierre Wynants of Comme chez Soi in Brussels, also refers to the classic French tradition, which stems from Escoffier and Bocuse. He does introduce Belgian products and methods of preparation, like *witloof* (Belgian endives), *stoemp*, and beer recipes.[7]

The French character of haute cuisine in Brussels has always been highly appreciated by travel guides, which have assigned French cuisine the highest status. Already in 1804, a travel guide compared a Brussels restaurant to the best Parisian one, as occurred repeatedly throughout the nineteenth and twentieth centuries. Quite telling is that Henri Gault and Christian Millau, the French culinary journalists who coined the term *nouvelle cuisine* for the innovations of the 1970s, deeply appreciated the way Belgian restaurants cooked *à la française*, even claiming that Belgian cuisine is only a regional French cuisine. The Michelin guide (first issue on France in 1900 and on Belgium in 1904) became the most prominent manual after World War II, establishing the culinary norm in Europe and the star system. Belgian restaurants generally did and do well in these guides. They obtained 79 stars in 2001 and 91 stars in 2007 (but *only* 89 in 2008, which, according to culinary journalists, has various causes, among which is cooks' loyalty to classic French cuisine and Michelin's goal to refresh its image by stressing innovation). Belgians love to believe that Belgium has the most Michelin stars per inhabitant in the world (although these little red books cover only a handful of countries or cities). Nowadays, the GaultMillau guide to Belgian restaurants tends to be more influential than the Michelin (the 2008 issue of the former has a print run of 47,000 copies).[8]

Belgian Cuisine

Not all restaurants in Belgium have been influenced by the French. Throughout the nineteenth century many restaurants, brasseries, cafés, and cabarets had a German, English, or Swiss ambiance. This would appear in the restaurant names (for example, Restaurant Bavaria, Taverne Anglo-Belge, or Café Suisse), as well as in the food and beverages, the latter being particularly English and German beers. Up to 1870, the German influence was important, not in the top layer of eating out—which was French—but in the estaminets (common pubs) or brasseries where more simple meals and menus were offered. In the late 1870s a guide tagged Brussels as the "Munich of Belgium" for its beer passion and mentioned that Belgians drank beer three times a day while enjoying rich dishes in simple, cozy places. In the 1890s some fancy Italian and Jewish restaurants appeared in Antwerp and Brussels, and in the course of the twentieth century many more ethnic restaurants were opened. Today, Resto.be mentions about 80 different ethnic cuisines in Belgium, including Thai, Japanese, Indian, Middle Eastern, Turkish, Armenian, Ethiopian, Moroccan, Jamaican, Cajun, Brazilian, North American, and nearly every European cuisine. Chinese restaurants, for example, have been present in Antwerp since the late 1950s, serving cheap meals to students, sailors, and the local Chinese community. Italian, Greek, Portuguese, and Spanish restaurants emerged in the Walloon and Limburg mining areas in the 1960s, while Moroccan and Turkish restaurants appeared in the larger cities in the 1970s and in many Belgian towns and villages in the 1980s. At first, they served food at very moderate prices to their community and adventurous Belgians, but since the late 1980s some of these places have turned into fancy and (sometimes very) expensive restaurants that specialize in allegedly authentic food. Resto.be lists two Italian, one Chinese, and four international restaurants in the top category in terms of prices. Since 2003 the Italian Istituto per il commercio estero (Institute for Foreign Trade) gives labels to Italian restaurants outside Italy that conform to genuine Italian food norms. Italian restaurants in Belgium were the first to receive these labels, and today some 40 Italian restaurants in Belgium are labeled as such.[9]

Regarding Belgian cuisine in Belgian restaurants and Belgian gourmet dining, Resto.be classifies 3,219 restaurants as Belgian, that is, 21 percent of the total number in the database, along with 17 restaurants serving Flemish cuisine (but none classified as Walloon or Brussels). Looking closer, many of these restaurants label themselves as *cuisine Franco-Belge* (or *Belgo-Française*), although some stick to a pure Belgian cuisine with exclusive attention to local dishes and ingredients. Moving to the higher price categories, however, almost all restaurants are labeled as Belgian–French cuisine.

Until the 1890s, gastronomic restaurants disregarded any reference to local dishes, ingredients, or methods of preparation, the French influence being absolutely dominant. This clearly appeared during international exhibitions and World's fairs that were frequently organized in Belgian cities and that were visited by tens of thousands of Belgians and foreigners. Such occasions generally allowed a country to put itself on the map in terms of industrial or artistic performance. There is no trace of Belgian cuisine at international fairs prior to 1890: travel guides, culinary journalists, or professionals in the catering business hardly mentioned local dishes up to the 1900s. The 1891 Baedeker guide, however, did hint at local food when it wrote, "Lastly, we should mention as good restaurants, particularly visited by Belgians, those small places North of the Grand'Place, where people primarily have oysters, steak and pork, and drink wine and beer."[10] The guide is referring to the lively quarter that nowadays is known as the *Ilot sacré* ("the small holy island"), where since the 1800s estaminets, butchers, food traders, bakers, cafés, and cabarets merged into one culinary locus.[11]

Prior to 1900, the *Ilot sacré* never had a gastronomic reputation: it was too popular, too rude, and too Belgian. Its fame was firmly established in the 1920s and 1930s, when many more plain restaurants settled there,

"Menu Belge," rue des Bouchers in Brussels, 2008, showing the construction of Belgianness through national dishes. Inside the restaurant, menus look different and are, in particular, more expensive. Courtesy of the author.

such as Aux Armes de Bruxelles (established in 1921), or expanded, such as Chez Léon (established in 1893). Culinary journalists then enthusiastically described these restaurants as places where Belgians and foreigners adored eating informally and copiously, enjoying mussels with *frites*, *carbonnades à la flamande* (a beef stew with beer), or *waterzooi de poulet* (a souplike chicken dish with vegetables). Beer was typically drunk, and prices were moderate. This area grew noticeably with the arrival of more restaurants, snack bars, fast-food eateries, and cafés (some have a dubious reputation). Typical for the *Ilot sacré* is the Belgian atmosphere of restaurants, which stress "Belgium" and even "Brussels" as food brands. This is seen in the names of restaurants (Le Vieux Bruxelles, for example), the colors (green and red form the Brussels banner), and especially in the menus and advertisement posters that propose rabbit with *Kriek* (the sour beer with cherries), *salade liègeoise* (potatoes with vegetables and bacon), *waterzooi, lottes panées au spéculaus* (fish breaded in crumbs of cinnamon cookies), *stoemp* (mashed potatoes with vegetables), *boudin* with apple compote, *ballekens à la Marolienne* (meatballs in tomato sauce; *de Marollen* being a popular Brussels quarter), and many other old and new *plats belges typiques* (typical Belgian dishes). Some of these had been served in the estaminets of the poorer town quarters in the early nineteenth century, and some were prepared in petty bourgeois kitchens, but others are quite recent creations that are promoted as authentic and traditional.

Around 1900, fancy restaurants started to change. Local dishes appeared, which led to the present-day reputation of Belgian restaurants. The French periodical *Le Figaro Illustré* of 1910 contains a zealous approbation of Flemish, Walloon, and Brussels dishes. Listed are *blinde vinken* (or *oiseaux sans tête* in French, which is minced, mildly seasoned meat wrapped in a thin slice of beef, see the recipe in Chapter 4), *choesels* (beef or veal pancreas and other offal—including oxtail—often in Madeira sauce), *rijstpap* (dessert of rice boiled in milk with honey and spices), *bouquettes* (pancakes made of buckwheat), *waterzooi, carbonnades à la flamande*, rabbit with prunes, and *moules marinières* (mussels with herbs and white wine). Once these were dishes of the lower and especially middle classes, a long tradition in many kitchens. Yet, *Le Figaro Illustré* was utterly enthusiastic about the exquisite flavors that the giants of French gastronomy would have loved. Moreover, Belgian cuisine utilized vegetables, such as celery, *witloof* (Belgian endives), *jets de houblon* (hop shoots), and various cabbages, that were long forgotten in France. These observations reflected innovations in Belgian fancy restaurants that moved local dishes and ingredients to the fore, which was totally unheard of prior to 1900. This is a nice example of the upgrading of popular cuisine to fancy cuisine, with, of course, different accents in the method of preparation and presentation, turning a common ingredient into a genuine luxury product. This had happened with oysters and shrimp at the end of the eighteenth century.

At least three elements may explain this breakthrough of Belgian dishes in the haute cuisine. First, Parisian gourmets had always shown interest in regional dishes; with Auguste Escoffier, trained in the Provence, this interest in the *cuisine du terroir* (local cuisine), with the emphasis on freshness, authenticity, and lightness, expanded. Thus, around 1900, many chefs and culinary critics in France (and Europe) explored regional cuisines as a possible contribution to fancy cooking. Traditional Belgian recipes became part of this quest for innovation. Second, the Belgian chefs, as well as the diners, wanted to establish a proper haute cuisine that, after almost a century of French hegemony, would make a difference. This may be linked to nationalistic sentiments as well as to the creation of a market niche. Since the French haute cuisine became available in grand hotels all over Europe (and the world), chefs and restaurant owners wished to revamp fancy cooking. Third, and crucially, for Belgium, World War I caused huge material and immaterial damage in Belgium, leading to a wave of international solidarity with Belgium, as well as to vehement nationalistic sentiments within the country. This put Belgium on the international map much more than before, and foreigners wished to learn about the culture of the country, while Belgians sought to construct a national culture.

Belgian chefs eagerly responded to the increasing interest in Belgian cuisine. Therefore, in the 1920s, menus of fancy restaurants differed drastically from menus of the 1900s in that they contained Belgian ingredients and dishes. This change was certified by the comments of the renowned *Larousse gastronomique*, published in 1938 and giving the state of the culinary art.[12] With regard to Belgian cuisine it said (p. 403), "Belgian are gourmets . . . but although they have adopted with great enthusiasm the delicacies of French cuisine, Belgians remained true to their old national dishes" and further, "The numerous French visitors do appreciate these dishes straight away, because even in the posh restaurants the menu includes Belgian dishes like *anguille au vert* [eel with vegetables], *carbonnades à la flamande* (with the famous Belgian *Geuze*), *choesels*, and above all, the much appreciated *waterzooi de poulet à la gantoise*." Appreciation of the fortunate mix between French haute cuisine and Belgian ingredients and dishes may be seen in travel and restaurant guides since the 1950s. One telling example is the comment by Gault and Millau, who wrote that the Belgian cuisine "ingeniously marries the charms of the local recipes to the wonders of the best dishes of our great [French] cuisine."[13]

Today, most fancy Belgian restaurants offer this mix of classic haute cuisine and local specials. Pierre Wynants, chef and owner of the Brussels Comme chez Soi (two Michelin stars in 2008), for example, declares that he cooks in the classic French way but with local ingredients and an international touch. In addition to Escoffier's solid basis, he uses Belgian endives, cilantro, ham from the Ardennes, cumin, Belgian beers, and Belgian cheeses. Outside Brussels, this Belgian influence would also be labeled as Belgian, with many local references (for example, *à la flamande, façon de Liège, coucou de Malines, truites de la Semois*—Liège and Malines being towns in Wallonia and Flanders, and Semois a river in the Ardennes).

In most fancy restaurants in Belgium, the diner highly appreciates this mix of the classic French haute cuisine, Belgian specialties, and a light international touch (with Asian spices or trendy molecular gastronomy). Belgians and foreigners adore dining in the luxury restaurants and are willing to pay a lot of money for a meal. Prices are far from modest now. Referring to *Notre classique*, Comme chez Soi's "standard" menu that exists since the late 1960s, the price rose by 300 percent between 1976 and 2006 (from 16 euros to 67 euros). This increase is caused by the inflation rate and the labor cost that remains high in luxury cooking. In 2007 two other menus may be chosen next to *Notre classique*: the *Saison* (the Seasonal) (131 euros) and the *Dégustation* (the Gourmet) (168 euros), which offer more courses, dishes, choices, and refinement. In fancy restaurants the diner not only buys an exquisite meal and outstanding wines but also a grand experience and a great story.

Mashed Potatoes with Brussels Sprouts (*stoemp met spruitjes* or *stoemp aux choux de Bruxelles*)

This has been labeled a typical Belgian dish. It may be served with salted bacon; it is prepared in many homes, but increasingly also in Belgian restaurants and recently in some top restaurants.

4 medium-sized onions
1 green cabbage (weighing about 1 pound)
10 big carrots
5 big turnips
4 stalks celery
leeks (0.55 lb / 250 g)
1 pound Brussels sprouts
7 tablespoons butter, melted
6 cups chicken stock
bouquet garni of thyme, bay leaves, and parsley
2 1/4 pounds potatoes
salt and pepper

Clean and wash the vegetables. Mince the onions and the green cabbage very fine, and chop the carrots, turnips, celery, and leeks into coarse chunks. Cut the Brussels sprouts in two. Put a large pot on low heat and melt the butter, then add all the vegetables to sweat (*suer*) for 10 minutes (meanwhile, stir regularly). Then, add the chicken broth, the bouquet garni, and some salt and pepper. Heat until boiling, cover the pot, reduce the heat, and leave for about 30 minutes. Peel and cut the potatoes into little pieces, and put these into the pot; cook for another 20 minutes, stirring regularly. Finally, heat the pot and stir vigorously, and add salt and pepper. Serve really hot.

Mores of Eating Out

The food, decorum, and personnel of restaurants have been discussed, but two other players should be stressed as well: the patrons and the journalists. They form, with the chefs, the golden trio of the business. Belgium became a rich country in the twentieth century. Eating for pleasure has been one of the favorite interests of bankers, entrepreneurs, traders, and their entourage. The brasseries allowed petty bourgeois to enjoy fancy food in restaurants, too. These targeted a less wealthy clientele, but their standards of quality are high, serving a *cuisine bourgeoise* with full plates. Together with the diners in the more popular places, like those of the *Ilot sacré*, many Belgians thus regularly enjoy a restaurant meal. Families, friends, colleagues, and couples often eat out, whether for a business lunch, a romantic dinner, a birthday, or, simply, spending time together. At such occasions, prices often are not really important, and it is common among friends to share the bill equally without calculating what each diner had.

Many foreigners love to eat in Belgium's fancy restaurants too. In the nineteenth century there were German, Dutch, and English business-people; French and Polish refugees; artists from all over Europe; and in general many people enjoying the liberal atmosphere of the city. In the twentieth century tourists and students joined them. This cosmopolitan character was a crucial enticement in the decision to make Brussels the de facto capital of the European Union in the 1950s. Today, thousands of employees of organizations of the European Union in Brussels, coming from 25 different countries and generally enjoying a comfortable salary, mostly have gourmet tastes. Moreover, other international institutions have chosen Brussels or Belgium as headquarters, such as the North Atlantic Treaty Organization, while many multinationals use Belgium as a stepping-stone, for conducting business throughout Europe. As a result, a myriad of languages are to be heard in the restaurants in Belgium.

The high interest in eating out by Belgians, foreigners living in Belgium, and tourists not only is apparent in busy or comfortable restaurants on Tuesday, Friday, and Saturday nights as well as Sunday noon, but also shows in the enormous curiosity about restaurant guides; culinary information in newspapers, magazines, and Web sites; and chefs. The nouvelle cuisine of the 1970s pushed chefs to leave their kitchens and meet the clientele in the dining room. Generally, patrons love this, but cooks dislike it. Belgian chefs have done more than just entering the *salle:* they willingly appear in books and magazines and on television. The contest for the year's best cook, organized by the Club Prosper Montagné,[14] is hot news in papers and magazines nowadays, although it has existed since 1952. Chefs publish books, are frequently interviewed in magazines, and have their own television shows. For example, every week Guy Van Cauteren, chef of Laurierblad (one Michelin star), prepares, explains, and discusses food on *Vitaya TV*, and Piet Huysentruyt, the former owner of a one-star Michelin restaurant, appears on *VTM-television* in a series called *SOS–Piet*, giving advice to desperate home cooks. In 2008, the VTM program *Mijn restaurant* (My restaurant) was a tremendous hit: young cooks wanting to start a business of their own were judged by a professional jury as well as by the general public.

Less amusing is the century-old Michelin guide, with a somewhat antique reputation now, although it leads every year to much media fuss about the loss or gain of stars. This was particularly the case when Comme chez Soi lost one star (of three) in December 2006, which brought about discussions and comments in cafés, trams, and shops, thus showing the impact of the phenomenon of Michelin stars and, indeed, a general interest in eating out in fancy restaurants. Other restaurant guides, like *Henry Lemaire* (1957), *Gault & Millau* (1965), and *Guide Delta* (1977), appear every year with evaluations of Belgian restaurants, giving rise to many comparisons between them by the clientele and professionals.[15] Along with these local guides, the standard foreign travel guides for Belgium, such as *The Rough Guide, Lonely Planet*, or *Frommer's*, contain simple or detailed information and suggestions, sometimes with a refreshing outside look and sometimes a baffling naïve one.

Culinary journalists not only write restaurant guides, they also publish in special sections of newspapers and magazines. Since the 1970s, the weekly *Knack—Le Vif* has made itself quite a reputation by printing restaurants reviews ("Knack knows where to dine"), which have recently been collected in the *Guide des restaurants Knack—Le Vif. The Bulletin,* a Brussels English-language weekly magazine since 1962, pays attention to wining and dining in Belgium. Most of these magazines and guides have Web sites that often offer more information than the paper guides. DeltaWeb, for example, lists almost 4,600 restaurants in Belgium, classified by price, cuisine, location, and the like. This Web site also presents the week's discovery, it invites patrons to write critiques and anecdotes, and it publishes the top-10 of virtually visited restaurants, along with its own evaluation of the restaurants. Resto.be does not evaluate restaurants but opens its pages to the customers. Patrons' critiques are particularly enlightening, ranking the quality of the food, the service, and the general atmosphere quite severely. For example, in 2007 a customer wrote about a cozy restaurant in Ghent that the food was "Nice, original and fresh, but far too expensive, and coming in too small portions. Service was very poor, the red wine was served far too cold, and not all patrons were served at once! Should be better." This shows that restaurant eating is a serious matter, indeed. Eating out in Belgium may be summarized with the words of Gault and Millau, who wrote in 1965, "It is easy to eat marvelously well and extremely badly."[16] This is still valid nowadays; a golden rule should be applied to avoid bad places: eat where the locals eat. Dining out well in Belgium (as elsewhere) is not primarily a matter of the check, but of a good nose.

There are common features of eating out in Belgium. Bread is always abundant and close by, second helpings of *pommes frites* are free, and the choice is wide. But there is more. Fancy restaurants affect the way food is prepared, presented, and named in snack bars and cafeterias, and this influence appears much more quickly than a decade ago. Haute cuisine seems to be *everywhere*: not just in the street but also in the media and the everyday talk of the common people. This presence leads to diffusion of the restaurant culture, to which the food in sandwich bars and cafeterias indeed testifies. If the Belgian eating-out culture is what it is today, it is because of the general and great consideration given to food, both for pleasure and during the workday.

NOTES

1. *Panel des consommateurs* (Brussels: Institut Economique Agricole, 1988).

2. See Yves Segers, "Food Recommendations, Tradition and Change in a Flemish Cookbook: Ons Kookboek, 1920–2000," *Appetite* 45.1 (2005): 4–14.

3. The change in meaning from the English *sandwich* to the Belgian *sandwich* should be studied: when did this word appear in Belgium, what did it represent precisely, and is it still used in an environment where the English language is much more present?

4. In Belgium the four-leaf clover (launched in 1967) is a well-known concept related to well-balanced and healthy food (see Chapter 8).

5. Resto.be claims to be the largest online Belgian restaurant guide. It offers search possibilities by region, type of cuisine, price, and name of the restaurant, as well as online reservations and some critiques by customers; see http://www.resto.be/ware/index.jsp?lg=EN (accessed October 25, 2007).

6. August Escoffier, *Le guide culinaire, aide-mémoire de cuisine pratique* (Paris: Art Culinaire, 1903).

7. Both chefs were interviewed recently; for a full report, see Peter Scholliers, "Propos culinaire: Tradition et innovation au *Comme chez Soi* depuis les années '70. Entretien avec Pierre Wynants," *Les Cahiers de la Fonderie* 34 (2006): 54–62.

8. Guide Michelin. *Belgique/België, Luxembourg 2008* (Paris and Brussels: Michelin, 2008).

9. See Ristorante Italiano (Istituto nazionale per il commercio estero) http://www.ristorante-italiano.be for the list of restaurants, quality norms, recipes, and more.

10. Karl Baedeker, *Belgique et Hollande y compris le Luxembourg. Manuel du voyageur* (Paris and Leipzig: Baedeker, 1891), 11.

11. See Commune libre de l'Ilot sacré (Free district of the Ilot sacré), http://www.ilotsacre.be/site/en/default_en.htm/.

12. Prosper Montagné and Alfred Gottschalk, *Larousse gastronomique* (Paris: Imprimerie Larousse, 1938), with a preface by A. Escoffier, which has appeared in many frequently revised editions and translations. For an English edition, see, for example, Jenifer Harvey Lang, ed., *Larousse Gastronomique: The New American Edition of the World's Greatest Culinary Encyclopedia* (New York: Crown, 1988).

13. Henri Gault and Christian Millau, *Guide Julliard de Bruxelles* (Paris: Julliard, 1965), 27.

14. For the Club Prosper Montagné-Belgium (named after the chef and writer, 1865–1948), see http://www.clubprospermontagne.be/cpm/.

15. Nowadays, the (paper) restaurant guides have become available on Web sites: French and Dutch versions are available at http://www.gaultmillau.be/, http://www.henry.lemaire.be, and http://www.deltaweb.be.

16. Gault and Millau, *Guide Julliard*, 43.

6

Special Occasions

In the past, stringent traditions regulated eating and drinking during celebrations in Belgium. Restrictions on drinking alcohol were mostly connected to the numerous Catholic festivities throughout the year. There were about 40 "high days" in Belgium in the past, but regulations in the 1780s limited this number. Today, only six Catholic celebration days remain as public holidays: Easter, Ascension Day, Pentecost, the Assumption of Mary (August 15), All Saints' Day (November 1), and Christmas (December 25). As a consequence of the increasing presence of other religions in Belgium, predominantly Islam, some favor making Islamic celebrations official (for example, *Id al-Fitr*, or the popular Sugar Feast, at the end of Ramadan). In the course of the nineteenth and twentieth centuries, new feasts appeared as a consequence of social, national, and regional identity construction. Hence, Labor Day (May 1), the *fête nationale* (National day, July 21), and Armistice Day (November 11) were added to the list of public holidays. Together with January 1, Belgians now have 10 official holidays, when shops, schools, and firms are closed. "Bridging," that is, taking a day off when a public holiday precedes or follows the weekend by one day, is very popular and is occasionally the outcome of shop-floor negotiations between employer and employees. Along with these national public holidays, each of the three Belgian regions (or four, including the small German speaking one) has its own commemorative day that is not yet a public holiday but that sometimes leads to lively feasting, with parades, speeches, and receptions.

Of course, Belgians do not celebrate only the official holidays. In addition to these days, which aim to foster religious and regional communities, local feasts have been revived, which often relate to work and which contribute to intimate group identity. For example, the end of harvest was celebrated in all of the country's villages in late August and early September, and since the 1920s the Limburg miners held their feast on Saint Barbara's Day (December 4). According to ethnologists, a renewed wave of local celebrations emerged in the early 1950s and particularly in the 1970s, which has led to a "feasting culture" nowadays, meaning that virtually every village and city district has its feast.[1] These feasts are labeled, for example, "Witches' walk," "Nobles' celebration," "Donkey feast," "Festival of this year's men," or "Giants' stroll." Moreover, there are innumerable Christmas markets, religious processions, and Bruegel feasts (a kind of fancy fair with a lot of food) all over the country throughout the year. Nowadays, these have taken on a new style and name. Outdated folk dance evenings are now trendy *boombals* (parties with live folk music), and the *pensenkermis* (literally, the "fair of sausages") gave way to the *buurtbbq* (neighborhood barbecue). So far the largest neighborhood barbecue occurred in Antwerp in August 2002: at the occasion of the start of a large public works project, the city organized a free barbecue party for thousands of feasting people. This recent wave of feasts "of the people," with the rediscovery of old customs or the creation of new practices, may be seen as a response to growing globalization (labeled "western homogenization" in the 1980s and "Americanization" in the 1990s), aiming to foster community bonds.

Further collective celebrating occurs during carnival (in February), at the time of a child's First and Holy Communion or similar rituals (April or May), on Mother's Day (May 13) or Father's Day (June 10), and for *Sinterklaas* or *Saint-Nicolas* (a children's holiday, December 6). Recently, Valentine's Day (February 14), Grandparents' Day (November 18), and Halloween (October 31) have become occasions for collective feasting, but there is opposition against their too-radical commercialization (which also occurs with regard to other holidays, notably, Christmas).[2] Also, there are individual and private festivities connected to family life (births, birthdays, weddings) and work and study (promotions, end of exams), and there are celebrations by the many clubs and associations (sports, arts, hobbies, politics). Finally, the recurring dinner parties with family and friends should be mentioned, which have only largely spread since the 1950s to become a very frequent way of partying in the 1980s when networks of friends gradually renewed the customary bonding with the family and neighbors. Today, no Belgian can escape from the country's feasting mindset, which tourist guides and folkloric accounts love to emphasize, often referring to centuries-old traditions that appear in paintings by Pieter Bruegel (1525–1569), such as *The Village Wedding Feast* (1568), or Jacob Jordaens (1593–1678), such as *The King Drinks* (c. 1640). To all this, one final special occasion should be added: the paid vacation.

FESTIVE EATING

All of the aforementioned public and private occasions include food in diverse forms and quantities, whether plain street eating or homemade haute cuisine. An average year means 10 festive dinners for the Belgian, with at least five *grand* meals (Christmas Eve, New Year's Eve, one's birthday, Easter, and a life-cycle ritual like a communion or wedding). Along with these important meals that affect the individual and the individual's nearest and dearest, many local feasts take place, with plenty of plain drinking and eating, whether inside or outside the house. As is the case with eating out in restaurants, several social variables have a bearing on the spending on at-home celebrations. There is no information about the frequency of feasting or about the money spent during such occasions, but it may be assumed that the higher the income, the greater the spending on at-home feasting. An indication of this may be found in the money spent on wine and liquor (below 23 percent alcohol content by volume) to be consumed at home: in 2005 the highest-income group spent 667 euros per family per year, the lowest only 106 euros, which is 6.3 times less (with the Belgian average being 300 euros). A lot of this money is spent on champagne, of which Belgians are the fifth highest per-capita consumers in the world (following France, Luxembourg, and French overseas regions).[3] Of course, not all these drinks are imbibed at parties, but the implication of a link between income and partying is clear. This suggests that some people are heavy partiers, experienced in sophisticated dining and wining, and aiming to innovate. It also indicates that other people only rarely celebrate (or not at all), having special foods that may appear utterly banal to others.

Since the mid-1990s, the traditions and rules of the older celebrations have tended to totally disappear. Fasting and its corollary, excessive eating, are virtually gone, whereas only traces remain in the link between feasts and the eating of particular food (such as fresh eggs on Easter). On Easter lots of little chocolate eggs are eaten, while at the end of February a very old tradition lives on with the *Krakelingenworp* in the town of Geraardsbergen (East Flanders): 10,000 little, round breads (like a donut) are thrown into the public, to cheer the coming of spring. One little bread contains a paper that is good for one piece of gold worth 750 euros. Another relic of old times at the same occasion is the drinking of a glass of wine that contains a tiny living fish (this custom is increasingly protested).

Old traditions remain (or are rediscovered) during carnival feasts (Mardi Gras), which are organized in about one-third of the Belgian communes in February, including famous parades such as those of Aalst (East Flanders, going back to the sixteenth century but with an annual parade since 1851), Binche (Hainault, maybe appearing in the fourteenth century; in 2003 it was put on UNESCO's world heritage list), or Hasselt (Limburg, established in 1947). While making fun of the rich and famous via decorated floats, funny masks, and clothing, thousands of people eat pancakes (prepared with beer in Binche), waffles, and pies but also eels, mussels, smoutebollen (doughnut balls; beignets or croustillons in French), and sausages in little breads, while they consume quarts of beer. Smoutebollen are strongly linked to the kermis or la kermesse, which is a fair with lots of children's attractions and food stalls that travels around the country, staying for about two weeks in different towns and villages.[4] Waffles, frites, caricollen (sea snails boiled in bouillon), cake, and doughnut balls—with lots of powdered sugar—are frequently consumed. The sweet smell of the doughnuts suffices for every Belgian to evoke the fun and abundance of fairgrounds. Large, kitschy decorated booths (with Rococo, Breughel-like, and flashy ornaments) sell the smoutebollen, which are eaten while walking around or sitting in a large space next to the booth, where beverages are sold as well. Some of these booths have gained an outstanding culinary reputation, having been active for generations in this business, going back to the 1890s. In some regions, doughnut balls are prepared at home for particular occasions such as the coming of the kermis to the village, a birthday party, or the annual carnival.

Doughnut Balls (*smoutebollen* or *beignets*)

1 2/3 cup flour

1/3 cup milk

1 tablespoon yeast

1 egg

1 teaspoon sugar

1/2 teaspoon salt

1 small bottle *witbier* (white beer, Hoegaerden type)

2 tablespoons butter

oil for deep-frying

Dissolve the yeast in the lukewarm milk and add the flour (sifting it well). Separate the egg, and add the egg yolk, sugar, salt, and beer to the milk-and-flour mixture, stir well, and add the melted butter. Then, beat the egg white and fold it gently into the dough. Cover the dough, and let rise until its volume has doubled (keep it out of the cold). Heat the oil to 350°F. Very gently stir the dough, then drop teaspoonfuls of the dough gently into the frying oil until it is golden brown (which takes about one minute). Use a slotted spoon to remove the doughnuts from the fryer, lay on a paper-towel covered plate to absorb excess oil, and serve with powdered sugar.

Most festive occasions today have only faint traces of old traditions. Like in many European countries the weakening of the old ways is linked to the general decline in religious practices and beliefs (although Islamic Belgians of Moroccan or Turkish roots hold on to religious rules). In the 1960s 52 percent of Belgians stated that they attended mass on Sunday, but in 2004 this had dropped to a mere 10 percent.[5] This suggests a continuation of the erosion of Catholic rituals that had started in the late nineteenth century, although many Belgians still conform to tradition, in that christenings, communions, weddings, and funerals are performed within the Catholic community. Belgian's declining religiosity implies the loss of traditional eating and drinking associated with Easter, Christmas, and other Catholic holidays. Since the 1950s the increasing purchasing power of Belgians has allowed them to abandon the traditional fasting and the correlated short-lived excesses after breaking the fast, while growing individualization has freed people from long-established community constraints.

Nonetheless, a growing trend aims to safeguard traditional ways of celebrating and, particularly, of eating. This is not linked to religious concerns but rather to matters of culinary heritage. Magazines, books, associations, and Web sites pay a lot of attention to culinary customs, with special enthusiasm when grand feasts are nearing (particularly in the last week of the year). Via various blogs, people recall how feasts of the 1950s and 1960s used to be, often rejecting present-day novelties and pleading for keeping allegedly old dishes and ways of doing things. Nowadays, some want to reinstate the ancient habit of eating turkey at Christmas (which was only introduced in the 1960s). The Academie voor Streekgebonden Gastronomie (Academy for Regional Gastronomy) wishes to be the keeper of the recipes for all Belgian regional dishes, assembling them on a Web site, but has no particular interest in festive food.[6] In 2007, the academy was awarded the Prize of Taste by the Flemish government for its continuous endeavors to preserve Belgian culinary heritage.

It is difficult to propose a hierarchy of Belgian feasts in terms of eating and drinking, since huge attention is paid to food during almost every special occasion in Belgium. Since the 1970s, people tend to celebrate in restaurants or special places with catering services much more than before, which helps to explain the growing expenditure on eating out (see Chapter 5). Of course, some feasts are much more important than others when it comes to drinking and eating. Mother's Day, Father's Day, Grandparents' Day, Labor Day, or the *fête nationale* are not particularly culinary peaks, while Christmas and New Year's Eve are. A common distinction is between special occasions associated with the life cycle (birth, rites of passage such as the first communion, promotion at work, wedding, retirement, death) and those associated with the cycle of the year (New Year's, Easter, Christmas, etc.), although this neglects the increasingly popular friends' parties. In this chapter, a somewhat artificial division will be made between small, intimate feasts and bigger, grand celebrations. Also, one section will discuss eating during vacations in Belgium. At every occasion, whether big or small, and whatever the occasion or the number of people, Belgians love to eat, and they devote substantial amounts of time to discussing the menu, choosing the wine, finding the appropriate ingredients, and beautifying the house.

INTIMATE FEASTING

Giving birth is a very intimate affair, but often the young parents wish to share their joy with family and friends. Until the early 1950s, infants were generally delivered at home, and most people did not see birth as an occasion to feast. Nowadays, specialized hospitals are preferred, and a celebration is always appropriate. In the first days after a birth, close family and friends visit the young parents, and often a bottle of champagne is opened, unless the young father invites the guests to a nearby café for drinks. Religious families baptize the baby, and the baptism is accompanied by presenting *doopsuiker* or *dragée de baptême* (sugared almonds and chocolates, nicely wrapped in a small paper box), which the parents present to visitors. In villages until the early 1960s the baptism was followed by a tour of almost all of the pubs of the parish, but nowadays young parents invite close family members and friends to a festive home meal. Hosting this event may cause the parents some concern, as appears from a specialized Web site for parents.[7] Some posts on this site include a new mother asking for help about what to cook during the *doopfeest* (baptismal feast). An experienced mother replies to serve food that can be prepared the day before, unless a barbecue with the young father or grandfather as cook would help. If one can afford it, a caterer would be best, though. But, in any case, the young mother should enjoy this day.

Peach melba, the dessert created by chef August Escoffier for soprano Nellie Melba at the London Savoy Hotel, 1892. It consists of peaches, raspberry coulis, and vanilla ice cream. Courtesy of the author.

Another woman replies that she just served coffee with cake from the *pâtissier* (pastry cook), another announces that she will prepare pasta with various homemade sauces, and yet another mother advises that it would be best to keep the worries minimal (and the house clean) by renting a special room and hiring a caterer's services. These replies show that there is no standard menu for christening parties anymore, whereas between about 1930 and 1970 very often a *koffietafel* (literally, coffee table) was offered to family and close neighbors, which consisted of sweet foods such as cake, cookies, and raisin bread, with coffee (and, for the men, a *jenever*, that is, a little glass of gin).

In general, rites of passage give rise to plentiful eating and drinking, providing the opportunity to families to gather and to renew or intensify ties (although old and new quarrels may, of course, surface as well). Christian families celebrate First and Holy Communion, whereas nonbelievers have the Spring Feast and the Feast of the Secular Youth. A mother of a 12-year-old girl doing her Holy Communion explained in 2004 that a friend of hers, an experienced cook, prepared a rather customary meal for

20 guests.[8] They started with champagne and toast with smoked salmon and asparagus. Croquettes with North Sea shrimp came next, followed by asparagus cream soup. The main course was roasted duck with *pommes frites* (French fries), and the dessert was ice cream with strawberries or peaches and whipped cream. Coffee and cookies ended the meal. The children had a slightly adapted menu, with *bitterballen* (a type of croquette) and *bouchées à la reine* (chicken pieces in cream sauce with mushrooms, presented in pastry). In fact, this menu does not differ much from a menu of the 1950s, which included soup, roast beef with vegetables, *ijslam* (ice lamb, that is, ice cream in the form of a little lamb lying down, as the symbol of Christ; when cut, it starts "bleeding" with grenadine), and cake, although the champagne was missing in the 1950s. A woman who had her First Communion in the early 1950s recalls on her blog that "those were genuine feasts, not styled and no blah blah," but so much work with the moving of the furniture; the preparing, cooking, and serving of the food; the coming and going of busy women with glasses, plates, forks, and dishes; the aunts, nieces, brothers, and grandparents chatting incessantly with the occasional squabble caused by the wine, liquors, and beers.[9] However, nowadays there seem to be no fixed rules with regard to the food at communion feasts, which may mirror perfectly well the trend toward innovation (even the ice cream lamb seems to have vanished). This is illustrated by a meal that was prepared in 2005 by a group of amateur cooks for the communion of the daughter of one of them: cappuccino of Belgian asparagus (a very light, whipped cream of asparagus), risotto made with grilled scallop shells, tapenade, eggplant in a wrapping with *pommes frites*, and tortillas with young vegetables.[10]

Children's birthday parties appeared in the 1970s. Prior to this date, the child's favorite dish was prepared with extra dessert and soft drinks, but only family members would be present. Today, parties for young children involve careful preparation with appropriate entertainment, decorations, and food, so much so that specialized magazines, Web sites, and professionals assist the parents. For example, the Association of Socialist Women has a page on its Web site called "Surviving a Children's Party," providing tips relating to all practical matters and possible perils.[11] With regard to the food—which is of crucial importance for the party's success—two options are suggested: the classic, consisting of pancakes, waffles, and cake with hot or cold cocoa, and the trendy one, of *pommes frites* with *curryworst* (skinless, deep-fried, somewhat spicy sausage). Whatever option is chosen, *fruit saté* (small pieces of fresh fruit on a stick), fruit juice, and water are supposed to keep the children healthy and away from Coca-Cola. This advice differs from the request of a 12-year-old, in a blog message to her parents, to allow her to have "a pajama party with potato chips and candy and so much more," thus expressing the actual culinary desires at parties of this age group.

For adult birthdays, the trend is eating out. Yet, a birthday is a great occasion to prepare a special menu at home, allowing family members to cook as a token of appreciation, thus turning the meal into a gift. Since the 1930s, cookbooks for the common household include tips and ideas for "anniversary" cooking. The Belgo-Dutch cookbook *Ik kan koken* (I can cook; 1951), for example, states that the meal should consist of three parts but that, according to the financial means of the family, each part may be extended.[12] A well-off household, thus, may have a starter that includes soup and cold and hot *entrée* (appetizer), followed by fish with potatoes and vegetables, meat with vegetables, and *croquettes*, and, most essential, roasted game or fowl with compote. The dessert consists of ice cream or pudding, followed by cheese and, finally, by fresh fruit. Strong coffee with cookies concludes the meal. In fact, this menu imitates the classic 1930s Escoffier meal, with the same sequence of dishes. In the 1970s and 1980s, cookbooks tend to simplify the food at parties. The 1972 edition of *Ons kookboek* suggests, for example, that guests should not sit down at the table but should be able to move and savor without restraint a cold buffet including roasted chicken, fine fish (salmon, smoked trout, and turbot), various savory pastries, slices of roast beef and ham, tomatoes filled with shrimp, ham rolls with asparagus, various salads and cold sauces (e.g., mayonnaise, tartar sauce), and assorted little breads.

Duchess's Potatoes (*hertoginneaardappelen* or *pommes duchesses*)

1 pound potatoes

1 egg white

1 1/2 tablespoons butter

1 cup milk

salt and pepper

nutmeg

Peel the potatoes and boil them in plenty of salted water. When done, set them aside for two to three minutes; meanwhile, heat the milk. Then, mash the potatoes well and add the hot milk, butter, and spices until a soft puree appears. Beat the egg white until frothy. Put the potato mixture into a pastry bag and pipe regular shapes (for example, little roses) onto a buttered ovenproof dish; spread the egg white on the potato shapes, and put into the oven till the potatoes obtain a nice brownish color (only a few minutes). Serve as a decorative element with a meat or fish dish.

Returning to children's feasts and eating, mention should be made of *Sinterklaas* or *Saint-Nicolas* on December 6. This is an old, intimate feast that goes back to the 1850s, when songs were composed that are still very popular. Yet, the legend of Saint Nicolas as the rescuer of three little girls has roots in the tenth century. Presents for children are essential (particularly nowadays when quite expensive toys are given, which receives increasing criticism—although not from the children), but food has always played a role. Dozens of stories and images depict the coming of Saint Nicolas.[13] The Good *Sint* (Saint) and his helper, *Zwarte Piet* (Black Peter), go out at night to put the presents in chimneys of houses where children live. Zwarte Piet has a huge book with information about all children, and those who have been nice get presents and candy, but those who have been bad are punished. Presents end up in the children's shoes, which are placed near the chimney (or another convenient place; even a heater might do today) on December 5. The nature of presents has changed over time, of course, but candy in all forms remains a genuine treat. Since the late nineteenth century, chocolate has been a favorite, but marzipan and gingerbread cookies (*speculaas* in Dutch or *spéculoos* in French) are still very popular. All candies are in the shape of Saint Nicolas, his white horse, Zwarte Piet, or a little pink piggy, the latter representing old ideas about ethics, survival during winter, and fecundity. Chocolate coins, wrapped in golden paper and put in a little bag, have been popular for more than a century now. In the 1960s, parents saw oranges and, later, tangerines as an alternative to the many candy bars, chocolates, and other sweets. Children have preferred the sweets, for to them *Sinterklaas* starts a great month of much more candy eating.[14]

Crepes (*pannenkoeken* or *crêpes*)

4 cups fine wheat flour

1 quart milk

1/4 cup white sugar

2 eggs

1 1/2 tablespoons fresh yeast

salt

butter (for baking)

Put the flour in a large bowl, add salt, and make a well in the middle. Dissolve the yeast in some lukewarm milk, add the sugar, and pour into the well; mix this gently. Whip the eggs (both yolk and white) well, and stir into the flour mixture. Add the rest of the milk and mix well to get rid of lumps. Leave the bowl in a warm spot until the batter volume has doubled. Put some butter in a pan, heat on medium high, and drop a spoonful of dough into it; spread this well. Cook the crepe for about two minutes until it is golden brown on one side, and then turn it and cook for another two to three minutes. Serve hot, with sugar, syrup, jam, or butter.

Inviting friends over for dinner, a post–World War II phenomenon for most Belgians, has become important and now challenges the old networks of family and neighbors. It is customary to respect a sequence of mutual visits and to never enter the hosts' house empty-handed (flowers, pralines, and wine being usual but nowadays somewhat outdated). Belgians are not known for inviting strangers into their homes, but once a friend is made, culinary copiousness awaits. Most men used to meet in pubs for drinks, and women would have a quick cup of coffee at home, chatting with friends. Up to the 1960s only the richer people would regularly invite guests for lunch and, mostly, dinner. This was a matter of "gourmet networking": the more important the company, the finer the food, and it was unthinkable to serve the same food twice to the same diners. Some of the rules of these classy friends' dinners appeared in popular cookbooks and women's magazines after World War II, as if the common people needed to be educated in how to entertain friends. Magazines and cookbooks would explain about *zakouskis* (*amuse-bouche* and *toasts canapés*, or cocktail snacks), the serving of aperitifs (e.g., vermouth, cocktails), the sequence and nature of dishes, the do's and don'ts. One bit of advice, for example, was to avoid frequently serving one's favorite dish, even though it might be excellent. Guests may think that they are not sufficiently appreciated if the cook did not do her (or, recently, his) best.

Moreover, since the 1960s, magazines, cookbooks, television programs, and, later, Web sites increasingly assist the cook of the house with countless tips on how to amaze guests with new and daring dishes. "Innovate" is the key word, hence a never-ending series of Italian, Spanish, Indian, African, authentic, fusion, *terroir* (regional), or other styles of dishes and snacks is presented. Public Flemish television, for example, started in 1955 with a cooking program (only two years after the beginning of broadcasting in Belgium, which stresses the importance of food in the country). *Kwart-eefje* appeared in the 1960s, *Kijk en kook* in the 1970s, *Kwizien* and *Krokant* in the 1980s, *1000 seconden* in the 1990s, and *Gentse waterzooi* and *Penelope* today.[15] The programs reveal an unambiguous evolution with regard to approach (from educational to edutainment), cooks (from professionals to popular entertainers), regions (from local and French to global), and content (from down-to-earth to extravagant).[16] They leave the viewer with the impression of a nation that not only is obsessed by

The *Trios des entrées* (the trio of starters), with three variations on salmon, the grand opening of a special dinner at a fancy restaurant, 2007. Courtesy of the author.

good cooking but is also totally oriented toward culinary innovation and experimentation.

BIG OCCASIONS

Nowadays, weddings are mostly celebrated in special places; people rent a hall and pay for a caterer to organize two or even three subsequent events: the meal of the newly wed couple with their parents and the immediate family (always out-of-the-ordinary food), the wedding reception for a wide range of guests from various spheres (plenty of drinks—including champagne, of course—and fancy snacks), and the evening party with dancing (again, plenty of drinks are served, mostly beer and cocktails, and tapas or canapés in the late hours). Some couples prefer the intimacy of a meal in a restaurant, inviting close family and friends, but others would stick to a big reception and offer drinks and plenty of nibbles. Again, there are no rules with regard to organization or food, with the one exception of striving for originality. The following two menus of recent weddings clearly show this.

The first is called the "Bruegel buffet" and has no specific order (except for the dessert):[17] tomato cream soup with little meatballs, a cartwheel (or a big, round construction) of little breads with ham, cheese, and salami, roasted pork with mustard, blood sausage with compote, meatballs with cherries, chicken with onion and tomato, various vegetables, mashed potatoes with carrots (*stoemp*), and plain potatoes; the dessert buffet contains

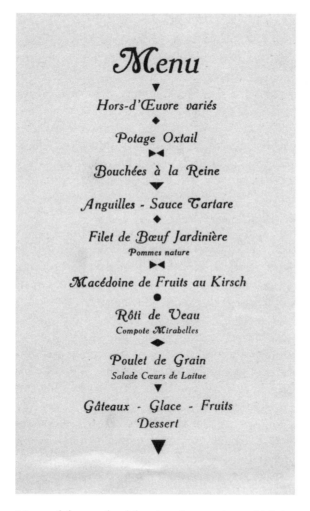

Menu

▼

Hors-d'Œuvre variés

◆

Potage Oxtail

▶◀

Bouchées à la Reine

▼

Anguilles - Sauce Tartare

◆

Filet de Bœuf Jardinière
Pommes nature

▶◀

Macédoine de Fruits au Kirsch

●

Rôti de Veau
Compote Mirabelles

◆

Poulet de Grain
Salade Cœurs de Laitue

▼

Gâteaux - Glace - Fruits
Dessert

▼

Menu of the meal celebrating the marriage of Mademoiselle Cécile B. with Monsieur François O., Anderlecht (suburb of Brussels), August 1936. This menu represents a very traditional organization of a fancy meal, as it was conceived in France in the 1850s. Courtesy of the author.

rice pudding, chocolate mousse, fresh fruit, apple pie, prunes and rice, and a selection of soft Belgian cheeses. Coffee and tea are offered to end the meal, and wine, beer, and soft drinks *à volonté* (free refills). This menu has, of course, little connection to the *actual* foods of the sixteenth century (when, for example, chocolate, tomatoes, and potatoes were largely unknown), but it is the idea of bucolic, copious eating and drinking that matters. The second menu is more sophisticated. The starter is a home-cooked salmon on lettuce with cranberry vinaigrette, followed by Agnes Sorel cream. A lime sorbet with champagne offers a short break before the roasted turkey in cream sauce and oyster mushrooms are served. A surprise dessert and coffee with biscuits end the meal. Château Plaisance 2003 and Domaine du Théron (2000) accompany the dinner.[18] This menu again reflects the classic French sequence of a meal, with the sorbet as a moment of rest and the roast as the climax of the meal.

Before the late 1970s, most Belgians celebrated a wedding at home or in a nearby café. Of course, today some people still celebrate a wedding at home for various reasons (e.g., exclusivity or financial restraints). Up to the 1970s, the meal expressed the joy and the status of the family according to their financial means. In most cases, including the more modest income groups, the menu would bear traces of fancy food in that the number, sequence, and nature of dishes would reflect opulent eating. For example, a wedding of a lower-middle-class couple in 1971 included crab cocktail (a classic in those days), cream of asparagus soup (again, a classic), salmon à la mousseline, roast beef with cranberries, melon with ham (another classic), roasted chicken with lettuce, ice cream, and coffee with cookies. An average cook could easily prepare these dishes, which show the typical organization of the Escoffier meal (with the inevitable roast as the pinnacle). Going back further in time, most wedding feasts were foremost a matter of plenty, not of refinement. Thus, familiar pricey food such as sausages, beef, pork, or chicken (that was truly expensive until the 1950s) was eaten. Opulent eating at wedding feasts has been a very old tradition, so much so that Emperor Charles V dictated in 1531 that wedding feasts had to be limited to 40 guests. In 1711, Emperor Joseph II repeated this restriction, adding that the feast should end after two days.

Eating out with a large party in order to celebrate a wedding anniversary would only be done in symbolic years such as the tin (10 years of marriage), silver (25 years), or golden (50 years) wedding anniversaries. Three to four decades ago, such an anniversary was generally celebrated at home, and the house's façade was decorated. The meal was prepared at home, often with the help of aunts or grandmothers, with the emphasis on quantity. Classics of those days were crab cocktail, asparagus cream soup, roast beef with a "garland" of vegetables (mostly peas, carrots, cauliflower, and beans, all cooked thoroughly), and ice cream. All other anniversaries would be limited to the couple or the direct family and friends. Eating in and eating out, then, are both possible, of course, but when people are eating at home, a special dish is prepared, something that is either familiar and meaningful to the couple or very innovative. The same goes for celebrating a promotion at work, the happy conclusion of studies, or any personal happy occasion, although eating out has lately gained enormous popularity at such occasions. At work, one event or another (a promotion, retirement, or birthday) is frequently celebrated with a drink and some cake, unless one of the colleagues really puts great effort into it by bringing homemade pastry or a special dish.

Crab Cocktail (*krabcocktail* or *salade de crabe*)

1 can of crab or lobster

2 to 4 eggs

1 tomato

1 lemon

parsley

lettuce

cocktail sauce

4 teaspoons mayonnaise

1 teaspoon Worcestershire sauce

chili pepper

1 teaspoon ketchup

1 teaspoon cognac

Start by making the cocktail sauce. Mix the mayonnaise and Worcestershire sauce; add some chili pepper and the ketchup. Stir well, and add the cognac; put in the fridge. Open the can of crab and drain the liquid off. Boil the eggs, let cool, and then peel the shells off. Cut the tomato into small pieces and the eggs into eight long slices. Take four large but flat glasses (with a wide mouth); put the lettuce on the bottom, followed by a layer of tomato pieces, and then the crabmeat. Adorn with the egg slices (place them standing up around the crabmeat) and the rest of the tomato. Top with some cocktail sauce; garnish with a tiny slice of lemon and some parsley.

Most of the discussion has concerned exceptional plentiful eating that occurs only occasionally in a lifetime, but some big festive meals occur annually. Easter used to be one of these moments of excessive eating, following a 40-day period of fasting (one meal per day and no meat or fish). Because Lent has largely disappeared since the 1950s, the significance of Easter as a privileged moment of excessive eating has diminished strongly. However, many people feel the coming of spring as a moment of "renewal" (of nature and the body, but also of refreshing the house and buying new clothes); they wish to get rid of winter and thus fast to some degree. To them, Easter offers an opportunity to stop fasting. In older times, food was abundant after the frugality of Lent, and people enjoyed the availability of lots of meat, dairy products, and fish at a relatively low price. This, of course, added to the festive ambiance. Symbolic food was largely consumed, particularly eggs, which represented life and regeneration. The yolks of fresh eggs were "blown out" and the outside decorated, which is still done today. Often, this egg decorating is a family activity, but increasingly specialized firms paint hard-boiled eggs. Another relatively old and persisting tradition is the Easter egg hunt: boiled, wooden, and chocolate eggs are hidden for the children to find in the yard or inside the house. In 2006 a grandfather wrote on his blog that the moment when his grandchildren go out to seek the eggs is one of the nicest moments in life to him. The importance of eggs also appears in the many Easter recipes. One Web site offers two dozen recipes with eggs, including starters, main courses, and desserts, such as egg salad, omelet, filled eggs, egg with salmon, scrambled eggs with truffles, and zabaglione.[19] For 2007 this Web site proposed a "typical" Easter menu that oozes tradition: scrambled eggs on toast, melon with ham from Parma, asparagus cream, grandmother's rabbit, and fruit salad. Each dish in this menu appeared in 1930s cookbooks.

Grandmother's Rabbit (*konijn op grootmoeders wijze* or *lapin grand-mère*)

Serves four.

1 rabbit, cut into pieces

butter (for frying)

2 cups brown beer

1 onion

salt and pepper

nutmeg

vinegar

Put the pieces of rabbit in a pan with water and add some vinegar. Marinate for two hours. Then, take the rabbit out and dry thoroughly. Fry the meat in the butter until brown, then put in the beer and the minced onion. Add salt, pepper, and nutmeg. Leave to simmer for two hours. Serve with croquettes and apple slices that have been baked in the oven, with butter and soft sugar, until a brown crust appears.

The biggest festive meals in Belgium are those around Christmas and New Year's. Generally, Christmas Eve, Christmas, and New Year's Day are spent with family and close friends at home, while New Year's Eve is often spent with friends eating out. Of course, many people also eat at home on New Year's Eve, staying up until midnight and watching television, while some people may go out on Christmas Eve. More and more, people who can afford it visit foreign countries during these days, although this is still a small minority.

In December 2007 a survey found that 89 percent of the interviewees celebrated Christmas, and 77 percent celebrated New Year's Eve, which is an increase from the previous year.[20] Most merrymakers are people in their thirties, living in middle-sized towns, and in families of three to four people. *Bruxellois* (inhabitants of Brussels), people older than 65 years, and people living alone rarely celebrate. For Christmas, 90 percent of the people celebrate by eating a meal with the family, and only 2 percent eat out. On New Year's Eve, only 61 percent of merrymakers have a meal with their family, and friends are invited for this more often than for Christmas. Moreover, 16 percent dine out and 30 percent celebrate the New Year in bars, nightclubs, or dance halls (the latter particularly by people between 18 and 29 years old). Christmas in Belgium is indeed a family occasion, for which an average of 14 guests, all family members, gather. For Christmas people spend less than for New Year's (124 euros and 136 euros, respectively, all expenditures included), which is due to the fact that more people go to restaurants, clubs, and bars on December 31. For New Year's Eve, the lowest-income group spends 28 euros on presents, the highest 56 euros, with the average being 41 euros, which shows important social differences. This survey also reveals that most Belgians cook for Christmas (72 percent), while a minority uses a professional caterer (12 percent). A trend that is gaining popularity among young families is "co-cooking," or group cooking (15 percent).

Most people prepare familiar food (60 percent), although they search for inspiration in cookbooks, Web sites, and magazines. Christmas dinners are rather traditional, with turkey, shellfish, salmon, game, and foie gras, and especially wine and champagne (for New Year's Eve the latter is consumed by no less than 77 percent of the interviewees). "Exotic foods" seduce only 10 percent of Belgian Christmas cooks. Finally, the questionnaire asked about the existence of "Bob." This Bob is a person who does not drink alcohol and is the designated driver.[21] For Christmas and New Year's Eve, only about one-fourth of the interviewees mentioned the presence of Bob, with large regional and social differences (Brussels, 11 percent; Flemish towns, 36 percent; Wallonia, 15 percent; and Flemish villages, 9 percent). These percentages reflect different partying habits.

Following strict traditions today is rare. For example, the number of people attending midnight mass on Christmas Eve is shrinking, which allows more flexible celebrating. The flexibility means that staying in and partying at home on Christmas Eve, Christmas, New Year's Eve, or New Year's Day becomes a cause of serious concern for the cook: what to prepare? It is also a matter of serious concern for the diner: how much to eat and drink? Since the early twentieth century, women's magazines and special sections of newspapers informed cooks about Christmas dinners, and since the late 1970s, these media stress the danger of overeating. In December 2006, a Flemish newspaper offered a series of guidelines for surviving December's festive eating, stressing that the average dinner provided about 3,000 calories per person, even without the habitual snacking and alcohol consumption in between. Some people eat abundantly on December 24 and 25 and on December 31 and January 1. Between December 24 and January 1, the average Belgian gains 8.8 pounds.[22]

Since the 1970s, magazines and newspapers emphasize innovation with regard to the December feasts: the latest aperitif, an out-of-the-ordinary soup, or a fashionable dessert. In December 1978, for example, the women's magazine *Libelle* proposed exotic alternatives to the eternal stuffed turkey or the *canard flambé* (duck flambé) ("for those who prefer innovations"), suggesting *Planter's Punch, Pimentade* (sauce based on chili pepper), or braised zucchini, which contain unusual ingredients such as ginger, hot pepper, guavas, or coconut milk (which could only be bought in specialty shops).

Some cookbooks contain the more classic Christmas dinner. *Ik kan koken* (1951) publishes two Christmas menus, a simple and an extensive one. The first contains a light bouillon with jelly of egg, turkey (or goose) with compote and *pommes duchesses*, and plum pudding, whereas the more elaborate menu includes oysters, consommé, lemon sole with mashed potatoes, goose with compote and sweet chestnuts, vegetables, plum pudding, cheese, fruit, coffee with sweets and cookies, and liquor or cognac. To emphasize the classics, the cookbook states, "Traditional Christmas ingredients are turkey, goose, duck or chicken, and plum pudding."[23] This sentence refers to a classic Anglo-Saxon Christmas dinner but hardly to Belgian Christmas traditions. Up to the early twentieth century, these were limited in most families to attending mass, coziness around the stove, the singing of Christmas carols, the baking of cake or bread (with milk and honey) in the form of a reclining infant, and the drinking of beer and *jenever* (the Christmas tree and father Christmas only spread after 1945). Richer families would celebrate Christmas within the intimate circle. Until the 1900s, for example, the Belgian king and queen dined together on Christmas, without eating anything extraordinary.

Nowadays, Web sites and blogs provide an avalanche of suggestions, recipes, and ideas, and they contain questions and cries for help that show insecurity and panic. Yet, they offer plenty of fascinating information about present-day worries and solutions with regard to December's festive dinners. In early September 2007, a woman posted a "rescue-me" message on the Web site of *Femistyle*, asking for help with regard to the Christmas Eve menu she was supposed to serve to 16 people.[24] In the days following her request, she received about 50 replies, some making jokes about this early worry and others showing empathy, but all suggesting an idea, recipe, or drink. Among the repliers was a man who stressed that he never cooked at such occasions but that he was happy to contribute by listing the food he had enjoyed during past Christmas dinners. Appetizers included quiche, hot and cold goat cheese on toast, little rolls of salmon with Boursin-cheese, toast with foie gras, stuffed cherry tomatoes, dishes of North Sea shrimp and freshly made mayonnaise, tomato with buffalo mozzarella, and little bowls of spicy soup. Starters consisted of all sorts of soup (including soup of Camembert cheese), salad with hot goat cheese and bacon, roasted fish with a mousse of celery and fennel, homemade sesame crackers, *coulis* (or puree) of tomato and basil, and raisin bread toast with goose pâté and red onion jam. With regard to the main dish this gourmet wrote, "Traditionally, we always have game although I'd prefer something else. . . ." The party has had roasted wild pork with *poivrade* (pepper sauce) and mustard sauce, garland of four vegetables and little roasted potatoes, leg of lamb with steamed vegetables (Belgian endives, haricots with bacon, small carrots, Brussels sprouts), croquettes with wild-game sauce, roe filet with chanterelles and *röstis* (baked potato slices), roasted duck with steamed apple and a tangerine sauce with cranberries, and venison with mashed potatoes and winter vegetables. A classic dessert was the cheese plate; a buffet with mango ice, small glasses of sabayon, crème brulée, and chocolate mousse; and the inevitable *bûche de noël* (a cream cake in the shape of a wooden log, commonly known as Yule log). This seems to be an inventory of recent Belgian Christmas Eve dinners, reflecting classic as well as innovative fancy food.

Cooks, by and large women, have somewhat different approaches. They can be divided into two groups: those who wish to have a relatively easy

task and settle on a fondue of meat or fish, and those who prefer to stand
out via sophisticated preparations. One participant in the blog discussion argued in favor of a meat fondue: "almost no work, and you sit with
the company, enjoying as much as everybody else." A survey in December 2006 by one of the big retailers in Belgium established a difference
between Flemish and Walloon Christmas feasts, in that Flemish households generally served champagne, asparagus soup, meat fondue, and the
Christmas cake, while Walloon families have champagne, *pâté de foie*
(liver paste), turkey, cheese, and *bûche de noël*. A participant in a blog
discussion on the Web site of a women's magazine argued in October 2007
that cooking skills and, indeed, honor were at stake, writing, "This year,
I'll cook for my family, which is nice, but there will be nine adults and
four teenagers. Moreover, they all are gourmets, and it will certainly not
suffice if I'd serve them a nice cheese plate or gourmet [i.e., some kind of
fondue], because they wouldn't accept it (to them, this simply isn't festive
eating). So, I need to score, preferably with a five-course dinner. Anybody
out there with ideas for a genuine festive dinner that I can handle? "[25]

Christmas cooks in need of help can visit specialized Web sites, among
which is the site of public television in Flanders, which in 2006 was totally
oriented toward innovation and amazement. An "alternative" Christmas
dinner is suggested in collaboration with a professional chef. The meal
is "scientifically acceptable," echoing the molecular cuisine as well as
health concerns: a light vegetable bouillon with chili pepper, peanuts,
and chocolate as a starter, followed by guinea fowl steamed in cola, and,
as dessert, Belgian endives with coffee and chocolate ice cream.[26] More
familiar menus can be found in magazines and on Web sites, though.
Receptjes.be, a popular "collection of free, simple and tasty recipes" with
4,000 hits a day in 2007 and particularly addressing middle-class women,
proposes customary Christmas menus that contain such genuine classics
as, for example, stuffed turkey and cranberries, steamed apples, and croquettes, melon with ham from Parma, or pork tenderloin with Port wine.[27]
However, this Web site also proposes more daring dishes and combinations, like lettuce with little bits of roasted spicy chicken, bell pepper
soup, lobster with herbs or monkfish with almonds and Russian potatoes.
Again, rules hardly exist, and cooks may readily experiment according to
the family's tastes, ways, and wishes.

At 6 P.M. on December 24, 2006, Kamiano, a Christian center for
homeless people in Antwerp that serves an average of 350 meals a day,
offered a Christmas meal to about 500 people. It started with a salmon
mousse, followed by a cream of forest mushrooms. The main course was
rabbit stew with cranberries and *pommes duchesses,* and the meal ended

Rich people on holiday at the seaside resort of Blankenberge, 1921, enjoying an ice cream. Courtesy of
the author.

with a Christmas cake. All diners were extremely satisfied.[28] This menu
resembled the one proposed by bourgeois cookbooks of the 1950s, thus
illustrating the increased accessibility to fancy food since then (of course,
on special occasions). Similar initiatives were taken in many other towns
too, showing the special atmosphere of the Christmas feast (although the
food was not always as sophisticated as in Antwerp).

The festive spirit is very different on New Year's Eve and January 1.
In general, people tend to go out more than for Christmas, and partying at restaurants and clubs is popular. However, since the year 2000
home parties with friends and family became a new trend, which worries
restaurant owners but delights caterers. For example, in 2007 a specialized caterer, Traditions nouvelles, supplied a *chef à domicile* (a chef who

does the cooking at one's home), providing a posh dinner for 50 euros per person (not including drinks), which contained smoked trout with fried orange, eggplant flan with caviar, foie gras, mousse of "homardized" fish, cassoulet with scallop shells sauce mousseline, roasted duck *en croûte balsamique* (crust with balsamic vinegar), and iced nougat with Baileys. It was advised to make reservations in advance.[29] The increase in home parties on December 31 is explained by rising restaurant prices, alcohol checkpoints on the road, and the striving for "pure coziness" that is hardly provided in restaurants, where the *réveillon* (New Year's Eve) is often qualified as artificial. When staying in, the majority of people cook themselves, just like with Christmas.

In general, the New Year's Eve dinner is less elaborate than the Christmas meal. Moreover, New Year's Eve is far less a family affair than Christmas, which implies that family members tend to have different activities and food on December 31. Blogs inform about this. Femistyle.be and Jim.be relate to housewives and teenagers respectively, and while the latter concentrates on "eating and, especially, drinking a lot" as well as on the key question "Where to party?," the former deals with recipes, advice about calories, and creative cooking. Since 2000, a new trend has appeared: cooking together, which is more popular on New Year's Eve than on Christmas Eve. In December 2006, a blogger on Femistyle.be launched the question "What will you eat during the feasts," to which a woman replied, "On New Year's Eve there will be ten of us, and everybody will prepare a dish. We don't know what will be prepared, and this may of course cause big surprises. Together with my friend, I'm in charge of the appetizers and the starter. It'll be simple but very tasty." Another blogger wrote, "We'll do the cooking all together, because it's the coziness that matters, then."[30]

Despite differences in style, form, and content, there seem to be some common features in Belgians' home parties on December 31. Half of them start with champagne and *zakouskis*, have foie gras as a starter, and fondue or grilled meat (in Flanders, beef and poultry; in Wallonia, game) as a main dish, with ice cream for dessert. Thirty percent of the Belgians spent between 10 and 15 euros per person, 50 percent between 15 and 25 euros, and 20 percent spent more than 25 euros on the food. Asked about their preferences, women shoppers replied that they were searching for something original but not too daring, like scampi, lobster, or crab, arguing that "It's a special day and we eat well, and I don't care much about expenses; it's the *réveillon* and we'll enjoy." However, one out of five inhabitants of the bigger cities do not celebrate New Year's Eve: they cannot afford it, they live alone and have no friends, they are too old, or they simply do not care.[31] The latter sentiment is also often expressed by teenagers ("New Year's Eve? I don't care, I hate it!"). It seems as if people are a little bit tired of eating copiously for New Year's Eve and January 1, although most Belgians would not even think of abolishing the dinners on those days.

VACATIONS IN BELGIUM

Quite particular eating practices occur during vacations. Since 1936 most wage earners in Belgium have paid holidays, amounting at present to a maximum of 24 days (which is less than in most surrounding countries), in addition to the 10 public holidays. July and August are the most popular vacation period, although since the 1980s vacations are spread more equally over the year. Nowadays, school holidays regulate the timing of vacations, with two weeks in December and around Easter, one week in February and November, and two months during summer.

If in 1985 half of the Belgians spent their vacations at home, nowadays three-quarters of them make one or more trips lasting several days during the year.[32] After the drop in 2002 following the shock of events on September 11, 2001, both inland and international tourism are growing ever more. Short trips (of fewer than four nights) are mostly made within the country and are becoming more frequent. Yet, because of the increasingly growing interest in short trips abroad (next to the ever-popular Paris, so-called city trips have become very trendy, including places such as Barcelona, Berlin, Prague, or Rome), the percentage of short inland trips fell from 62 percent in 1998 to 55 percent in 2005. Longer vacations (more than four nights away) are overwhelmingly spent abroad, with France by far being the most popular (followed by Spain, Italy, Turkey, and Austria). Just like in other European countries, Belgians' considerable traveling abroad since the 1960s contributes substantially to the swift introduction of foreign foodways into everyday cooking. However, one-fifth of Belgians still prefer Belgium as the location for their longer holiday. Most Belgians take their car for traveling (driving within Belgium or to nearby France, Germany, or the Netherlands), but the airplane is increasingly used (flying to New York, Egypt, China, and other trendy places), while traveling by train remains insignificant (with 5 percent of all holiday trips).

When staying in Belgium, the coast (45 percent) and the Ardennes (20 percent) are by far the most popular places for Belgians. The coast is about 40 miles long, with large, sandy beaches and dunes where hotels, campgrounds, and apartment blocks have chaotically appeared, turning the coastline into one of the ugliest of Europe. Belgians (as well as many tourists from France, Germany, the Netherlands, and the United Kingdom) love to spend time on the hectic beaches and in the crowded streets of Ostend, Blankenberge, or Koksijde. The Ardennes offers more tranquility, with picturesque places such as Durbuy, Dinant, or Rochefort.

When vacationing in Belgium, most Belgians appreciate a familiar environment, meaning that they prefer by far to spend the holiday in a rented apartment (22 percent), their second residence (19 percent), or with friends (9 percent); these places provide the customary facilities for cooking, cleaning, and leisure (including television). Only a minority would check into a hotel (12 percent). Apartments in "all-inclusive" resorts (with restaurants, tropical swimming pools, playgrounds, cafés, and amusement halls), bed and breakfasts, and agro-tourism farms have become popular since the 1980s (15 percent), but Belgians have little interest in camping (5 percent) and sport camps (6 percent). Not all of them, of course, enjoy vacations to the same extent. Along with differences with regard to age and household composition, unequal incomes lead to hugely different spending during vacations, revealing a very substantial inequality. In 2005 the highest-income group spent no less than 20 times more than the lowest-income group. Moreover, high-income groups spent significantly more on foreign trips than the low-income groups.

For those traveling abroad, as well as for those taking an inland holiday or staying at home, eating is always special during vacations. This takes very different forms. People may have more time to shop, cook, and eat and may become more complacent with regard to meals in terms of organization, timing, and content. At the same time, the busy holiday plans may leave less time for eating, and fast food may do. Both the coast and the Ardennes have several gastronomic restaurants (the small town of Knokke, for example, has three restaurants with a Michelin star), and undoubtedly many tourists enjoy having a gastronomic experience during vacations. A handful of them can do this daily and others do this just once during the holiday, but most of the tourists simply use the kitchen of their apartment or the little heating device of their camper, preparing the food they are accustomed to. Thus, holiday meals generally do not differ much from daily home cooking, except for the more casual organization and timing.

In the 1950s, with the emergence of mass tourism, to ease the housewife's shopping and cooking burden, plain convenience foods could be bought from a takeout restaurant or retailer. Homemade soup, *pommes frites*, or very plain meat dishes could be purchased. With the general increase in the sophistication of food in Belgium since the 1960s, the supply by caterers and in supermarkets rose significantly. For example, Traiteur

De Groote in Knokke, established as a simple fishmonger in 1924, offered in 2008 a very rich and varied selection of ready-made dishes, including classics such as shrimp croquettes and smoked salmon mousse but also pastry of poultry, pork Orloff, and lobster à l'armoricaine (a sauce made with cognac, cream, white wine, and hebrs), to be carried out or delivered to homes, all at relatively high prices. A more moderately priced caterer is the recently established De Ton in Ostend, providing a daily dish for 5 euros (in the week of December 10, 2007, dishes offered were Chinese chicken with rice, hamburger with *pommes frites*, beef stew (*hutsepot*), fish with vegetable sauce and potatoes, stew of poultry and mushrooms, pork à la milanaise, or in the Milanese way, with tomato sauce and ham, all to be carried out). This caterer also sells soup by the liter (about one quart, for one euro), which recalls the old 1950s custom.

Day-trippers on the beach or in the woods of the Ardennes love to picnic whenever the weather is nice. According to a journalist with long experience in picnicking, the ideal picnic is spread over the day with continuous eating of fine foods and drinking of cool wines, using a heater to slightly grill the little breads that are filled with smoked salmon, Ganda ham (dried and salted ham from the region of Ghent), or Camembert cheese with nuts. The eating and drinking alternate with chatting, playing games, and snoozing. Doing this is not just a matter of relaxation, but it is claimed to be the instinctive way of living with a reference to humans' deepest wish to be one with nature.[33] Opposed to this romantic view is the more widespread association of tourists' picnicking with cheap and tasteless eating, captured by the term *frigoboxtoerist* (literally, the tourist with a cool box), that was launched by the mayor of fancy Knokke in the early 1990s, who wished to get rid of the moderately spending day-trippers. Belgian, foreign, rich, and poor tourists enjoy eating waffles and ice cream throughout the day. Quite famous is Mother Siska, an eatery established in the 1880s that specializes in heart-shaped waffles with butter, fruit, or whipped cream.

The food eaten on special occasions not only mirrors the general development of the Belgian diet, but also shapes it in that many home cooks wish to excel in preparing special food for festive meals. This leads to a continuous quest for new tastes, combinations, dishes, and ingredients when the festive days come into sight. Web sites, magazines, television programs, books, and specialized sections of newspapers are oriented toward guiding the home cook in this search. Often, new festive dishes have been tried out on the close family some days before the actual feast. If the meal was a success, particular dishes or ingredients may make their way into the daily cooking of the family. Festive eating, thus, introduces and diffuses new things. This contrasts with old traditions, when most feasts were linked to particular foods. Still, the aim at the new, original, and peculiar leaves space for old traditions (albeit introduced a couple of decades and even years ago). Moreover, many people prefer to stick to familiar festive food with such classics as asparagus, game, lobster, croquettes, salmon or turbot, cranberries, foie gras, and, most certainly, champagne.

NOTES

1. Stefaan Top, *Kalender van de Vlaamse feesten* (Kapellen, Belgium: Helios, 1986).

2. Dimitri Mortelmans and Sofie Damen, "Attitudes on Commercialization and Anti-Commercialization reactions on Gift Giving Occasions in Belgium," *Journal of Consumer Behaviour* 1.2 (2001): 156–173.

3. In 2004, champagne consumption per capita reached 0.8 gallons (2.9 liters) in France, 0.3 gallons (1.3 l) in Luxembourg, 0.25 gallons (0.9 l) in Belgium, 0.13 gallons (0.5 l) in the United Kingdom, and 0.02 gallons (0.07 l) in the United States. See, the champagne pages, http://www.champagneinfo.net/Commercie/ChampagneConsumptieinCijfers/tabid/189/Default.aspx (accessed November 12, 2007).

4. Full information on the Belgian kermis (where, when, what?) is to be found at Fête-foraine/Kermis-feest, http://www.fete-foraine.be/ (accessed November 20, 2007).

5. "Le Belge boude la messe, pas la foi," *Le Soir*, October 2, 2004, 8–9.

6. The Academie voor Streekgebonden Gastronomie has an inventory of Belgian ingredients and dishes (so far only in Dutch), which is available at http://www.asg.be/nederlands/Gastronomie/frameset_gastronomie.htm (accessed November 5, 2007).

7. See 9Maand/9Mois (Nine Months), http://www.9maand.be/forum/archief/reactions/41123 (accessed November 3, 2007).

8. See Brussels Onderwijspunt (Brussels Education Center), http://www.bop.vgc.be/tijdschriften/wablieft/wab471/Wa71sam1.txt (accessed November 4, 2007).

9. See De kindertjes (the little children), http://dekindertjes.skynetblogs.be/post/3378981/plechtige-communie (accessed November 4, 2007).

10. See Hapjestiem (characterized by the enthusiastic amateur cook as "Intimate cooking for ultimate pleasure"), http://hapjestiem.skynetblogs.be/post/1132909/ik-eerste-communie-jij-eerste-communiet-wij-e/ (accessed November 4, 2007).

11. See Viva, Socialistische vrouwenvereniging, http://www.viva-svv.be/Viva/WatDoenWe/GezinRelatiesOpvoeding/Dossiers/kinderfeest2.htm (accessed November 3, 2007).

12. P. J. Sarels van Rijn, *Ik kan koken* (Antwerp and Leiden: Van Tuyl & Sijthoff's, 1951), 106–109.

13. Rita Ghesquière, *Van Nicolaas van Myra tot Sinterklaas* (Leuven, Belgium: Davidsfonds, 1989).

14. A specialized *Sinterklaas* Web site is http://blog.seniorennet.be/ pierre2005/archief.php?ID=3; it is available only in Dutch but includes many photographs.

15. The archive of *Gentse waterzooi*, listing all recipes, is to be found at http://www.een.be/televisie1_master/programmas/e_gent_archief/index.shtml (accessed August 3, 2008).

16. Anne Widart, *Kookprogramma's in evolutie* (master's thesis, Vrije Universiteit Brussel, 2005).

17. Dagboek familie Cornelis (Diary of the Cornelis family), http://www. familie-cornelis.be/Huwelijk_dagboek.html/ (accessed November 9, 2007).

18. Wendy & Sven, http://www.svencipido.be/wijtrouwen/huwelijk.aspx/ (accessed November 9, 2007).

19. See Eenvoudige en lekkere recepten (Simple and flavorful recipes), http://www.receptjes.be/menu_pasen.html (accessed November 11, 2007).

20. *Eindejaarsfeesten* (Brussels: OIVO, 2007). See also the Web site of the Centre de recherche et d'information des organistations des consommateurs, http://www.crioc.be/FR/.

21. "Bob" appeared during a nationwide promotion campaign in 1995. Because of its general success (it actually led to a change in mentality), the European Commission adopted it in 2001 and supports it since then. The 2007 Belgian campaign used the slogan "No party without Bob" (see Bob, http://www. bob.be/fr/campagne/campagne2.htm).

22. "Hoe de feestmaaltijd overleven?" [How to survive the feast?], *De Morgen*, December 1, 2006.

23. Sarels van Rijn, *Ik kan koken*, 111.

24. *Femistyle* is an e-magazine for the "trendy woman," published since 2000 and containing sections on fashion, travel, food, children, and the like; it can be found at http://www.femistyle.be/ubbthreads/ubbthreads.php?ubb=showflat& Number=470739&fpart=1 (accessed November 15, 2007).

25. See Libelle, http://forum.libelle.be/viewtopic.php?t=319402 (accessed November 16, 2007).

26. See TV-Eén (TV one), http://www.een.be/televisie1_master/program mas/e_hoez_zozitdat_kerstmenu/index.shtml (accessed November 16, 2007).

27. See Eenvoudige en lekkere recepten (Simple and flavorful recipes), http://www.receptjes.be/menu_kerst.html (accessed November 10, 2007).

28. "Kamiano trakteert armen op kerstdiner in Sint-Andrieskerk" [Kamiano treats poor people to Christmas dinner in the church of Sint-Andries], *De Standaard*, December 26, 2006.

29. Traditions nouvelles (New traditions), http://www.traditions-nouvelles. be/?nouvelan/ (accessed November 18, 2007).

30. Femistyle, http://www.femistyle.be/ubbthreads/ubbthreads.php/ubb/showthreaded/Number/288081/site_id/0 (accessed November 18, 2007).

31. See RTBF, http://old.rtbf.be/rtbf_2000/ (accessed November 18, 2007). RTBF is the French-speaking public radio and television station in Belgium.

32. All information in the following is derived from official surveys about Belgian tourism practices; see http://statbel.fgov.be/figures/d34_nl.asp#2 and http://statbel.fgov.be/press/fl026_nl.asp (accessed December 5, 2007).

33. "Buiten eten en drinken" [Outdoors eating and drinking], De Standaard, August 6, 2005.

7

Diet and Health

Today in Belgium, food is on sale 24 hours a day, and most Belgians may eat whatever, whenever, and wherever they want. Compared with the past, this is a drastic change. If the pre–World War II food-related problems are viewed in terms of shortage and imbalance (with lack of calories, vitamins, and protein, leading to loss of weight and strength, edema, anemia, lethargy, and, for children, slow growth), the post-1950 abundance has caused problems of a new kind related to body shape and health: being overweight and obese increases the risk of diabetes, cardiovascular diseases, hypertension and stroke, and some cancers. Naturally, this health concern scores high on the agenda of nutritionists, doctors, and public health workers. With the health concern comes the worry about *safe* food. Consumers, too, are concerned about health and dieting. In bookstores the cookbooks are in the same section as the diet and health books. Both genres boast high sales. This chapter discusses three connected phenomena that have greatly interested Belgians recently: food safety, being overweight, and body ideals.

FOOD SAFETY

In May 1999, Belgian television news announced that dioxin had contaminated some food. Few people cared. Within a week, however, all Belgians knew the word *dioxin*, realized it was bad (it is part of a dangerous chemical group that causes cancer), and believed that the entire Belgian food chain was poisoned. One government minister warned against dioxin pollution of groundwater due to excrement from chickens that had been fed polluted fodder. Newspapers reported that supermarkets removed eggs and milk from their shelves but soon also cured meats, fresh meat, cheese, mayonnaise, ice cream, chocolate, yogurt, and all foods containing eggs or milk. "What's for dinner tonight?" became a dreadful question that made people wonder about the origin and safety of their food. What would mothers serve to their children? Could friends be invited for dinner? Was it okay to eat in restaurants and cafeterias? Within two weeks, a cornerstone of society crumbled with people actually witnessing it. Shoppers responded by buying fish and frozen food or eating lots of bread with vegetable soup. In addition, some nonfood products, such as shampoos and beauty creams with animal fat, were banned from the shops' shelves too. By early June 1999 Belgians' deep-seated distrust went beyond food, involving public authorities and the press. Everybody was talking about the "dioxin crisis," and genuine panic surfaced.

Many food-processing firms stopped production. Companies stockpiled food, losing lots of money. Some went bankrupt within a couple of weeks (such as chocolatier Van Dyck, who had started business in 1988 with entirely new equipment, producing small pralines in the shape of fish). During the first weeks of June, thousands of pounds of fresh and cured meat were destroyed. Export of all Belgian food, whether contaminated or not, was curtailed, and some countries prohibited the import and sale of Belgian food, disregarding the nature, origin, or date of production. Russia, for example, barred the import of pork and poultry in May and of all meats in June 1999. This caused commotion in Belgium. It is generally believed that food inspection mechanisms in Russia are not as sophisticated as in Belgium, and many people suspected that Russia made use of the crisis in Belgium to protect the Russian meat processing industry. Nevertheless, some other countries also banned Belgian products, and, in any case, consumers throughout the world started to doubt the quality and safety of Belgian food. On June 6, the New York Times wrote that "It is Europe's worst food scandal since the mad cow disease in 1996."[1]

Belgian authorities were totally unprepared for the events. Food security experts could not trace the origin of the contamination, for they lacked the necessary means to react instantly (much later, it was found that a feed producer had used contaminated products). Moreover, several food bureaus worked alongside each other. On top of that, some specialists said that there was no danger at all because of the microscopic doses of dioxin that spread into the food chain, while others claimed that all dioxin had already been consumed without causing many health troubles, although still other experts warned that more poisoning was to come. Valuable time was lost, and the specialists could not inform the government nor reassure the public. In late May, Belgian politicians worried about the nearing general elections on June 13; most of them were busy campaigning throughout the country, addressing problems of gross domestic product, unemployment, or pension insurance. Members of the majority were rather confident in the blissful outcome of the elections, ignoring the impact of the crisis. The government took some crisis measures such as prohibiting the sale of all eggs. As a result, the crisis was reinforced because many people believed that the crisis was bigger than presented by ministers or nutritionists. So, a public authority had detected a tangible food problem, but it was totally unable to resolve the problem, thus aggravating the crisis. Still, some newspapers warned against the "madness of the day." *De Standaard*, for example, wrote on June 4, "Reason is totally lost in this drama. We are in a phase of hysteria, of madness," and "The ministers' hesitation has made this crisis beyond any control."[2] Two ministers quit their jobs in those days, hoping to prevent a further political debacle. In vain: the elections of June 13 caused an earthquake in Belgian politics, which made international news.[3] All observers agreed that the dioxin crisis was the main reason, since it had become the top item in political debates and commentaries, with members of the opposition accusing the government of slackness, naïveté, and incompetence.

The new government, the first without Christian Democrats for decades, wished to act firmly and to restore the public's trust in food as soon as possible. The size and nature of the *poisoning* had to be known; therefore, immediate measures were taken. However, only after a couple of weeks it became clear that the actual size of the food pollution was far less than feared (only years later, food experts accepted that dioxin had indeed struck the food chain, but to such a negligible extent that no harm was done). For many Belgians, the July vacations meant escaping the infected Belgian food supply, to come back a couple of weeks later, hoping the crisis was over.

The government sought to prevent similar food fears in the future and set up a wholly new organization under the responsibility of one minister, the Federal Agency for the Safety of the Food Chain.[4] Financial support and powers were greatly increased, which led to rising efficacy, as was proven during another food affair in 2002 when contamination with polychlorinated biphenyl (PCB) was traced within a couple of days, and no panic or anxiety arose among the public. The Federal Agency for the Safety of the Food Chain applies European legislation and guidelines;[5] monitors all producers, importers, and sellers of food; delivers safety certificates; and may close down risky producers, traders, or restaurants. The latter is done recurrently, which is acclaimed by newspapers, although they criticize the severity of some regulations when these jeopardize the traditional (so-called unsanitary) production mode of small artisans. Because the public's trust had to be restored as soon as possible, the setting up of the agency was promptly announced in July 1999, emphasizing the unprecedented coordination, efficiency, and rapidity (not to secure economic interests, but public health). The agency's tasks were very much oriented toward the consumers, including the publication of a monthly newsletter, the setting up of a system to send in complaints (which Belgians increasingly do), and the regular announcement of test results. The agency is the watchdog, which is acknowledged and appreciated by many observers.[6] The launching of the agency had the desired effect. If newspapers had announced in late June "Panic in Dairy Sector" or "Tens of Thousands of Firms in Trouble Due to Dioxin," headlines in early July were "Milk, Butter, Eggs, Cheese, and Meat Are Safe!" or "Agency Will Watch over Food Chain." By the end of July 1999, the food scare was over. The dioxin episode lasted for about two months, and, as appeared later, there had never been any danger. Yet, it shows the immense, almost unmanageable impact of fear related to food, which may surface at any moment.

The Coca-Cola incident of 1999 illustrates this. In late June 1999 some pupils at several schools in Flanders and northern France became ill after drinking Coca-Cola from a vending machine. They experienced headache, weak knees, heart palpitations, and nausea. Within hours after the news had been on national radio and television, many more students fell ill, and after one day 250 people, both youngsters and adults, were reported to be sick. The Coca-Cola Company, food experts, and public authorities claimed that this was a clear example of mass psychogenic illness, with an insignificant trigger (a bad smell) that caused panic. Still, Coca-Cola was forced to withdraw all its products from the shops, leading to a loss of $103 million (in 1999 dollars). Months later, it appeared that there was indeed a problem with phenol and bad carbon acid gas but that there had been no reason for far-reaching measures. Within the following year Coca-Cola had to deal with consumers' continued skepticism. Two good things came out of the dioxin and Coca-Cola crises: more efficient monitoring of the entire food chain and higher sensitivity on the part of the public, the institutions, and producers with regard to matters of food safety and quality.

The Vlaams centrum voor agro- en visserijmarketing (VLAM, the Flemish center for agricultural and fishery marketing) provides a good example of the manifold initiatives that emerged after the 1999 dioxin affair.[7] VLAM's first aim is the promotion of Flemish food in Belgium and abroad, and it is therefore clear that safe food is a main concern.[8] In early July 1999 VLAM started a campaign against the "fear of dioxin on your plate," aiming to restore consumer confidence in food. Since then, many projects emphasize the quality and rich taste of Flemish products, as well as reassuring consumers about the safety regulations for the entire food chain. "Tasty products from our land" is the catchphrase of VLAM's home page, which highlights the flavor of products by giving recipes, cooking hints, cooking demonstrations, favorite dishes and ingredients, and kitchen jargon.[9] VLAM's home page also contains a long list of links to bureaus that deal with food safety and quality. Flandria, for example, grants quality labels for fruit and vegetables, as Meesterlyck does for cured meats, Meritus for beef, or Integrale Kwaliteitszorg Melk (Integral Care for the Quality of Milk).[10] All of these bureaus stress aspects of sanitation, monitoring, and trust, emphasizing "transparent control," "a quality assurance scheme," or "quality and safety from the fodder trough to your plate." Hoeveproducten.be (Farmers' products) takes this to an extreme, listing 10 reasons to buy directly from the farmer: the first reason is trust (followed by the farmer's story, authenticity, openness, quality, freshness, etc.).[11] Through direct contact, one learns to know the farmer better, which establishes a bond of trust, which echoes the complete loss of trust in 1999. Equally, streekproduct.be (Regional products) wishes to promote local, honest, quality, tasty, and safe food products. This bureau delivers labels, stating that "Only with a label is one certain about the origin." Hence, the bureau has three labels for products, referring to the geographical origin, the guaranteed traditional special product, and the original name of the product.[12] Finally, food safety is a great concern of the Nutritional Information Centre (NICE) that was established in 1992 but has expanded widely since the 1999 dioxin crisis, offering three divisions: information for the professional, the general public, and the teacher/researcher.[13]

Nowadays, Belgian producers, traders, and official authorities use a meticulous inspection system for the entire food chain, and everything possible is done to maintain trust. Consumers' organizations, like Test-Aankoop (Test-Purchase) or Gezondheid.be (Health.be), closely watch the official bureaus, like the Federal Agency for the Safety of the Food Chain. They, too, analyze food. For example, in 2007, analyses by Test-Aankoop of 684 foodstuffs showed that about 270 products were not entirely satisfactory and that some contained pesticides (vegetables), benzene (soda drinks), or sulfur (red wine). These findings are largely presented in Belgian newspapers[14] but do not cause panic. On the contrary, they add to the general sentiment of alertness.

Finally, big retailers have learned from the food crises. When it comes to safe food, 49 percent of Belgians trust farmers (direct purchases at farms), 39 percent trust supermarkets, only 29 percent rely on vendors at markets and a mere 22 percent trust corner shop.[15] These figures are low, and particularly supermarkets aim at increasing the bond of trust between them and shoppers (shoppers' trust in supermarkets in neighboring countries is much higher). Through leaflets and Web sites, supermarkets provide lots of information about their efforts to secure safe food: continuous monitoring of the whole food chain, full information via labels, announcement of the origin of the food, customers' help desk, and so on. The German-based ALDI chain, for example, explains its principle ("top quality and low price") by stressing the nonstop monitoring and effort for quality "that is confirmed through multiple, independent analyses." Delhaize stresses the fact that it knows all its suppliers. Some have expanded the quantity of organic foods offered for sale. Others, as, for example, Colruyt, opened special organic stores, and today there are four Bio-Planet stores, where no fewer than 7,000 organic (food and nonfood) products are on sale, all of which are certified to meet the highest standards and are monitored by Colruyt and official bodies. This responds to the public's interest in organic food, which emerged marginally in the early 1970s to gain success in the 1990s. Today, 60 percent of the Belgians regularly buy organic food (particularly young and more highly educated people). Only a minority of 7 percent, however, always purchases organic food, especially vegetables, fruit, and eggs.

Before the 1999 dioxin episode Belgium had a well-established food inspection system. There have been regular periods of food scares due to shortages that led to rising prices, growing inequality, hunger for some (or many, depending on the extent of scarcity), and increasing mortality. Regularly, such crises went along with various types of food fraud, such as adding crushed field beans or inedible materials, such as sand, to wheat or rye flour, or mixing plain water with milk (and chalk, to get rid of the bluish aspect of watered-down milk). Such fraud was mostly harmless in terms of health (but was of course punished for dishonest trade). Often, "bad" food was simply food past its prime that dishonest traders wished to camouflage by adding spices or natural colorants. With the arrival of more sophisticated additives in the nineteenth century, like chemical colorants or preservers, things became more complicated. By then, food fraud not only appeared to be deceitful, but it also could seriously damage health and even cause death. Regularly, newspapers reported about sudden food problems, mostly with bread, which was the main food for most Belgians. Pharmacists and physicians performed analyses of flour, bread,

Poids et santé (weight and health), two new features of interwar Belgium, particularly relating to middle and upper classes. From *Le Patriote Illustré*, January 19, 1930, p. 96. Courtesy of the author.

beer, water, wine, and other foodstuffs. Some of these scientists were fully trusted, but others were not, and they had a reputation for being crude moneymakers.

In order to cope with the increasingly sophisticated frauds and to provide official and objective advice about food safety, the Brussels administration set up a municipal chemical laboratory in 1856, which was the first of this type in Europe. It still exists today. Right from the start it performed well, analyzing a growing number of foods and employing an increasing number of people. Initially, primarily bread and flour were analyzed, but by the turn of the century much more diverse and even luxury foods were examined, thus showing the shift in food consumption in the second half of the century. The proportion of adulterated samples fluctuated strongly, with about 10 percent in the 1870s and 1910s but 25 percent in the 1880s (a period when agriculture had troubles, and profits of producers and traders fell). In the twentieth century, fraudulent food fell below 10 percent of analyzed samples. Much of the activity of the Brussels municipal laboratory aimed at reassuring the public. As in 1999, the launching of measures and the outcome of tests were announced in the press and on posters throughout the city. Also, the public was invited to collaborate actively with the laboratory's work: a suspect can of sardines, wine with a bizarre color or smell, and dubious butter were to be brought to the laboratory where a free test was performed. The mayor personally sent a letter with the result of the analysis to the citizen, as well as a copy to the press, showing the adequate functioning of the laboratory. All was oriented toward maintaining trust. Many European cities took the Brussels laboratory as a model.

Alongside local initiatives, national legislation existed too. In 1830 Belgium adopted older (French and Dutch) laws with regard to fraud, with the stress on the economic context. In 1890 an entirely new law was passed, which led to the establishment of a national bureau of food inspection and the setting up of state-run laboratories. Emphasis shifted to the monitoring of food quality and safety. More refined legislation appeared in the twentieth century, and laboratories were given more means and personnel. In 1999, however, the dioxin catastrophe was so crushing that the many local, regional, and national initiatives appeared to be inadequate. Paradoxically, in 1999 health was hardly threatened, whereas food impurities and food frauds in the nineteenth century (and before) surely caused serious health trouble.

WEIGHT AND OBESITY

In earlier times, lack and imbalance of food caused the biggest health problems, but today the abundance of food leads to health problems. Just like in other European countries, public authorities, doctors' associations, nutritionists, and consumers' organizations in Belgium tackle health problems related to the abundance of food. Belgians' weight has become a public problem. Today, 52.5 percent of the Belgians are considered to have "normal" weight according to the body mass index (BMI, or the relation between weight and height of a person). Belgians score on par with the Danes (55%) and the Italians (54%) but better than the Czechs (46%) and much better than Americans (35%) or the British (33%).

"Normal" refers to a BMI between 18.5 and 25; below 18.5 is seen as undernourished, 25 to 30 qualifies as overweight, and 30 to 40 is obese. Since the 1980s all over the world the number of obese people has tended to increase rapidly, in Third World countries as well as in the West. In 1997, 9 percent of Belgian adults were obese, but in 2007, the proportion reached 12.7 percent. With regard to surrounding countries, Belgium is doing well compared to Germany (19% of Germans are considered to be obese) and the United Kingdom (24%) but poorly compared to France (11%), the Netherlands (10%), and Italy (9%). Within the past 10 years, the increase in the number of obese adults in Belgium (+4%) is moderate compared with the United Kingdom (+13%) and the United States (+16%), but it is more than the Italian, French, and Dutch increase.[16] Puzzlingly, in Belgium, more women than men are obese, which differs from the situation in most other European countries.

The growing obesity in the past decade worries nutritionists, doctors, and health workers in Belgium, as in other countries. This is echoed in the news media. "Why Are We Too Fat?," "One Adult out of Two Copes with Being Overweight," or "World Hunger Diminishes, but Gluttony Expands" are some of the headlines of recent news articles in Belgium. Often, these present the average Belgian as an irresponsible, nonstop eater of unhealthy food who exercises far too little, has a poor social life, barely has a hobby, takes too much time for cooking and eating, drinks too much alcohol, smokes a lot, watches too much television, and risks dying from cardiovascular diseases, stroke, or cancer. Altering this image, and particularly the image of obese people, is one of the reasons of existence of the Association belge des patients obèses (Belgian Association of Obese Patients) that, among other things, aims to establish obesity as a medical condition. This would allow obese people to tap into the medical insurance system. This association launched the First National Day Against Obesity in May 2008.

In 2004 the Scientific Institute of Public Health, an official bureau of the Ministry of Health, conducted a national survey in Belgium to understand the size of the problem. It led to the establishment of a National Food and Health Plan, 2005–2010.[17] The plan starts off with the finding that the average life expectancy in Belgium is increasing and reaches 75.9 years for men and 81.7 years for women (in 2003). However, this favorable trend is put under heavy pressure by the fact that the way of life has greatly changed: the use of the car, comfortable homes, television, central heating, declining working time, and so on have made Belgians lazy, or, at least, put them into poor physical condition. In particular, the diet has totally changed, with the large supply of relatively cheap food and drinks that contain too much fat and sugar. The combination of an easygoing life with a rich diet has led to the fact that "obesity has become one of the major health problems in Europe," as the report amply stresses.

In Belgium, women pose a bigger problem than men with regard to weight: more women than men are obese. This, however, only appears after the age of 44 years. Moreover, there are regional differences between Flanders and Wallonia, with Walloon men being much more obese than Flemish men (throughout all age groups). Finally, social differences characterize the obesity pattern in Belgium: the lower the income and the level of education, the higher the risk for obesity. This may explain the difference between Flanders and Wallonia, since incomes in Wallonia are generally lower than in Flanders. An explanation why Belgian women over 44 years of age are generally heavier than their sisters in most European countries is yet to be found.

The study reveals many aspects of self-perceptions of Belgians with regard to food and health. It appears that only a small minority of men and women are aware that being overweight may cause cardiovascular problems. They are somewhat better informed about risks related to hypertension and in general well aware of the high cholesterol level that may come with being overweight. When asked about their self-image, men and women tend to underestimate their weight. Sixty percent of women see themselves at a normal weight, but only 50 percent of men have this self-image. Elderly people tend to underestimate their weight more than younger people. When interviewed about their concern with their body weight, men seem to be much less concerned than women: 45 percent are indifferent about it (against 33 percent of the women). Inversely, more women than men actually wish to lose weight (30 and 20 percent, respectively).

Belgians have many ways of trying to losing weight. Slimming products (such as laxatives) are popular among 40 percent of men and 33 percent of women, but starting exercise, or simply more physical efforts like using the stairs instead of the elevator, is hardly considered (only 3 percent of men and 7 percent of women). A minority of Belgians (about 10 percent) calls on a doctor for help with losing weight. Stomach reduction has gained popularity. Obesity surgery (stomach reducing, stomach ring) increased by 75 percent in Belgium between 2001 and 2007, and particularly women choose it (80 percent of the total number). Most of them are happy with the result: while the average BMI reaches 40 prior to the surgery, it attains 27 points after the treatment. Doctors and patients see this as a genuine success. If about one-third of the patients complain about side effects (high blood pressure, diabetes) within the first months after surgery, most of the grievances disappear after a year.

The most popular way of losing weight is dieting. During the 2004 survey, 17 percent of the interviewees were trying to lose weight, with slightly more women than men and definitely more elderly people than youngsters. This proportion includes people who diet for purely health reasons (like diabetes patients, for example). Dieting takes many forms: eating less in general, eating less sweet and/or fat food, eating more fruit and vegetables, skipping meals, starting with diet products, and/or following, strictly or loosely, the latest fad in dieting, whether this be Montignac or Atkins. In 2000, Koen Crucke, a popular Flemish tenor, actor, and television figure, published *33 kilo later*, where he reported on his struggle with being overweight. He lost more than 66 pounds without having to forgo his daily glass of champagne and other delicacies. Naturally, many Belgians wished to find out how Crucke did this: the book sold 150,000 copies and went through 22 editions.

Dieting is big business, to which manifold magazines, books, Internet sites, professional advisors, and charlatans testify. On the Internet numerous highly specialized, well-elaborated, and "guaranteed" diets can be found: the fruit diet, the bread diet, the one with soup, the Mayo-diet, the Ahorn diet, the Canada diet, the Heller diet, the Scarsdale diet, the Moerman diet, the blood-type diet. Some Internet sites offer adequate information on these (and other) diets, like Gezondheid.be, which supplies the visitor with information on all health matters and particularly on food, being overweight, and dieting. There are, however, countless Internet dieting sites of various kinds, among which are dubious ones. Almost all of them are linked to commercial activities. *Dieetlijn*, for example, is part of the magazine *Goed gevoel* (Good feeling), promoting itself as the "Most Interactive Online Dieting Program of Flanders." It offers the possibility to calculate one's BMI and gives dieting advice, but it also supplies the guidance of experts for a fee of 75 euros per year. *Gezond Vermageren* (Losing weight in a healthy way) tempts the visitor with "Searching for *the* Diet that Does Work?" and proposes the book *The Advanced Dieting System* for only 27 euros. *Afslanken* (Slimming) sells pills that will surely work "Without Dieting, Hunger, Heavy Excercise or that Horrible Yo-Yo Effect." One little bottle costs 59.5 euros.[18] Dieting is really big business.

Fricandeau of Veal with Parsley Sauce, a Dish for Those on a Diet

3 slices of stale wheat bread

1/2 cup fresh parsley

3 cloves garlic

4 tablespoons olive oil

salt and pepper

2 pounds veal fricandeau (larded veal roasted and glazed in its own juice)

1 pound asparagus

Cut off the crust of the loaves, and crumble the bread into a pot; wash, dry, and chop the parsley; add the chopped parsley, garlic, and two teaspoons of the olive oil to the bread. Mix this well, and add salt and pepper. Heat the oven to 400°F (200°C). Make one or two deep incisions in the veal, and fill with the bread mixture (press it well). Smear the veal with the remaining oil. Prepare the asparagus (wash gently and cut off the hard ends), put them into a casserole dish, and add some water. On top of this, put the veal. Put the casserole in the oven for about 40 minutes (until the meat is brownish). Serve with bread or potatoes.

Public authorities are very much aware of the complexity of problems associated with being overweight, especially the awkward reactions of the public (indifference, rejection, or offense). This is why the National Plan suggests several initiatives. The main recommendation is quite simple: there should be a good balance between food intake and physical effort. Miners and athletes may consume up to 7,000 calories per day, and they will not become heavy. So, for most Belgians, it suffices to exercise somewhat more, and a great deal of the problem with being overweight would

Blijf fit, eet gezond (Stay fit, eat healthy): An advertisement for a margarine, emphasizing the high vitamin content. From *Het Rijk der Vrouw*, September 22, 1976, pp. 38–39. Courtesy of the author.

6me Année   AVRIL 1932   Nº 57

La Cuisine

Ah, les bonnes frites
à l'Huile Impériale!

PRIX : Fr. 1.25   Revue Mensuelle
de la Parfaite Maîtresse de Maison

"Ah, the tasty *frites* made with Impérial oil" appeared
on the April 1932 cover of *La Cuisine* ("the monthly
for the perfect housewife") as a reaction to the emerging awareness of high fat content of *frites* prepared
with lard. Courtesy of the author.

problems leading to being overweight. For example, hotel and cooking
schools should include notions of healthy food in their program (much
more so than has been done so far). Finally, and perhaps crucially, full
attention should be devoted to "vulnerable" groups, in particular, to infants, children, and elderly people. Particularly children cause great concern. Recently, they show an alarming increase in average weight, which
in many cases will lead to being overweight as an adult. The National

disappear. Recommendations are modest:
utes suffices. Ten years ago, food recommei
toward physical activity. Recently, fast-fo
shift toward a balance between eating and a
for example, promotes its business by makin
sportswoman who won several golden meda
under the heading, "It's what I eat and wha
matters, she says, implying, of course, that h
shakes do no harm as long as there is sufficien

The National Plan, however, realizes that it
ply suggest more physical activity; therefore, it l
that aimed at various domains of Belgian socie
the ideal diet that is presented in the food pyr
base (1 1/2 quarts of liquids, preferably water), a :
of grain products and substitutes (2/3 lb. potatoes,
brown bread), fruit and vegetables (each about 2/
dairy products (2.8 ounces) and meat and fish (3.
a small miscellaneous "group" of not strictly nece
cookies, alcohol, chocolate, or pastry. A pyramid sh
food consumption would, however, be an odd, in
much of the wrong food (meat, grain products, alc
little of the good food (vegetables, fruit, milk, water

Hoping not to upset overweight people, the plan
mendations to achieve the ideal of the food pyramid.
should be appropriately informed ("in clear language
of the nutritional inquiry. Hence, in early 2005, the
health organized a press conference to announce the
being overweight and obesity, stressing the results of t
vealing the new strategy. Not only scientists were to be
committee but also representatives of the food industi
general information is of course important, it is even
to create a positive attitude toward habits of good eati
Thus, stress is put on eating breakfast regularly, drinkin
and milk, and eating fruit but limiting candy, breakfast (
or sodas. An "advertising code" was launched in May 20(
agreement between producers, retailers, consumers' ass
the government to limit advertisements that encourage n
special agency, Flanders' Food, was set up to support this
of the plan; it evolved into a specialized, scientific bureau
information about safe food.[19] Next, and closely connected
ous point, all people involved in the food system should be

Plan, therefore, suggests a campaign to increase the breastfeeding of babies, which is an excellent way to maintain an infant's ideal weight. Most attention, however, is focused on children between 6 and 14 years. Regular breakfasts, eating with parents (or under guidance), having sufficient fruit and vegetables, and limiting candy, potato chips, and soft drinks are the recommendations.

ORIGIN OF THE SLIM FIGURE

The first warnings about obesity, fatty diets, and unhealthy foods appeared in the 1920s. Before then, obesity had not been an issue. Around 1900, medical studies revealed that one-third of adult male workers with full-time jobs had sufficient food, whereas about one-third lacked this, and another third had more than enough to eat. Compared with the heavy workload of most workers in those days, caloric intake was hardly adequate, even for workers with a daily intake of 5,000 calories or more. Yet, manuals used in schools suggest the limitation of food excess, with the focus on balancing the household budget, not health or body shape.

Frites with mayonnaise today. Courtesy of Andrea Carita.

Still, these schoolbooks stress the need of plentiful food. Louisa Mathieu, for example, wrote in 1906 that healthy food is characterized by good quality (by which she meant fresh and unadulterated food), variety (both with regard to ingredients and preparation), digestibility (regular eating), and satisfactory quantity. She preferred abundant, healthy, and solid food, "because it is through food that man maintains and augments his strength, and he will thus be able to work and produce more, and have higher wages."[20] This reflects mid-nineteenth century concerns of European medical doctors, entrepreneurs, and public administrators, who all knew about the relationship between sufficient and varied food (especially meat) and work performance. Of course, it also refers to times when too little food was a bigger problem than too much food. Cauderlier and De Gouy, who had published the thriving Belgian cookbooks of the late nineteenth century, meant for a bourgeois public, make no mention of dieting. They advise to have sufficient food in order to permit people "with a good appetite" to eat as much as they wish.

In the early 1920s, medical reports observed moderate amelioration of the workers' average diet compared to the 1900s, because of the increase in meat consumption. However, almost half of the adult male workers had insufficient caloric intake, which was more than in pre-1914 inquiries. This changed radically by the end of the decade, when an economic boom led to wage increases and full employment. Qualitative and further quantitative expansions appeared, such as more fresh and cured meats, canned fish, dairy products, chocolate, pastries, and other processed foods.

In the late 1920s, a new discourse emerged in women's magazines, consumers' journals, and manuals for schools: for the first time the danger of too much food was mentioned. In 1928, for example, one cookbook bluntly stated that abundant food does not nourish man, but it kills him![21] In 1934 La Cuisine et la Femme (The kitchen and the woman) (the "monthly of the perfect housewife") paid attention to the problem of being overweight, writing that it had no intention to plead for vegetarianism but that, in general, Belgians ate too much meat and too few vegetables, despite the fact that vegetables were both healthy and tasty. Vegetables should be prepared well, though, which meant that they must not be overcooked or drowned in salt. Still, in the same period, this magazine advised its readers to "satisfy your husband's gluttony" for the sake of harmony within the family and the influence that cooking gives to women. La Famille Prévoyante (The Prepared Family, the monthly of the socialist insurance fund), stressed the fact that industrial workers were wary of vegetables because they preferred their customary diet. This consisted of steak, beef stew (carbonnades à la flamande), and frites (fries) at noon, and bread (with jam) and coffee (with sugar) in the morning and the evening. The journal stressed the need for educating the worker and his wife, not by asking her to refine her cooking ("It is, unfortunately, hardly the time to play bourgeois games," which testifies to the severe economic crisis of the 1930s), but by encouraging her to prepare cheap, tasty, and healthy food. By the end of the 1930s, many cookbooks and household books suggested a reduction in the consumption of meat, cheese, and eggs, in order to stop the "growing army of sufferers from arthritis and vascular hardening." Women's magazines, aiming at a bourgeois public, started to pay attention to the slim figure, which was a new concept about the modern, active, and fashionable housewife. In 1935, thus, *La Cuisine et la Femme* recommended, "Take that cup of tea around 5 P.M., but please, if you want to maintain your slim line or simply your good health, ladies, leave the pastries, chocolates and cookies untouched."[22]

Within two decades, the average Belgian evolved from an eater who had hardly enough food into someone who needed to worry about too much food. This Belgian not only knew about health implications of too much food, but he or particularly she was increasingly concerned about the ideal of the slim body. The latter started among women in bourgeois circles but little by little spread throughout all social layers. Since then, except for the sinister war years in the 1940s, many Belgians never stopped worrying about too much sugar, meat, cream, pastry, sweets, soft drinks, potato chips, and the like. Calories started to rule the lives of thousands of people.

In the 1950s medical authorities started to worry as well. They intensively conducted studies to learn about the actual food intake of factory workers, athletes, schoolchildren, or elderly people. These investigations led to identical results: too much meat, charcuterie, eggs, *frites*, butter, precooked dishes, pastries, white bread, and beer or soft drinks and too little vegetables, potatoes, margarine, fruits, skim milk, young cheese, or dark bread. A broader conclusion was to call on public authorities to finance research, start a national information campaign, set up an expert bureau, and enlist nutritionists in cafeterias of schools, offices, and factories. Gradually, all this was achieved from the 1960s onward, which was a decade later than in most surrounding countries. Workers' food conservatism was often criticized, although it was explained that food provides energy that gives strength and, consequently, a good wage. Having enough food, thus, guaranteed an income, even if the job required less energy. Moreover, some people do not consider being overweight as a problem, viewing the surplus as a reservoir that may help them through future misfortunes like job loss, rising food prices, or serious illness. To some people, thus, overeating provides security.

The workers' wives and daughters, however, unreservedly discovered the slimming and dieting. In 1960, *Bij de Haard* (the women farmers' monthly magazine) paid attention to this trend: in the West, people no longer were hungry but could eat whatever they liked, hence the overeating and the new trend toward dieting. *Bij de Haard* advised readers to see a doctor before starting a diet and, especially, not to think too readily that one is too heavy. But, of course, how to resist the image of the slender woman, as she appeared in movies, advertisements, and television? Since the 1960s, women's magazines and cookbooks have paradoxically combined an interest in gourmet cooking with dieting advice. If Belgian cookbooks of the 1950s and early 1960s paid attention to healthy food by publishing the *Voedingsmiddelentabel* (the table of nutritional values) and detailed information on the digestive system, cookery books of the late 1960s were much more practical, with mixed interest in both health and body shape.

Ons kookboek, for example, started in the early 1960s by publishing health and body weight recommendations that appeared at the very beginning of the book.[23] The "slice of five" was presented, which contained five food categories (milk; vegetables and fruit; meat, cheese, fish, and eggs; butter and margarine; and bread); it sufficed to eat one food of each category daily to have a healthy diet. In the 1970s, the four-leaf clover and the meal disc nutritional guides were introduced, which resembled very much the slice of five. In those days, large posters with edifying images of what to eat appeared in many school and factory cafeterias. In the 1980s, *Ons kookboek* adopted the food triangle (or food pyramid), which represented a definite break with previous recommendations: a clear hierarchy of foods was implied, with a broad base (water) and a tiny top (gratuitous food). *Ons kookboek* echoed the findings and recommendations of public health bureaus, such as the Scientific Institute of Public Health. Following the conclusions of the 2004 national diet investigation, this cookbook will most likely introduce the active food triangle in its coming edition, which stresses the need for physical movement.

Consumer movements appeared with the working-class cooperatives of the late nineteenth century and gained influence in the 1920s, when women organized within farmers' associations, political movements (*mutualités*, or social security funds), and leagues for the protection of the family. They all aimed at having safe food and fair trade but neglected the consequences of too much food. An independent organization appeared in 1957, Test-Aankoop (Test-Purchase), which compared products.[24] Copying American and British examples, this organization published a magazine in which products' strong and weak points were presented, ending with a best-buy recommendation that often led (and still leads) to reactions by producers, traders, and the public. Test-Aankoop wishes to inform, defend, and represent the consumer, and it has gained a lot of renown since the 1950s. The organization is represented in the Raad voor het verbruik (Council of Consumption), the official bureau that was set up in 1964 to advise the government and the parliament in matters of consumption (fair advertising, for example). Test-Aankoop pays a lot of attention to food. In the 1960s, the quality, taste, and price of mayonnaise, frozen peas, or canned tuna fish were compared; in the 2000s foods, snacks, and eating places are still compared, but information is also provided about food safety, labels (including their shortcomings and mysteries), new products and trends, dieting medications (and their dangers), kitchen hygiene, losing weight, light products, dieting advice in books and magazines, and so on. Alongside Test-Aankoop, many more consumers' organizations deal with food, overweight issues, dieting, and food security, among which is the Centre de recherche et d'information des organisations de consommateurs (the Center of Research and Information of the Consumers' Organizations) that was established in 1976 and aims to coordinate and advise all Belgian consumers' associations.[25]

Since World War II, a drastic change has occurred with regard to food security: the peril no longer lies in shortage but rather in abundance of food. Along came problems of overweight and obesity, immense interest in health and dieting, and multiple recommendations from nutritionists, experts, and health workers. The public authority's influence on what Belgians eat has largely increased in terms of safety monitoring, information, and recommendations. Belgians nowadays eat more safely than ever before, and, above all, they are much more informed about the tiniest food risk, food safety procedures in supermarkets, organic foods in cafeterias, and dieting schemes. Yet, despite the greater sensitivity regarding health and safety of food, recent crises have shown the very feeble trust most people have in the food chain. For some, eating copiously provides the badly needed security in today's uncertain times.

NOTES

1. "Food Scare Is Leaving Tables Bare in Belgium," *New York Times*, June 6, 1999.

2. "Waanzin!" [Madness!], *De Standaard*, June 4, 1999.

3. For example, "Voters React to Dioxin Scandal: Belgium's Leaders Rebuked at Polls," *International Herald Tribune*, June 14, 1999.

4. This agency took off in January 2000. For its mission, see The Food Agency, http://www.afsca.be/home/home/home_en.asp (accessed March 3, 2008). An adequate survey of its history and functioning is G. Houins, *Belgian Approach of the Safety of the Food Chain* (January 2007), to be downloaded at the English pages of the Agency's Web site, http://www.favv-afsca.fgov.be/home/home/home_en.asp. An excellent portal for health matters related to food is provided at the Federal Health, Food Chain Safety, and Environment Web site, https://portal.health.fgov.be (see "Food Safety") (accessed August 4, 2008).

5. The European regulations with regard to food safety can be found on the Web page "Food Safety from the Farm to the Fork," http://ec.europa.eu/food/index_en.htm (accessed August 4, 2008).

6. In 2008 a Flemish newspaper recalled the episode of the June 1999 elections, concluding that the dioxin crisis had one but important positive effect, that is, the launching of the Federal Agency for the Safety of the Food Chain (*Het Nieuwsblad*, January 21, 2008), 11.

7. The Walloon equivalent is the Agence Wallonne pour la promotion d'une agriculture de qualité (The Walloon agency for promoting a qualitative agriculture) (http://apaqw.horus.be/code/default.asp), offering quite similar services to VLAM.

8. VLAM is commissioned by the Flemish government and the "business community," providing information, assisting producers and traders, and delivering labels; see http://www.vlam.be/index_en.phtml.

9. Lekker van bij ons (Tasty food from our region), http://www.lekkervanbijons.be (accessed March 6, 2008).

10. Flandria, http://www.flandria.vlam.be/pro/index_en.phtml; Meesterlyck (Masterly), http://www.meesterlyck.be; Meritus, http://www.meritus.be; Integrale Kwaliteitszorg Melk (Integral Care for the Quality of Milk), http://www.ikm.be/home_en.phtml (all accessed March 6, 2008).

11. Hoeveproducten (Farmers products), http://www.hoeveproducten.be (accessed March 6, 2008).

12. Streekproducten (Regional products), http://www.streekproducten.be (accessed March 5, 2008).

13. Nutritional Information Centre, http://www.nice-info.be (accessed March 6, 2008), with a full English version.

14. For example, "Drie producten per dag uit de rekken gehaald" [Three products per day are removed from the shelves], *De Standaard*, January 26, 2008, 12.

15. *Consumers in Europe: Facts and Figures* (Luxemburg: European Community, 2001), 64.

16. Global Database on Body Mass Index (by the World Health Organization), http://www.who.int/bmi/index.jsp (accessed February 20, 2008).

17. *De Belgische voedselconsumptiepeiling 2004* (Brussels: Wetenschappelijk Instituut Volksgezondheid, 2006). See also Epidemiology Unit (Scientific Institute of Public Health), http://www.iph.fgov.be/epidemio/.

18. Vermageren (Losing weight), http://www.vermageren.com; Dieetlijn (Dieting Line), http://dieetlijn.goedgevoel.be; Afslanken (Slimming), http://www.afslanken.com (all accessed March 8, 2008).

19. Flanders' Food, ("The Competitive and Innovative Pool of the Flemish Agribusiness"), http://www.flandersfood.com (accessed March 8, 2008).

20. Louisa Mathieu, *Notions d'économie domestique pour les écoles normales d'institutrices* (Verviers: A. Hermann, 1906), 98–99.

21. P. Mertens and M. De Beuscher, *Huishoudkunde. Voedingsleer* (Antwerp: De Bièvre, 1928), 264.

22. J. Etienne, "Restons jeunes. Que faut-il manger?" [Let's stay young. What do we eat?], *La cuisine et la femme*, April 1935, 24.

23. Yves Segers, "Food Recommendations, Tradition and Change in a Flemish Cookbook: Ons Kookboek, 1920–2000," *Appetite* 45.1 (2005): 5.

24. Test-Aankoop/Test-Achat (Test-Purchase) http://www.test-achat.be (accessed March 21, 2008).

25. Onderzoeks- en informatiecentrum van de verbruiksorganisaties / Centre de recherche et d'information des organisations de consommateurs (the Center of Research and Information of the Consumers' Organizations) http://www.oivo.be (accessed March 23, 2008).

Glossary

beenhouwer/boucher Butcher. Sells meat, charcuterie, and often sandwiches.

blinde vinken/oiseau sans tête Ground meat wrapped in a slice of veal or beef.

boterham met plattekaas Slice of bread with white cheese, radish, and herbs.

boterham/tartine Slice of bread with butter (or margarine), cut in two, and put one on top of the other.

bouquet-garni Bundle of herbs (thyme, bay leaf, and parsley) to be put in soup or broth to add flavor.

carnaval/karnaval Mardi Gras.

cervela(a)t Dry sausage of pork, beef, and flour; early form of fast food.

chapelure Dried and ground (stale) bread; breadcrumbs.

charcuterie/fijne vleeswaren Cured meats made of beef and especially pork (e.g., ham, sausages, pâtés, salamis).

choesels Stew of pancreas of veal, kidneys, tail, and other organ meats.

confitures Jam of (mostly) fruit; sometimes made of vegetables.

dame blanche Vanilla ice cream topped with hot chocolate and whipped cream.

estaminet Café or pub.

filet américain/américain préparé   Steak tartare (raw ground meat with herbs and egg).

filter/café-filtre   Plastic container filled with ground coffee for one cup; it makes a somewhat stronger coffee.

friet/frites   Short for *pommes frites,* "French fries."

gaufres liègeoises/Luikse wafels   Soft waffles from Liège, served with coarse sugar.

gehakt/haché   Ground meat (pork, veal, or beef), slightly seasoned.

gewonnen brood (wentelteefjes)/pain perdu   "Gained" (or recuperated) bread: slices of day-old bread, soaked in milk and beaten egg, fried in butter.

gratin   Cheese on top of a dish, put in the oven to melt.

hopscheuten   Hop shoots, a delicacy that may replace truffles. To be eaten in May.

jenever/genièvre   Gin; liquor made of grain and flavored with juniper berries.

kalfskop/tête de veau   Meat of boiled calf's head, with spices (sometimes truffles).

kermis/kermesse   Fancy fair, carnival.

mosselen/moules   Mussels, often served with fries.

pannekoek/crèpe   Pancake or crepe.

pékèt   *Genièvre* from the Liège region.

peperkoek/pain d'épices   Gingerbread.

pistolet   Round, little bread made of wheat flour, crusty on the outside, eaten on Sunday mornings with butter or as fast food (with cheese, ham, or *américain*).

pommes frites   French fries.

praline   Small chocolate candy with various fillings.

rozijnenbrood (krentenbrood)/pain cramique   Bread made of white flour, milk, and raisins.

salade liègeoise   Mixed dish with lots of potatoes, beans, vinegar, and bacon.

sandwich   Little oval, very soft bread, made of wheat (for its use, see **pistolet**).

smoutebollen/beignets   Dough balls fried in fat or oil, served with sugar.

speculaas/spéculaus   Spiced, dark brown cookie; ginger bread cookie.

stoemp   Mashed potatoes with crushed vegetables; often served with bacon.

toast cannibale   Raw minced beef with capers, Worcestershire sauce, pickles, small onions, salt, and pepper, all on a toast.

tomaat met garnalen/tomate aux crevettes   Fresh tomato with North Sea shrimp, lettuce, and mayonnaise.

waterzooi   Consommé with bits of chicken or fish.

witloof/chicons   Belgian endives.

Resource Guide

WEB SITES

General

The Food Time Line (1999), http://www.foodtimeline.org. L. Olver's chrono-
logical collection of food products, dishes, recipes, links.
Medieval & Renaissance Food Homepage, http://www.pbm.com/~lindahl/food.
html. Primary sources, articles/publications, individual recipes, fourteenth–
eighteenth centuries.
Plant Trivia Time Line, http://www.huntington.org/BotanicalDiv/Timeline.
html. "World history from the viewpoint of a botanist," chronology of
food, with short bibliography.
The World on a Plate (1994), http://www.globalgourmet.com/destinations/. Very
general introduction to world cuisine.

Belgian Surveys, Recipes

Behive. An e-zine featuring Belgian culture. Foodhub, http://www.behive.be/
food/. Includes recipes, specials, and information on beer and restaurants.
Belgian Recipes, Fast and Easy Belgian Recipes (2004), http://www.belgian-
recipes.be/index.html. Translation of the quite popular Flemish Web site
Receptjes.be, maintained by M. Meeuwes, organized by type (starters,
lunch, dessert, soup, etc.), and with a collection of so-called traditional
recipes.
Belgium, Gourmet Food and Gastronomy (2006), http://www.belgium-tourism.net
/contenus/belgium__gourmet_food_and_gastronomy/en/64.html. By the Office de Promotion du Tourisme de Wallonie et de Bruxelles (Tourist Office

for Wallonia and Brussels); links to specialized sites about beer, gastronomy, specialties, and restaurants.

Belgium Cooking, http://www.archaeolink.com/belgium_cooking_anthropology_ of_.htm. Part of Cooking around the World—Anthropology of Food; a collection of Internet sites related to Belgium and its cuisine.

Belgourmet, http://belgourmet.com/keuken/belrec/rec24/html. Antwerp-based site, with a collection of links to Belgian recipes including rabbit, endives, waffles, mussels, and more.

La Bonne Cuisine: Toute la Gastronomie en ligne (in French), http://www.la bonnecuisine.be/. Regional cuisine, recipes, food "dossiers."

La Cuisine de Claudine (1996, in French), http://www.wallonie.com/cuisine/. Traditional and daily cooking in Wallonia, with recipes for desserts, special dishes, and pastries.

Epicurien (2004, in French), http://www.epicurien.be/default.asp. Belgian recipes, information about beer; newsletters, and readers' comments.

Food (2005), http://209.213.221.5/food.htm. Official site of the Belgian Tourist Office in the Americas; information about products and ingredients, food events, gourmet tours, recipes, restaurants, and more.

Kookkroniek (2006, in Dutch), http://www.kookkroniek.be. Practical and easily usable search engine for recipes; glossary, cooking tips.

Receptjes.be (2004, in Dutch), http://www.receptjes.be/. "Belgian recipes," the original Dutch version of *Belgian Recipes* (2004).

Recipes4us: Belgium (1999), http://www.recipes4us.co.uk/Belgian%20Recipes. htm. Part of a more general Internet site; starters, appetizers, (classic) main courses, desserts; culinary information and some history.

Sally's Place. Ethnic Cuisine: Belgium, http://www.sallys-place.com/food/cuisi nes/belgium.htm. By L. Seibert Pappas; historical overview, personal experiences, recipes.

Topchef (in Dutch, stopped in 2008), http://www.topchef.be/index.php. Glossary, recipes, documentaries, home-cooking videos, business lunches.

Webchef (2007, in Dutch), http://www.webchef.be. 135,000 recipes from Belgium and Europe.

Eating Out

La Bonne Table (in French), http://www.labonnetable.be/. Restaurant guide and reviews, new restaurants.

Guide Henry Lemaire (2007, in French and Dutch), http://www.henry-lemaire. be/. E-version of the restaurant guide.

Op restaurant (in Dutch), http://www.oprestaurant.be. Monthly menus of about 30 Flemish restaurants, menus for special occasions.

Resto.be (in English, Dutch, and French), http://www.resto.be/ware/index.jsp. More than 16,000 restaurants on the Internet (August 2008); search by name, province, town, cuisine, or budget; top 10 per town; news and newsletters; recipes.

Restopages. The Internet Guide of Restaurants in Belgium (2005), http://www.
restopages.be/en/. Search by province and city, and style of eating.

Sensum. Restaurants with Style in Brussels, Flanders and Wallonia (2004),
http://www.sensum.be/en/. Restaurants from A to Z, restaurant of the
week, newsletter, Restoblog.

Products and Ingredients

Appellation d'origine protégée, http://www.apaqw.be/code/pages.asp?Page=2931.
Information on geographically protected butter of the Ardennes, cheese
from Herve, ham from the Ardennes, and pâté from the Gaume region.

Beer Lovers. Belgium for Beer Lovers (2005), http://www.visitbelgium.com/
beer.htm. Official site of the Belgian Tourist Office in the Americas,
with information about breweries, abbey beers, festivals, and types of
beer.

Belgian Beer Paradise, http://www.beerparadise.be, Web site of the association of
Belgian brewers, with information about beer styles, way of serving, qualities and characteristics, the Brewers' House in Brussels.

Belgian Fries. The 100% Belgo Web Site (1997), http://www.fries.be/v4/index.
cfm. Photos of fries shacks, jokes, and cartoons.

Belgian Fries. The Original Belgian Fries Web Site (1995), http://www.bel
gianfries.com/. History, images, recipes, fries, and art; fries shacks.

Brussels Sprouts (2000), http://www.uga.edu/vegetable/brusselsprouts.html.
Characteristics, history, harvesting, preservation.

Charcuterie (fine meats) (2002, in Dutch and French), http://www.slagers
vlaanderen.be/index.html. Recipes, fairs, health matters.

Choco-Story, http://www.choco-story.be/map/en_map.htm. Bruges-based museum
of chocolate, brief history, recipes, events, and more.

Endives, http://www.belgianendive.com. Commercial pages for promoting sales
of endives, with recipes, brief history.

Flemish regional products, http://www.streekproduct.be/producten/index.
phtml?start=9. Provides the list of "recognized" regional products (including, for example, Brussels endives, *Filet d'Anvers* (smoked ham from beef),
or *Mattentaarten* (little cheese cakes).

Fromage de Herve, http://www.fromagedeherve.com/aindex.html. With information on the history, the production process, the producers, and "cheese
events."

Mattentaart (2007), http://www.mattentaart.be. Little cheese cakes (history,
producers, recipes).

Research and Reference

FOST (2006), http://www.vub.ac.be/FOST. Site of the Social and Cultural Food
Studies at the Vrije Universiteit Brussel, with information about research,
bibliography, links, meetings.

Historical Culinary & Brewing Documents Online, http://www.thousandeggs. com/cookbooks.html#DUTCH Cindy Renfrow's pages, with Low Country cookbooks from the fifteenth to the eighteenth centuries.

Kookhistorie (2002), http://www.kookhistorie.com. By Marleen Willebrands; transcription of historical cookbooks from the Low Countries, 1500–1800, with medieval food glossary.

Online Bibliography on the History of Agriculture and Food (2006, in Dutch), http://www.hetvirtueleland.be/cat/index_cat.asp?ID=300030100. By the Centre for Agricultural History, which presents stories, images, tools, and links related to Flemish agricultural history.

Organizations and Offices

Academy of Regional Gastronomy, http://www.asg.be/engels/frameset_engels. htm. "To promote the study of regional gastronomy," with information about events, publications, online bibliography.

Biosafety Server (2005), http://www.biosecurite.be/HomePage.html. Semiofficial board; all about food safety in Belgium.

Eurotoques.be, http://www.eurotoques-belgique.be/en/accueil. Association of Belgian chefs; information about events, members; news site.

The Food Agency, http://www.favv.be. Official board; all about food safety: events, news, publications, colloquia, general information to the public.

Gastronomica.be, http://www.gastronomica.be. Museum of gastronomy, library with online catalog.

Maîtres cuisiniers de Belgique (in Dutch and French), http://www.maitres cuisiniers.be. Association of Belgian chefs started in 1980; list of members, news.

Nutria—The Belgian Food Consumption Survey (2004), http://www.iph.fgov. be/nutria/. By the Scientific Institute of Public Health, Unit of Epidemiology; information about health, lifestyle, foods, food safety, links, and interactive search.

Office des produits wallons (in French), http://www.welcomonline.be/produits. wallons/INDEX.HTM. Commercial Web site to promote Walloon food products; addresses of producers with "typical" foods.

Portail Agriculture (2006, in French and Dutch), http://www.statbel.fgov.be/ port/agr_fr.asp. Official Web site of the Belgian government, with data on food production, trade, prices, agricultural employment, food safety, and so on.

Test—Achat [Alimentation] (2000, in French and Dutch), http://www.test-ach ats.be/alimentation/p15852.htm. Testing of wine and food, health and food safety, dossiers.

VLAM (2002), http://www.vlam.be/index_flash2.html. Flanders' board for promoting regional products.

Week van de smaak (2006, in French and Dutch), http://www.weekvandesmaak. be/. The Flemish Week of Taste, held in November; events, the yearly "city of taste" and "country of taste," photos.

MAGAZINES

Ambiance. De gastronomische referentie (in Dutch), http://www.ambiance.be. Succinct information about the magazine devoted to good dining and wining in Belgium (and the world).

Exquis Magazine (in Dutch and French), http://www.exquismagazine.be/.

Gastromania, le marché des saveurs (in French and Dutch), http://www.gastroma nia.be. E-guide for about 600 restaurants; lots of information about food.

Gastronomen.net (in Dutch), http://het.gastronomen.net/default.asp. Launched by *Knack–Magazine*; weekly menu, recipes, restaurant guide and restaurants reviews, drinks, healthy food, culinary glossary, cooking club, articles, books, and the interactive "Ask the Chef."

Libelle Lifestyle Magazine (in Dutch), http://www.libelle.be. Since 1945, *Libelle* publishes recipes, cooking tips, reports on foreign cuisines.

FILMS

Adoration (1986) by Olivier Smolders.
Bienvenue chez les Ch'tis (2008) by Danny Boom (Daniel Hamidou).
Bon appétit (2000) by Patrice Baudinet.
Camping Cosmos (1996) by Jan Buquoy.
Confituur (2005) by Lieven Debrouwer.
Décembre, mois des enfants (1957) by Henri Storck.
Fêtes de Belgique (1970–1971) by Henri Storck.
Les fleurs du malt (1999) by Dominique Loreau.
Les gestes du repas (1958) by Luc De Heusch.
Gourmandises (2004) by Roland Lethem.
Homard, champagne et ravioli (1992) by Jean-Philippe Luxen.
In Bruges (2008) by Martin McDonagh.
Jambon d'Ardenne (1977) by Benoît Lamy.
La kermesse héroïque (1935) by Jacques Feyder.
De keyzer van de smaak (2007) by Frank van Passel.
Les mille et une recettes du cuisinier amoureux (1995) by Nana Dzhordzhadze.
Muet comme une carpe (1987) by Boris Lehman.
Le mur (1998) by Alain Berliner.
Ober (2006) by Alex Van Warmerdam.
Plain Food (2007) by Isabelle Tollenaere.
Poulet—Poulet (2005) by Damien Chemin.
Les restaurants bruxellois (1919) by Hippolyte De Kempeneer.
Saute ma ville (1968) by Chantal Akerman.

Spa, richesse nationale (1953) by Paul Pichonnier.
Symphonie paysanne (1942–1944) by Henri Storck.
Tous à table (2001) by Ursula Meier.
TV-Dinner (2004) by Jan Swerts.
Vol-au-vent (1991) by Rudolf Mestdagh.

Selected Bibliography

GENERAL WORKS

Albala, Ken. *Food in Early Modern Europe*. Westport, CT: Greenwood Press, 2003.

Burnett, John, and Derek J. Oddy, eds. *The Origins and Development of Food Policies in Europe*. London: Leicester University Press, 1994.

De Vries, André. *Flanders: A Cultural History*. Oxford: Signal Books, 2007.

Freedman, Paul, ed. *Food, the History of Taste*. Berkeley: University of California Press, 2007.

Montanari, Massimo. *Food Is Culture*. New York: Columbia University Press, 2006.

Moulin, Léo. *L'Europe à table: Introduction à une psychosociologie des pratiques alimentaires*. Paris: Elsevier Séquoia, 1975.

Plouvier, Liliane. *L'Europe à table: Histoire et recettes*. 2 vols. Brussels: Editions Labor, 2003.

Scholliers, Peter, ed. *Food, Drink and Identity: Cooking, Eating and Drinking in Europe since the Middle Ages*. Oxford: Berg, 2001.

Teuteberg, Hans Jürgen, ed. *European Food History: A Research Review*. Leicester, England: Leicester University Press, 1992.

COOKBOOKS

Andrieu Delille, Jacques. *220 recettes de cuisine belge d'hier et d'aujourd'hui*. Paris: J. Grancher, 1981.

Blais, Denis, and André Plisnier. *Belgo Cookbook*. New York: Clarkson Potter, 2000.

Boon, Louis Paul. *Eten op zijn Vlaams*. Amsterdam: De Arbeiderspers, 1985.

Buren, Raymond. *Le goût de l'Ardenne: Cent et onze recettes traditionnelles*. Brussels: Vif éditions, 1995.

Center for Belgian Culture of Western Illinois. *Belgian Cook Book: Eet Smakelijk, Bon Appétit, Good Eating*. Moline, IL: The Center, 1978.

La cuisine au pays de Gambrinus: Les 300 meilleurs recettes de plats aromatisés à la bière. [Brussels?]: Chevalerie du Fourquet, 1955.

Cuisine d'aujourd'hui à la portée de tous. Brussels: Alliance agricole féminine, 1975.

De Dijn, Rosine. *Flanders: Treasure-House of the Occident*. Tielt, Belgium: Lannoo, 1993.

Demanet, Roger. *La bonne cuisine flamande*. Paris: Solar, 1990.

Denis, Marie. *La cuisine rustique en Flandre*. Forcalquier: R. Morel, 1970.

De Prins, Dirk. *La cuisine des Belges*. Paris: Editions du Chêne, 1995.

Gabriel, Jean-Pierre. *Wittamer, les heures et les jours: Les 100 meilleures recettes de l'atelier Wittamer*. Tielt, Belgium: Lannoo, 1994.

Gordon, Enid. *A Taste of the Belgian Provinces*. Brussels: Tuesday Group, 1982.

Gordon, Enid, and Midge Shirley. *The Belgian Cookbook*. London: Macdonald, 1983.

Halverhout, Heleen. *Dutch and Belgian Cooking: Traditional Dishes from the Low Countries*. New York: Garland, 1973.

Hamelecourt, Juliette Elkon. *A Belgian Cookbook*. New York: Farrar, Straus and Cudahy, 1958.

Hamelecourt, Juliette Elkon. *Trente cinq recettes de cuisine belge*. New York: Moretus Press, 1942.

Hazelton, Nika Standen. *The Belgian Cookbook*. New York: Atheneum, 1970.

Kreusch, Marcel, and Huguette van Dyck. *La cuisine de la Villa Lorraine et de l'Ecailler du Palais Royal*. Paris: Flammarion, 1984.

Loeber, Kris. *Apple Pie to Waterzooi*. Brussels: American Women's Club of Brussels, 1996.

Luck, Brian. *The Belgian Cook-Book*. Boston: IndyPublish.com, 2006.

Moulin, Léo, and Léon Léonard. *L'art de manger en Belgique: Trente portraits, trente maisons*. Antwerp: Esco Books, 1979.

Renard, Philippe, and Philippe Saenen. *La nouvelle cuisine Wallone*. Tournai, Belgium: Renaissance du Livre, 2002.

Van Waerebeek, Ruth, and Maria Robbins. *Everybody Eats Well in Belgium Cookbook*. New York: Workman, 1996.

Watts, Sarah Miles. *The Art of Belgian Cooking*. Garden City, NY: Doubleday, 1971.

"What's Cooking?" Special Issue, *The Low Countries* 13 (2005): 11–99.

Willems, Louis. *La cuisine belge de Louis Willems: Plus de 300 recettes et traditions culinaires du "plat pays" à déguster en famille ou entre amis*. Tournai, Belgium: Renaissance du Livre, 1999.

Wynants, Pierre, and Léon Léonard. *Comme Chez Soi: Creative Belgian Cuisine*. Brussels: Editions de La Truffe Noire, 1995.

CHAPTER 1

Arblaster, Paul. *A History of the Low Countries*. London: Palgrave, 2006.

Arnaud, Camille. *Une carte de restaurateur en MDXXXIII*. Trésors gastronomiques, no. 3. Brussels: Le Grenier du Collectionneur, 1988.

Barnes, Donna, and Peter G. Rose. *Matters of Taste: Food and Drink in Seventeenth-Century Dutch Art and Life*. Albany, NY: Syracuse University Press, 2002.

Beyers, Leen. "Creating Home: Food, Ethnicity and Gender among Italians in Belgium since 1946." *Food, Culture and Society* 11.1 (2008): 7–27.

Blom, J. C. H., and Emiel Lamberts. *History of the Low Countries*. New York: Berghahn Books, 1998.

Caluwé, Danielle. "The Use of Drinking Vessels in the Context of Dining and Communal Meals: Some Preliminary Thoughts Drawn on Archaeological Evidence from Medieval and Post-Medieval Periods in Flanders and the Duchy of Brabant." *Food & History* 4.1 (2006): 279–304.

Commission for Relief in Belgium. *Feeding 7,000,000 Destitute Belgians: The Remarkably Efficient Organization Created to Meet the Most Appalling Situation in the History of the World*. [Brussels]: CRB, 1915.

Cooremans, B. "The Roman Cemeteries of Tienen and Tongeren: Results from the Archaeobotanical Analysis of the Cremation Graves." *Vegetation History and Archaeology* 17 (2008): 3–13.

Deceulaer, Harald, and Frederik Verleysen. "Excessive Eating or Political Display? Guild Meals in the Southern Netherlands, Late 16th–Late 18th Centuries." *Food & History* 4.2 (2006): 165–185.

De Vlieger-De Wilde, Koen. *Adellijke levensstijl. Dienstpersoneel, consumptie en materiële leefwereld van Jan van Brouchoven en Livina de Beer, graaf en gravin van Bergeyck (ca. 1685–1740)*. Verhandelingen van de Koninklijke Vlaamse Academie van België voor Wetenschappen en Kunsten, no. 16. Brussels: Koninklijke Vlaamse Academie van België voor Wetenschappen en Kunsten, 2005.

De Vooght, Daniëlle. "Culinary Networks of Power. Dining with King Leopold II of Belgium (1865–1909)." *Food & History* 4.1 (2006): 85–104.

Ervynck, Anton, Wim Van Neer, Heide Hüster-Plogmann and Jörg Schibler, "Beyond Affluence: The Zooarchaeology of Luxury." *Word Archaeology* 34.3 (2003): 428–441.

Frey, Olivier. *La cuisine des Belges*. Tournai, Belgium: Renaissance du Livre, 2002.

Hachez, Henri. *La cuisine à travers l'histoire*. Brussels: Société belge de librairie, 1900.

Herrscher, Estelle, Hervé Bocherens, and Fréderique Valentin. "Reconstitution des comportements alimentaties aux époques historiques en Europe à partir de l'analyse isotopique d'ossements humains." *Revue Belge de Philologie et d'Histoire* 80.4 (2002): 1403–1422.

Hurlbut, Jesse D. *"Vive Bourgogne Est Nostre Cry": Ceremonial Entries of Philip the Good and Charles the Bold (1419–1477)*. Turnhout, Belgium: Brepols, 2001.

Jansen-Sieben, Ria, and Johanna-Maria Van Winter. *De keuken van de late Middeleeuwen. Een kookboek uit de Lage Landen.* Amsterdam: Bakker, 1989.

Janssens, Paul, and Siger Zeischka eds. *Dining Nobility: From the Dukes of Burgundy to the Belgian Royals.* Brussels: VUBPress, 2008.

Lepage, Yvan, and Jean Deligne. "Habitudes alimentaires en Belgique selon les revenus des ménages." In *La viande, un aliment, des symboles,* eds. M. Aubaille, M. Bernard, and P. Posquet, 145–158. Brussels: Edisad, 2004.

Libert, Marc. "Les habitutes alimentaires à la cour de Bruxelles au XVIIIe siècle." *Cahiers Bruxellois* 32 (1992): 61–84.

Lis, Catharina, and Hugo Soly. "Food Consumption in Antwerp between 1807 and 1859: A Contribution to the Standard of Living Debate." *Economic History Review* 30.3 (1977): 460–486.

Murray, James M. *Bruges, Cradle of Capitalism, 1280–1390.* Cambridge: Cambridge University Press, 2005.

Niesten, Eddie. *La Belgique cuisine!: Cauderlier et le premier siècle belge, 1830–1930.* Leuven, Belgium: Centre d'histoire agraire, 2004.

Paddleford, Clementine. *Belgium, a Land of Plenty; A Series of Articles on the Temptations of the Belgian Cuisine.* New York: Belgian Government Information Center, 1955.

Polet, C., and M. A. Katzenberg. "Reconstruction of the Diet in a Mediaeval Monastic Community from the Coast of Belgium." *Journal of Archaeological Science* 30 (2003): 525–534.

Polet, Caroline, and Rosine Orban. *Les dents et les ossements humains: Que mangeait-on au Moyen Age?* Typologie des sources du Moyen Age occidental, no. 84. Turnhout, Belgium: Brepols, 2001.

Schildermans, Jozef, Hilde Sels, and Marleen Willebrands. *Lieve schat, wat vind je lekker? Het Koocboec van Antonius Magirus (1612) en de Italiaanse keuken van de renaissance.* Leuven, Belgium: Davidsfonds, 2007.

Schokkaert, Erik, and Herman Van der Wee. "A Quantitative Study of Food Consumption in the Low Countries during the Sixteenth Century." *The Journal of European Economic History* 17.1 (1988): 131–158.

Scholliers, Peter. *Arm en rijk aan tafel. Tweehonderd jaar eetcultuur in België.* Berchem and Brussels: EPO & BRTN, 1993.

Scholliers, Peter. "Cuisine, Internationalism, Nationalism and Regionalism. The Role of Food in the Construction of Territorial Sentiments (Belgium, 1860s–2000s)." In *Regionalisierung europäischer Konsumkultur im 20. Jahrhundert,* ed. Hannes Siegrist and Manuel Schramm, 171–189. Leipzig, Germany: Leipziger Universitätsverlag, 2003.

Scholliers, Peter. "From the 'Crisis of Flanders' to Belgium's Social Question: Nutritional Landmarks of Transition in Industrializing Europe." *Food and Foodways* 5.2 (1992): 151–175.

Segers, Yves. "Food Recommendations, Tradition and Change in a Flemish Cookbook: Ons Kookboek, 1920–2000." *Appetite* 45.1 (2005): 4–14.

Segers, Yves. "Oysters and Rye Bread: Polarising Living Standards in Flanders, 1800–1860." *European Review of Economic History* 5.3 (2001): 301–336.

Souris, Christian. *La folle histoire de la cuisine wallonne*. Ottignies, Belgium: Quorum, 1995.

Stevens, I. *La cuisine au pays du Manneken Pis. Plats nationaux Belges du bon vieux temps*. Brussels: Ed. Gastronomiques Nova, 1946.

Thøfner, Margit. *A Common Art: Urban Ceremonial in Antwerp and Brussels during and after the Dutch Revolt*. Studies in Netherlandish Art and Cultural History, no. 7. Zwolle, The Netherlands: Waanders Publishers, 2007.

Vandenbroeke, Chris. *Agriculture et alimentation*. Ghent: Centre belge d'histoire rurale, 1975.

Van Hee, R. "Food and Health at the Time of Rubens: A Lecture Given at the ESPEN Congress, Antwerp 1991." *Clinical Nutrition* 11.4 (1992): 244–247.

Van Isacker, Karel, Raymond van Uytven, and J. Andriessen. *Antwerp: Twelve Centuries of History and Culture*. Antwerp: Fonds Mercator, 1986.

Van Otterloo, Anneke. "The Low Countries." In *The Cambridge World History of Food*. ed. K. F. Kipple and K. C. Ornelas, 2:1232–1240. Cambridge: Cambridge University Press, 2000.

Van Uytven, Raymond. *Production and Consumption in the Low Countries, 13th–16th Centuries*. Aldershot: Ashgate, 2001.

Van Winter, Johanna Maria. "The Low Countries in the Fifteenth and Sixteenth Centuries." In *Spices and Comfits: Collected Papers on Medieval Food*, 107–128. Totnes, UK: Prospect Books, 2007.

Verstraeten, Jean-Paul. *Ma mère son manger: Les souvenirs culinaires d'un bruxellois de classe moyenne de 1946 à nos jours*. Limelette, Belgium: Capucines, 1999.

Zeischka, Siger. "His Majesty, His Miners: Raoul Warocqué's Festivities and Guests." In *The Dining Nobility: From the Burgundian Dukes to the Belgian Royalty*, ed. Paul Janssens and Siger Zeischka, 123–135. Brussels: VUB-Press, 2008.

CHAPTER 2

Damme, Jef. *Ice Cream and Sorbet*. Tielt, Belgium: Lannoo, 1991.

Deglas, Christian, and Guy Derdelinckx. *The Classic Beers of Belgium*. Ann Arbor, MI: G. W. Kent, 1997.

Deweer, Hilde. *All Belgian Beers*. Oostkamp, Belgium: Stichting Kunstboek, 2007.

Dubrulle, Bernard. *Guide to Belgian Chocolate*. Brussels: Neocity, 2001.

Hieronymus, Stan. *Brew Like a Monk: Trappist, Abbey, and Strong Belgian Ales and How to Brew Them*. Boulder, CO: Brewers Publications, 2005.

Hobert, Liesbeth, and Felix Alen. *Witloof from Belgium*. Antwerp: The House of Books, 2003.

Jackson, Michael. *Michael Jackson's Great Beers of Belgium*. Philadelphia: Running Press, 1998.

Jacobs, Marc, and Jean Fraikin. "Belgium: Endives, Brussels Sprouts and Other Innovations." In *Culinary Cultures of Europe: Identity, Diversity and Dialogue*, ed. Darra Goldstein and Kathrin Merkle, 75–85. Strasbourg: Council of Europe Publishing, 2005.

Mommaerts, Myriam. *L'aventure du chocolat belge*. Braine-l'Alleud, Belgium: Collet, 1994.

Nelson, Max. *The Barbarian's Beverage: A History of Beer in Ancient Europe*. New York: Routledge, 2004.

Pirotte, Fernand. *La pomme de terre en Wallonie au XVIIIe siècle*. Liège, Belgium: Musée de la vie wallonne, 1976.

Scholliers, Peter. "From Elite Consumption to Mass Consumption: The Case of Chocolate in Belgium." In *Food Technology, Science and Marketing: European Diet in the Twentieth Century*, ed. Adel Den Hartog, 127–138. East Linton: Tuckwell Press, 1995.

Thoen, Cécile. *Grande eau-de-vie et petit péket: Distilleries et liquoristeries en Wallonie*. Brussels: Labor, 1996.

Unger, Richard W. *Beer in the Middle Ages and the Renaissance*. Philadelphia: University of Pennsylvania Press, 2004.

Vandenbroeke, Christian. "La culture de la pomme de terre en Belgique (XVIIe–XIXe siècles)." *Flaran* 12 (1990): 115–129.

Van Gelderen, Chantal. *Les trésors gourmands de Wallonie. À la dècouverte des produits d'exception du terroir wallon*. Tournai, Belgium: Renaissance du Livre, 1999.

Van Winter, Maria-Johanna. "Green Salads: An Innovation in the Diet of the Renaissance Period." In *Changing Tastes: Food Culture and the Process of Industrialization*, ed. Patricia Lysaght and Christine Burckhardt-Seebas, 182–190. Basel: Schweizerische Gesellschaft für Volkskunde, 2004.

Verbeke, W., and P. Van Kenhove. "Impact of Emotional Stability and Attitude on Consumption Decisions under Risk: The Coca-Cola Crisis in Belgium." *Journal of Health Communication* 7.5 (2002): 455–472.

Vines, G. "Brussels Sprouts: Why Evil-Smelling Greens Are So Good for You." *New Scientist* 2061/2062 (1996): 46.

Webb, Tim. *The Good Beer Guide to Belgium*. Saint-Albans, England: CAMRA Books, 2008.

Willems, Louis, Raymonde Claes, and Renaat Hubert van der Linden. *Patisserie: The Sweet Things in Life*. Antwerp: MIM Pub, 1988.

Woods, John, and Keith Rigley. *The Beers of Wallonia: Belgium's Best Kept Secret*. Bristol: Artisan, 1996.

CHAPTER 3

Crauwels, Danny, Ghislaine Vlieghe-Steps, and Jo Van Caenegem. "Philippe Cauderlier (1812–1887), Belgian Chef and Culinary Author: A Short Biography, His (Cook)books and Their Authorship." *Food & History* 3.1 (2005): 197–224.

Scholliers, Peter. "Anonymous Cooks and Waiters: Labour Market and Professional Status of Restaurant, Café and Hotel Personnel in Brussels, 1840s–1900s." *Food & History* 2.1 (2004): 137–165.

Scholliers, Peter. "Novelty and Tradition: The New Landscape for Gastronomy." In *Food, the History of Taste* ed. Paul Freedman, 332–357. Berkeley: University of California Press, 2007.

Van den Eeckhout, Patricia, and Peter Scholliers. "The Language of a Menu (Le Grand Hôtel, Brussels, 1926)." *Food & History* 1.1 (2003): 240–247.

Van Molle, Leen. "*Kulturkampf* in the Countryside: Agricultural Education, 1800–1940: A Multifaced Offensive." In *Land, Shops and Kitchens: Technology and the Food Chain in Twentieth-Century Europe*, ed. Carmen Sarasùa, Peter Scholliers, and Leen Van Molle, 139–169. Turnhout, Belgium: Brepols, 2005.

Vereecken C. A., K. Bobelijn, and L. Maes. "School Food Policy at Primary and Secondary Schools in Belgium-Flanders: Does It Influence Young People's Food Habits?" *European Journal of Clinical Nutrition* 59.2 (2005): 271–277.

CHAPTER 4

Cox B., N. Debacker, et al. *Food Consumption Survey, Belgium 2004* (Food Consumption Survey Interactive Analysis NUTRIA). Brussels: Unit of Epidemiology, Scientific Institute of Public Health, 2005.

Matthys, C. "Estimated Energy Intake, Macronutrient Intake and Meal Pattern of Flemish Adolescents." *European Journal of Clinical Nutrition* 57.2 (2003): 366–375.

Mestdag, Inge. "Disappearance of the Traditional Meal: Temporal, Social and Spatial Destructuration." *Appetite* 45.1 (2005): 62–74.

Mestdag, Inge. "Introducing Italian Cuisine into Flemish Home-Meal Cooking in the Twentieth Century: An Analysis of the Flemish Cooking Bible Ons Kookboek (1927–1999)." *Food & History* 1.1 (2003): 156–177.

Mestdag, Inge, and Jessie Vandeweyer. "Where Has Family Time Gone? In Search of Joint Family Activities and the Role of the Family Meal in 1966 and 1999." *Journal of Family History* 30.3 (2005): 304–323.

Scholliers, Peter. "Workers' Time for Cooking and Eating in Nineteenth- and Twentieth-Century Western Europe." *Food and Foodways* 6.3–4 (1996): 243–260.

Segers, Yves. "Food Recommendations, Tradition and Change in a Flemish Cookbook: Ons Kookboek, 1920–2000." *Appetite* 45.1 (2005): 5–12.

CHAPTER 5

Declerfayt, Raymond. *Bruxelles, à boire et à manger*. Brussels: Éditions Immobilières, 1962.

Jacobs, Marc, and Peter Scholliers, eds. *Eating Out in Europe: Picnics, Gourmet Dining, and Snacks since the Late Eighteenth Century*. Oxford: Berg, 2003.

Pang, Ching Lin. "Business Opportunity or Food Pornography? Chinese Restaurant Ventures in Antwerp." *International Journal of Entrepreneurial Behaviour and Research* 8.1/2 (2002): 148–161.

Scholliers, Peter. "Propos culinaires: Tradition et innovation au *Comme chez Soi* depuis les années '70. Entretien avec Pierre Wynants." *Les Cahiers de la Fonderie* 34 (2006): 54–62.

CHAPTER 6

Baker, Lucy. *Christmas in Belgium*. Chicago: World Book, 2002.
Piette, Albert. *Les jeux de la fête: rites et comportements festifs en Wallonie*. Paris: Publications de la Sorbonne, 1988.
Raymaekers, Jan. *België feest: Een geschiedenis van Bourgondisch tafelen*. Leuven, Belgium: Van Halewyck, 2005.
Roeck, A., J. Theuwissen, and J. Van Haver. *Vlaamse volkscultuur: Het traditionele volksleven*. Deurne, Belgium: Baart, 1982.
Vandenbroucke, Jacques, and Pierre Dandoy. *40 ans de fêtes de Wallonie à Namur: 1960–2000*. Brussels: L. Pire, 2000.

CHAPTER 7

Berg, Lisbet. "Trust in Food in the Age of Mad Cow Disease: A Comparative Study of Consumers' Evaluation of Food Safety in Belgium, Britain and Norway." *Appetite* 42.1 (2004): 21–32.
Bernard, Afred, Fabrice Broeckaert, Geert De Poorter, Ann De Cock, Cédric Hermans, Claude Saegerman and Gilbert Houins. "The Belgian PCB/ Dioxin Incident: Analysis of the Food Chain Contamination and Health Risk Evaluation." *Environmental Research* 88.1 (2002): 1–18.
De Henauw, Stefan, and G. De Backer. "Nutrient and Food Intakes in Selected Subgroups of Belgian Adults." *British Journal of Nutrition* 81 (1999): 37–42.
De Vroede, Maurice. "Primary Education and the Fight against Alcoholism in Belgium at the Turn of the Century." *History of Education Quarterly* 25.4 (1985): 483–497.
Janssens, J., L. Bruckers and J. Joossens. "Overweight, Obesity and Beer Consumption: Alcohol Drinking Habits in Belgium and Body Mass Index." *Archives of Public Health* 59.5–6 (2001): 223–238.
Rozin, P., C. Fischler, S. Imada, A. Sarubin and A. Wrzesniewski. "Attitudes to Food and the Role of Food in Life in the U.S.A., Japan, Flemish Belgium and France: Possible Implications for the Diet-Health Debate." *Appetite* 33.2 (1999): 163–180.
Staessen, L., S. De Henauw, D. De Bacquer, G. De Backer and C. Van Peteghem. "Fat Sources in the Belgian Diet." *Annals of Nutrition and Metabolism* 42.3 (1998): 138–150.
Verbeke, Wim, Jacques Viaene, and Olivier Guiot. "Health Communication and Consumer Behavior on Meat in Belgium: From BSE until Dioxin." *Journal of Health Communication* 4.4 (1999): 345–357.

Verbeke, W., R. W. Ward, and J. Viaene. "Probit Analysis of Fresh Meat Consumption in Belgium: Exploring BSE and Television Communication Impact." *Agribusiness* 16 (2000): 215–234.

Vereecken, C., K. Bobelijn and L. Maes "School Food Policy at Primary and Secondary Schools in Belgium-Flanders: Does It Influence Young People's Food Habits?" *European Journal of Clinical Nutrition* 59.2 (2005): 271–277.

Index

About the Author

PETER SCHOLLIERS is Professor of History at Vrije Universiteit Brussel. He specializes in European food history and has written numerous works on Belgian foodways.

Recent Titles in
Food Culture around the World

Food Culture in China
Jacqueline M. Newman

Food Culture in Great Britain
Laura Mason

Food Culture in Italy
Fabio Parasecoli

Food Culture in Spain
Xavier F. Medina

Food Culture in the Near East, Middle East, and North Africa
Peter Heine

Food Culture in Mexico
Janet Long-Solís and Luis Alberto Vargas

Food Culture in South America
José Raphael Lovera

Food Culture in the Caribbean
Lynn Marie Houston

Food Culture in Russia and Central Asia
Glenn R. Mack and Asele Surina

Food Culture in Sub-Saharan Africa
Fran Osseo-Asare

Food Culture in France
Julia Abramson

Food Culture in Germany
Ursula Heinzelmann

Food Culture in Southeast Asia
Penny Van Esterik